Wittgenstein on Language and Thought

D1610643

Wittgenstein on Language and Thought
The Philosophy of Content

Tim Thornton

Edinburgh University Press

For Lois, beloved

© Tim Thornton, 1998

Edinburgh University Press
22 George Square, Edinburgh

Typeset in 10½ on 12½ pt Goudy
by Hewer Text Ltd, Edinburgh, and
printed and bound in Great Britain
by the University Press, Cambridge

A CIP record for this book is available from the British Library

ISBN 0 7486 1107 X (hardback)
ISBN 0 7486 0938 5 (paperback)

Contents

Preface

This is a book about Wittgenstein's philosophy of content. The philosophy of content forms part of the philosophy of thought and language. It is not concerned with the development of a formal semantic theory, nor is it concerned with the qualitative character of thought. It deals instead with the intentionality of thought and language: how thoughts or utterances can be about something, can be true or false. This is the central theme of Wittgenstein's *Philosophical Investigations*.

Wittgenstein himself does not give a formal theory of meaning. Indeed, he offers principled arguments against explanatory philosophical theories. Nevertheless, my intention here is to draw out of the later writings a *systematic* account of the philosophy of content for two reasons. Firstly, organising Wittgenstein's arguments into a coherent account of content provides a map for navigating through the remarks that, by his own admission, run 'criss-cross in every direction'. Secondly, it helps locate his account of content in the contemporary debate. Because Wittgenstein scholarship has tended to concentrate on narrow internal matters of exegesis, his relevance to current discussion in the philosophy of mind and language has often been missed. This is a mistake. One of the key claims in this book is that Wittgenstein's arguments refute the current representationalist orthodoxy in the philosophy of content. Linguistic meaning cannot be explained as the result of the animation of otherwise dead signs by acts of understanding. Mental content cannot be explained as a result of free-standing internal mental representations.

The structure of the book is as follows. Chapter 1 sets the scene. It sets out six characteristics of content with which any philosophical account must deal. It then sets out strategic choices. Can linguistic meaning be explained as resulting from mental content or vice versa? Or is there no explanatory priority? Can content be explained in independent, causal terms? It then characterises the orthodox representationalist answer to these questions. Representationalism attempts to explain linguistic content as resulting from mental content and then to give a reductionist account of the latter. Mental content is 'naturalised' through the provision of a causal explanation of content. This takes the form of either a pure descriptive causal theory, such as Fodor's, or a teleological, or natural selective account, such as Millikan's. Both approaches share the assumption that mental content can be explained by postulating internal mental representations that stand in causal relations to things in the world. The chapter concludes by sketching out provisionally Wittgenstein's contrasting account of content. Words are not injected with meaning through acts of understanding. Instead their meaning is their use. Mental states are not internal free-standing states of the mind which have to be connected via mechanisms with the world but are intrinsically relational states.

Chapter 2 articulates Wittgenstein's destructive arguments against *explanatory* theories of content. It draws on two sections of the *Investigations*: the central and lengthy discussion of rules; and the later discussion of content-laden mental states, such as expectations. Wittgenstein's arguments here undermine any attempt to explain content by appeal to free-standing internal mental representations. No such account can accommodate the normativity of content. They either presuppose what they set out to explain or fail to sustain normativity. Wittgenstein's criticisms are then applied to descriptive and to teleological versions of causal theories of content.

Chapter 3 begins to examine Wittgenstein's alternative positive account of content. This is a form of philosophical minimalism. The negative arguments do not undermine the everyday platitudes that meaning *determines* correct use, or that thoughts determine what they are about. Thus, neither a sceptical interpretation, such as Kripke's, nor a constructivist one, such as Wright's, can be correct. What is undermined is any attempt to *explain* this determination in foundational or mechanical terms. Instead, the ability of language-users to self-ascribe understanding directly, albeit fallibly, and to understand the meaning of the utterances of others, in both cases without epistemic intermediaries, has to be presupposed. Any attempt to explain these abilities through underlying processes fails to sustain the normativity of content. Instead, the construal of mental states as free-standing internal states has to be abandoned.

Despite Wittgenstein's hostility to advancing *explanatory* theories in philosophy, his positive claims about content can be marshalled into a descriptive but minimalist 'theory of content' which is the subject of Chapter 4. This clarifies how content-laden mental states can be employed in the explanation of action without contradicting Wittgenstein's claim that understanding (action, for example) does not depend on interpreting bare sounds and movements. It also highlights the minimalist support that Wittgenstein provides for externalism. On the one hand, no further relation underpins or explains a person's ability to think about an object at any particular moment. On the other, the general ability to entertain empirical contents presupposes an ability to explain those contents using samples. Samples play a role in the individuation of content. But, because, on Wittgenstein's account, samples are used as representations, they can form part of a theory of sense.

Chapter 5 argues that Wittgenstein's account has important similarities to some of Davidson's writing on content. Davidson's philosophy of content comprises two elements: the philosophy of language of the field linguist; and the formal theory of meaning. Although the latter runs counter to Wittgenstein's account, the former can be interpreted as broadly Wittgensteinian. Davidson's arguments against the dualism of scheme and content can then be used to shed light on, and themselves be clarified by, Wittgensteinian minimalism. Both deny that any philosophically significant distinction can be drawn between language and the world. But Davidson also claims that the very idea of representation should be abandoned and, at times, suggests that it should be replaced by merely causal links between content and the world. The chapter concludes by showing how McDowell's criticism of any such picture can be defended using Wittgenstein but arguing that Davidson need not be so interpreted. In fact, it is possible to interpret Davidson along Wittgensteinian lines in which case there is no reason to deny that beliefs can represent the world.

Finally, Chapter 6 examines Wittgenstein's radical claims that causality has nothing to do with content, and that psychological regularity might arise out of physiological chaos. The most natural response to these claims is to say that they are false and do not follow from Wittgenstein's attack on the reduction of content to causal mechanisms. The chapter begins by examining Davidson's argument that reasons must be causes and his explanation of how this is possible through anomalous monism. Anomalous monism might be thought to constitute a possible reconciliation of Wittgenstein's arguments against the reduction of content with a plausible form of physicalism. Davidson's positive arguments for a causal construal of mental states are, however, unconvincing. Furthermore, anomalous monism is incompatible with Wittgenstein's account of content. It presupposes the very conception of mental states as free-standing internal states which Wittgenstein refutes. Davidson's account of content is compatible with Wittgenstein's, but his account of the metaphysics of mind is not. While this does not justify Wittgenstein's hostility to all forms of physicalism, it shows how his position is at least coherent.

I should like to thank Blackwells for permission to use material published as 'Intention, rule following and the strategic role of Wright's order of determination test', in *Philosophical Investigations* 20, 1997.

My understanding of Wittgenstein, the philosophy of content and metaphysics in general has benefited from discussions with Neil Gascoigne, Ross Harrison, Jim Hopkins, Greg Hunt, Nick Jardine, Peter Lipton, Michael Luntley, Ian Lyne, Brendan Wilson and the members of the University of Warwick Davidson Reading Group.

I am also grateful for the support and encouragement of Mij and Grahame Thornton and the regulars at the Swan Hotel.

CHAPTER 1

Rival Approaches in the Philosophy of Content

The purpose of this chapter is to set the scene for the more detailed discussion in the rest of the book. It does this, in four sections, by characterising the subject matter of the philosophy of content, the available strategies and the contrast between Wittgenstein's approach and the current 'representationalist' orthodoxy.

The first section sets out six pre-philosophical characteristics of linguistic meaning and mental content. These serve two purposes. They help to characterise what it is that the philosophy of content is concerned with. And they also serve as a benchmark for a satisfactory account of content. Any philosophical account of content that undermines one or more of these features has to justify this revision of our pre-philosophical understanding of content or be rejected as unsatisfactory.

The second section outlines two preliminary strategic choices for the philosophy of content. The first concerns the explanatory priority of linguistic meaning and mental content. Should linguistic meaning be explained as resulting from mental content, or vice versa, or should the same account be given of both with equal priority? The second choice concerns the kind of explanation or explication to which the philosophy of content should aspire. One approach is to attempt to give a reductionist analysis that avoids related intentional concepts in its explanation of content. The alternative is to accept that this is a false hope and instead to shed light on content using other related notions. Representationalism adopts the first order of explanatory priority – it attempts to explain linguistic meaning as resulting from mental content – and then attempts to reduce mental content to non-intentional concepts. Wittgenstein, by contrast, adopts either the second or third approach to explanatory priority and makes no attempt to reduce content to non-content-laden concepts.

The third and fourth sections contrast representationalist and Wittgensteinian approaches to content. I characterise representationalism using four key claims. But the underlying idea is that the content of mental states can be explained by the possession of *inner* mental representations. These possess natural, underived content or intentionality because of the causal relations in which they stand. The

1

meaning of linguistic items, written and spoken, is then explained as deriving from the content of mental states.

Wittgenstein, however, rejects any attempt to explain linguistic meaning as resulting from the animation of otherwise dead signs through mental acts of understanding. Instead, there can be no deeper explanation of meaning than the practical explanations of meanings that can be given in everyday contexts. His account, which is the subject of the rest of this book, is briefly summarised in the fourth section.

1 The Pre-philosophical Characteristics of Content

Before outlining the strategic choices that govern the philosophy of content and the contrasting representationalist and Wittgensteinian approaches, it is necessary first to give a rough pre-philosophical account of content. Because the central purpose of this book is to provide a philosophical account of content, this preliminary characterisation may seem redundant. Surely, it may be thought, a philosophical account will supersede any cruder pre-philosophical characterisation. But it is precisely a *pre*-philosophical characterisation that is necessary to guide the development and assessment of a philosophical account of the subject. This is not to say that the pre-philosophical characterisation is an immutable standard. According to most philosophers, philosophical analysis might revise some of our everyday concepts. But, even such revision would have to preserve some features of our everyday understanding of content to be recognised as a theory of it.

There are two parenthetical notes to this use of a pre-philosophical account of content:

- Wittgenstein did not share the widespread methodological assumption that philosophy can legitimately seek to revise everyday concepts. He claimed that it could only revise – or, more usually, destroy – *philosophical* theories or uses of words. But, because one of the purposes of this book is to present Wittgenstein's account of content from a contemporary perspective, this assumption will not play a decisive role in the discussion. The fact that a philosophical theory of content has revisionary consequences need not count against it. The *nature* of those consequences may.
- Setting out the key pre-philosophical characteristics of content as a standard for philosophical accounts might suggest that a firm distinction can be drawn between the pre-philosophical and the philosophical. (This is also presupposed by Wittgenstein's distinction between what can and cannot legitimately be revised.) In fact, in the case of the characteristics listed below, no sharp

distinction seems plausible. Few, if any, of the characteristics would be offered, even after reflection, by the 'man on the Clapham omnibus'. But this need not matter. The characteristics mark out features at the end of a spectrum between the pre-philosophical and the philosophical. They are not driven by particular philosophical or theoretical interests. And they are features that might be accepted by non-philosophers as true. They serve both to identify what the philosophy of content is about and as a standard in assessing particular accounts.

I shall focus on six features that any theory of content should account for:

- Content possesses 'aboutness' or intentionality.
- Content can be specified by a 'that-clause'.
- Content is normative.
- Content plays a role in an explanatory theory of speech and action.
- Content is structured.
- Content is asymmetrically accessible from both first and third person.

1.1   Content possesses intentionality

Throughout this book I shall use 'content' to refer to mental content and to linguistic meaning. What these have in common is the possession of intentionality or 'aboutness'. Content-laden *mental* states – such as beliefs, intentions and expectations – and *linguistic* entities – such as sentences and utterances – can be *about* distant or even non-existent states of affairs. In ascribing content to mental states or to groups of words, one ascribes this kind of general intentionality or 'aboutness'. In this broad philosophical sense, 'intentionality' refers to the capacity to be about something. This is a philosophical and non-standard use of the word. It should not be confused with the everyday sense of intentional which means deliberate or with an intention. Intentions in that other sense are merely instances of mental states with the broader property of intentionality. The intention that one will read more philosophy possesses the broader property of intentionality because it concerns, and is about, one's intended future reading practice.

   Another way of saying that mental states and sentences have intentional properties is to say that they have *semantic* properties. But semantics is also the name given to a regimented theory of the relation between the meaning of words and sentences in a language, and the connection between the truth of sentences and the referring properties of constituent words. The articulation of a semantic theory for language – or at least the general form of any such theory – is the goal of one philosophical approach to meaning which will be discussed in the fifth chapter. In this book, however, except where explicitly stated, semantics will stand for intentionality in general.

There is a long philosophical tradition, attributed to Brentano, that takes intentionality in this abstract general sense – the sense of 'aboutness' – to be the defining feature of the mental (Brentano 1995). Despite the close connections between the mind and intentionality, it is worth noting two qualifications of any such definition. Firstly, it should not be taken to imply that the only forms of intentionality are forms of mental content. Sentences and utterances also possess intentionality. Secondly, there are mental states, such as sensations, that lack intentionality. But, whether or not it can be used to define the mind, intentionality does define the subject matter of this book. I shall be concerned with linguistic meanings and with those mental states that possess intentionality or content.

1.2 Content can be specified by using an appropriate 'that-clause'

The content of the belief that Wittgenstein was a difficult fellow is, precisely, that *Wittgenstein was a difficult fellow*. The content of the hope that this book will clearly explain Wittgenstein's philosophy of content is that *this book will clearly explain Wittgenstein's philosophy of content*. Using the content is clearly not the only way of *referring* to mental states. The above examples might have been referred to as: the belief that I entertained cycling home last Thursday, and my current hope. But contents as specified by 'that-clauses' are necessary individuating properties of content-laden mental states. Such specification also unpacks the intentionality that mental states possess. My earlier belief about Wittgenstein not only concerns or is about him, it also ascribes to him a particular characteristic: being a difficult fellow. Both the object of the belief – the intentional object – and what is attributed to it are stated in the appropriate 'that-clause'.

Because content can be stated using a that-clause, it is also called *propositional* content. Content-laden mental states are propositional attitudes because they can be individuated as attitudes or relations towards propositions. For example, Neil's hope that pragmatism will return to fashion is an attitude of hopefulness that Neil has towards the proposition *pragmatism will return to fashion*. Neil is related, via a relation of hope, to that proposition. This form of analysis is clearly a move towards a philosophical rather than a pre-philosophical account of content. But it is a more less natural development from, and codification of, the claim that content is what is stated by a 'that' clause. Furthermore, I am simply assuming that a proposition is the meaning of a sentence – and thus what can be shared by sentences in different languages – and not offering a philosophical theory of propositions. (Thus, the corresponding claim that linguistic meaning comprises propositional content is trivial. Because propositions can be defined as sentence meanings, sentences obviously have propositional content.) The focus of this book is thus propositional content in general. (There is considerable philosophical debate about whether the content of content-laden states can *always* be specified using that-clauses, and thus whether it is always propositional. This debate will be touched on in the fourth and fifth chapters. For now, all that matters is that content can generally be specified in this way.)

1.3 Content is normative

Spelling out intentionality in terms of propositional content highlights a connection that will be of central importance. Propositional content is normative. Because I shall discuss this at some length in the next chapter, some brief preliminary remarks will suffice here. The normativity of content consists in part in the fact that words can be used correctly or incorrectly, and assertions or beliefs can be true or false. The meaning of a word or sentence determines the circumstances in which it would be correct to use it. The content of a belief *prescribes* the condition that has to obtain for it to be true. But other content-laden mental states are also normative in that they also prescribe what would satisfy them. Propositional attitudes specify a condition for the world to satisfy if the attitude is to be fulfilled. Wittgenstein links these various content-bearing phenomena with normativity in the following passage:

> A wish seems already to know what will or would satisfy it; a proposition, a thought, what makes it true – even when that thing is not there at all! Whence this *determining* of what is not yet there? This despotic demand? (Wittgenstein 1953: §437)

(This passage, however, also makes fun of one explanation of normativity. As I shall argue in later chapters, the fact that content-laden mental states are normative does not imply that they somehow, and magically, predict the future.)

1.4 Content plays a role in an explanatory theory of speech and action

The normativity of content-laden states is also reflected in the fourth pre-philosophical characteristic of content. The mental states ascribed in propositional attitude psychology are content-laden. Propositional attitude psychology is our everyday way of making sense of, explaining and predicting, other people's behaviour. We might explain the fact that Ian went to the bookshop by saying that he wished to buy yet another book by Husserl and believed that he could buy one by going to the bookshop. Because it is used in this everyday way it is often called *folk* psychology. It works by deploying a complex system of propositional attitudes to make sense of action and speech:

First reference is made to a particular *person*; then some *attitude* is ascribed to that person; finally a *content* is specified for that attitude. Assertions of this form tell us who has what attitude towards which proposition. By making and receiving such assertions we come (it seems) to understand other people: what they do, why they want such and such, what made them hope for so and so, and so forth. Varying the three elements in the *person-attitude-content* structure gives us a seemingly powerful system for describing the minds of others (and our own), a system both antique and ubiquitous. Thinking of this system as a (tacit and unformalized) theory, we can say that folk psychology is a theory that centrally employs an explanatory ontology of persons and contentful attitudes; with these basic theoretical resources it sets about its explanatory and descriptive work. (C. McGinn 1989: 120)

On the assumption that folk psychology can be characterised as a *theory*, there has been much recent philosophical debate about whether it is a good theory. I shall return to the question of its theoretical character in the fourth chapter. For now it is enough to note that folk psychology is a *systematic* interpretative stance, that it is used to explain behaviour and that it does this by ascribing content-laden mental states.

Linguistic meaning dovetails with this system in the following way. Utterances provide the most important evidence for the ascription of propositional attitudes because agents can *express* their mental states through language. The content of mental states can be put into words without remainder. There is considerable philosophical dispute – based in part on a difference of pre-philosophical intuitions – about whether mental states also possess qualitative characteristics that are ineffable. Wittgenstein provides arguments against such a possibility. What matters in this context, however, is the *content* of beliefs and the claim that that is fully expressible is less controversial.

(The philosophical debate mentioned earlier about whether the content of mental states can always be expressed using that-clauses has consequences for this point as well. Suppose that Grahame approves of the design of one particular grommet. He might express his belief by the sentence: 'This is a fine grommet'. In ascribing a belief to him, patient observers will have to pick out the right object of his thought. But, in this sort of case, while the description 'the most expensive grommet' may uniquely apply to the object of Grahame's fancy, he may not have realised that that is so. He just thinks 'This grommet . . .'. Thus, the object itself will play a role in determining the content of the thought. One way of putting this point is to say that this thought is not fully linguistically codifiable. This, however, should be understood as a philosophical claim about how thought is represented, whether in internal symbols in the head, for example. It does not counter the everyday claim that thoughts can be expressed in language, where the distinction between what is part of language and what is part of the world, generally plays no role. I shall return to the linguistic, or otherwise, status of samples in Chapter 4.)

1.5   Content is structured

The systematicity of folk psychology presupposes some relational structure between the content-laden mental states ascribed. I shall mention two such connections. One is that content is rationally structured. This is a claim forcefully stated by Frege (e.g., Frege 1964). Mental states stand in logical and rational relations to one another. They are consistent, inconsistent, justificatory, disconfirmatory and suchlike. These relations constitute another way in which content is normative. Holding one belief can justify holding another.

There is a second and distinct respect in which content is structured although this is clearly more of a philosophical claim, albeit one based on a powerful intuition. If one is able to understand the thought that a particular frog is green, one must also able be able to understand thoughts to the effect that things other than frogs are green and that other frogs have colours other than green. Obviously, this is not to say that one must actually *hold* that this is the case. (One may have good reasons to hold that there is only one frog and one green thing left in the world.) But the ability to *understand* the first thought presupposes the ability to understand these other thoughts because all turn on constituent abilities. The most influential statement of the claim, that understanding a thought or, more generally entertaining a propositional attitude, is a structured ability that systematically presupposes connections to other thoughts or propositional attitudes, is by Evans (Evans 1982: 100–5). Consequently it is often termed Evans's Generality Constraint. But the claim that content is systematic in this way is also emphasised by many others (e.g., Fodor 1987: 147–53).

Linguistic meaning is also systematic. When one comes to understand a language – rather than simply knowing some phrases from a phrase book – one understands how to construct grammatically correct sentences from constituent words. It is criterial of this sort of understanding that, if one can understand the sentence 'Simon loves Lesley', then one will necessarily understand the sentence 'Lesley loves Simon'. When one understands a language, one has a systematic ability to construct and to understand novel sentences that employ known words in new structures.

The systematicity of linguistic and mental content has given rise to two philosophical explanatory strategies that are worth noting here:

- **Compositional semantics** is the name given to an approach that, in its strongest form, claims that the best explanation of the systematicity of our linguistic understanding is that we have tacit knowledge of a grammatical theory which determines the meaning of sentences on the basis of their component parts. Weaker versions of this position merely claim that light can be shed on our ability through the provision of such a semantic theory. As an explanation of linguistic systematicity, compositional semantics faces two sorts of difficulty. One is the problem of providing a regimented semantic theory for natural languages. [One quoted example is the rule for adding the suffix 'ness' to colour words, which works well for blue, less for purple and not at all for magenta (Baker and Hacker 1984a: 327).] The other is to explain what exactly the explanatory role of the theory is supposed to be. It is an improbable candidate for tacit knowledge but, if it is not in some sense known, it is hard to say what explanation it can provide. I shall return to these issues in the discussion of Davidson in Chapter 5.

- **Language of thought hypothesis** is an ingredient of one form of representationalism. As I will describe below, some representationalists make use of the symmetry between thought and language to try to *explain* the systematicity of thought. The argument turns on the idea that the systematicity of language results from the compositional structure of sentences and thus, because thought is also systematic then the best explanation of the systematicity of thought is that the vehicles of thought – internal mental representations – also possess a compositional structure. I will return to the difficulties of this account later in this and in the next chapter.

The point of flagging these philosophical explanations here is to emphasise the following point. One need not subscribe to either to acknowledge the systematicity of language and thought that they attempt to explain.

1.6   Content is asymmetrically accessible from first and from third person perspective

Mental states can be ascribed to others on the basis of behavioural evidence. But they can also be self-ascribed on the basis of no evidence. Whereas someone else may infer, from my purposeful behaviour at the bar, that I intend to buy a pint of beer, I do not have to make any observations of my own behaviour to ascribe this intention to myself. It appears instead that I have direct unmediated access to my mental state that, while not always infallible, is reliable.

It is arguable that this asymmetry also applies to linguistic meaning. If the meaning of the words that someone else uses is obscure, I can normally ask them for an explanation of what they mean. Alternatively, I may attempt to infer the meaning from the linguistic and behavioural context of the words. (Perhaps the most influential image in recent philosophy of language is that of an anthropologist attempting to understand a native language from scratch. This idea is deployed by Wittgenstein, Quine and Davidson in their discussions of meaning.) Either way, I can rely on this 'evidence' to determine the meaning of the words that other people utter. But it is incoherent to suggest that I need to rely on any such evidence to determine the meaning of my own words. Thus, it seems that there is an asymmetry between first and third person access to linguistic meaning.

This brief sketch ignores some complications suggested in philosophical work on linguistic meaning. One is the distinction between linguistic meaning and speaker meaning. I may intend to say something but use words of communal language that have a different meaning. This distinction might seem to undermine first-person authority concerning *linguistic* meaning rather than merely speaker's intended meaning. Another complication is introduced by Putnam's idea of the division of linguistic labour (Putnam 1975). Speakers, he claims, need not know the meanings of their own words but can rely on the knowledge of experts who can distinguish, for example, between elm and beech trees. The fact that there can be local or occasional failures of first-person authority about linguistic meaning does not imply, however, that it could fail generally. Any evidence for the claim that a speaker were generally mistaken about meanings would really be evidence that she was not a speaker of any language or a speaker of a different language. Errors in meaning only make sense against a backdrop of correctness. Thus, asymmetry of access applies to linguistic meaning and mental to content alike.

1.7   The philosophy of content

Having summarised six key characteristics of linguistic meaning and mental content, I can put the central problem of the philosophy of content bluntly: how is all this possible? How can there be sentences, utterances and mental states that, aside from whatever other properties they possess, also possess intentionality, normativity and the rest?

What makes this question pressing and difficult is the divide that seems to exist between intentionality and the physical properties invoked to describe the behaviour of things in the world. A person can have many properties that can be so described by the physical sciences – height, mass, weight, charge, colour – but may also have the property of being hopeful about the next election, or desirous of a hoppy beer. Utterances have a particular duration and involve a range of frequencies but they may also concern distant or non-existent states of affairs. There does not seem, however, to be any continuity between these different sorts of property. Prima facie, no property that forms part of a purely physical description corresponds to being about something, and certainly not to being about something that never existed.

Thus, one of the motivations for asking how content is possible, how there can be intentionality, is to explain how it can be part of nature. How can such a mysterious property be integrated into a general and scientifically respectable account of the world? This book is concerned with Wittgenstein's response to this sort of question.

2 Strategic Choices for the Philosophical Elucidation of Content

The characteristics outlined in the last section concerned mental content and linguistic meaning. Both are alike – and unlike anything else – in possessing the property of intentionality. In this section, I shall set out two strategic choices for philosophical accounts. This will help to locate Wittgenstein's account of content and contrast it with representationalism:

- The first concerns explanatory priority of mental content and linguistic meaning. Should one begin by explaining how linguistic meaning results from mental content hoping then to explain mental content later? Or the other way round? Or should one attempt to account for both in the same way with equal explanatory priority?
- The second decision concerns the kind of account that is to be given. Should it be reductionist and explain the concept of content using concepts that do not themselves presuppose intentionality at all (such as via particular causal mechanisms)? Or should it more modestly assume that content-presupposing terms cannot be dispensed with?

2.1   The explanatory priority of mental content or linguistic meaning

Given that mental content and linguistic meaning share many of the same puzzling properties, there are, in principle, four distinct strategies that can be adopted concerning their explanatory priority:

- Assign explanatory priority to mental content and explain how linguistic meaning results from that.
- Assign explanatory priority to linguistic meaning and explain how mental content results from that.
- Explain mental content and linguistic meaning in the same way with equal priority.
- Explain mental content and linguistic meaning in different ways with equal priority.

The first option is the strategy adopted by representationalist theories. Their hope is that conditions can be specified concerning the mental states of speakers which are necessary and sufficient to establish linguistic meaning. The standard approach is to attempt to explain the meaning of sentences as an abstraction from the meaning of utterances made using them. The meaning of utterances is then supposed to be explained as deriving from the content of beliefs or other propositional attitudes that the utterances were intended to convey. Given the content of these mental states, the meaning of sentences can be derived and explained. A different and independent account would then have to be found of how mental states possess their content.

Examples of this strategy dominate contemporary philosophy of thought and language. This is partly the result of the influence of Grice's work (e.g., Grice 1969). Grice aimed to explain linguistic meaning as the result of speakers' beliefs and intentions. He attempted to articulate the conditions that have to be met for a speaker to intend to communicate a belief to an audience using a linguistic expression. The promise of the Gricean programme is that the meaning of conventional spoken words and sentences is explained as deriving from the content of the beliefs which the speaker intends to communicate and which the audience realises it is intended to share by means of established linguistic conventions. Thus, linguistic meaning can be explained in terms of a speaker's beliefs and intentions. Attempts based upon Grice's work to reduce in this way the two problems of linguistic meaning and mental content to a single problem of mental content are called 'intentional-based semantics'. As I will describe in the next sub section, intentional-based semantics is usually paired with a *reductionist* account of mental content.

There are three other strategies concerning explanatory priority but only two are practical. The second is to reverse the above order and to explain mental content in terms of linguistic meaning. The third is to ascribe priority to neither side and to explain both in the same neutral way. While these are clearly different in principle, in practice, it is difficult sharply to distinguish examples of them. In particular, it is unclear whether Wittgenstein's account is best regarded as an example of the second or third approach. The difficulty is this. Wittgenstein explicates linguistic meaning and mental content with equal priority in the same way. Nevertheless, he also argues that there is a conceptual dependence of thought on language. Unless one can speak a language, one is, to put it mildly, severely constrained in the thoughts that one can think. Thus, although he does not claim that thinking is a form of internal speaking – indeed, to the contrary, Wittgenstein provides explicit argument that it cannot be – the claim of conceptual dependence places him in the second camp, while the fact that mental and linguistic content are explicated on a par places him in the third. What is clear, however, is that he does not characterise linguistic content as merely a derivative of mental content. In this, his approach differs sharply from representationalist theories.

(There is also, in principle, a fourth possibility. One could assign no priority and offer two different and independent explanations of mental and linguistic content. Such a strategy has two clear practical disadvantages. Firstly, it assumes from the start that the task is twice as difficult as the other three approaches. It assumes that two different accounts of content have to be given rather than that one will serve for mind and for language. Secondly, it faces the problem of explaining how the two distinct forms of content are related. Given that the content of a belief can be expressed by a sentence, some account of this congruence is required. It is unsurprising that examples of this strategy are difficult to find.)

2.2   Reductionist and non-reductionist accounts

In addition to the question of explanatory priority there is also a second strategic decision to take. What should count as a successful analysis or explanation of content? Here the most important distinction is between reductionist and non-reductionist accounts. Reductionist accounts aim to explain content by showing how it derives from processes that can be described without using, and thus presupposing, any intentional concepts. The aim is that the puzzling features of content can be reduced to processes that are not puzzling. Fodor characterises this aim as follows:

> What we want at a minimum is something of the form 'R represents S' is true iff C where the vocabulary in which condition C is couched contains neither intentional nor semantic expressions. (Fodor 1991: 32)

Reductionism aims at giving necessary and sufficient conditions (or failing that at least sufficient conditions) for content that can themselves be stated without using intentional concepts. If this could be achieved, then it would provide a translation of the problematic intentional vocabulary into an unproblematic language, and thus resolve the philosophical difficulties. Intentional states would be shown to comprise or derive from non-intentional states.

This reductionist approach is sometimes called a 'naturalistic' account of content. Such a label reflects the belief that unless content can be explained in non-intentional terms, then it cannot be an unmysterious part of the natural world. Fodor gives a clear expression of this methodological assumption in the following passage:

> I suppose that sooner or later the physicists will complete the catalogue they've been compiling of the ultimate and irreducible properties of things. When they do, the likes of *spin*, *charm* and *charge* will perhaps appear upon their list. But *aboutness* surely won't; intentionality simply doesn't go that deep. It's hard to see . . . how one can be a Realist about intentionality without also being, to some extent or other, a Reductionist. If the semantic and intentional are real properties of things, it must be in virtue of their identity

with . . . properties that are *neither* intentional *nor* semantic. If aboutness is real, it must be really something else. (Fodor 1987: 97)

Fodor's claim is that, unless one can reduce or 'naturalise' the intentional, then one will be driven to deny that it really exists. The motivation for this claim appears to be that, if it is not reducible to something else, nothing as strange and magical as meaning could itself form part of a respectable account of the world. Failing reduction, one would be forced to adopt an anti-realist reconstrual of content as a strictly fallacious way of speaking, a hangover from the pre-scientific age or as a sort of secondary quality existing only in the eye of the beholder.

One representationalist strategy for the reduction of content is to combine the first view of explanatory priority described above with either a causal or a biological 'teleological' account of mental content. Linguistic meaning is explained as deriving from mental content and that is claimed to result from causal or 'teleological' processes. (The idea is that biological 'teleological' processes are not themselves intentional because, as we all now know, natural selection can explain biological 'teleology' as really the result of perfectly natural non-teleological causes. They are not in this sense genuinely goal directed or teleological.) I shall return to both causal and to teleological theories later in this chapter. But, as I will argue in the next chapter, there are good Wittgensteinian reasons for thinking that no such reduction could be carried out.

This would be a depressing conclusion if Fodor's assumption were mandatory. But it is not. Wittgenstein denies that reduction is possible. In this, he follows the tradition, dating back to Brentano, that argues that intentional concepts cannot be analysed in terms of, or reduced to, non-intentional concepts. There is a long philosophical tradition, attributed in part to an 1874 work by Brentano, that takes intentionality in this abstract general sense – the sense of aboutness – to be the defining feature of the mental (Brentano 1995). But, according to Wittgenstein, content is no less natural because it cannot be analysed in non-intentional terms. The denial that this makes them any less natural is a key aspect of Wittgenstein's philosophical minimalism. Later chapters will fill out the close connection between content and pre-linguistic natural abilities which Wittgenstein emphasises.

The fundamental strategic differences between a Wittgensteinian and a representationalist theory of content can now be plotted out. Representationalist theories assume that linguistic content is derived from mental content and that mental content can itself be given a reductionist explanation. Content or intentionality can be explained as resulting from processes that can be described in non-intentional 'naturalistic' terms. Wittgenstein's account, by contrast, denies that any such reduction is possible and accounts for mental content and linguistic meaning symmetrically. Nevertheless, the fact that content-laden processes cannot be reduced to non-content-laden ones does not show that content is any the less natural.

3 The Representationalist Orthodoxy

Having set out the preliminary strategic choices for the philosophy of content, the rest of this chapter will summarise two opposing approaches. The first is the representationalist approach which is the current orthodoxy in the philosophy of content. The second is the Wittgensteinian account which is the subject of this book and which is set out in more detail in the chapters that follow. By contrasting the Wittgensteinian and the representationalist approach in this preliminary way, I hope to highlight the basic claims of a Wittgensteinian account and bring out the radical nature of Wittgenstein's project.

Some of the key assumptions of representationalist theories of content can be found in the accounts of the mind given, among others, by Descartes and Locke. Modern representationalism, however, developed from functionalist theories of mind that originated in the 1960s. Functionalism claims that mental states are functional states that mediate causally between sensory inputs and behavioural outputs (see Block 1980). What instances of the same type of mental state have in common is a shared type of causal or functional role. This is a second-order property. Individual states may vary in their first-order physical properties while nevertheless playing the same functional role in a person or a population's mental economy.

Functionalism evolved as an answer to the ontological problem in the philosophy of mind. It has advantages over type-identity versions of behaviourism and physicalism:

- Type-identity versions of behaviourism identify types of mental state with types of behavioural disposition. But because a mental state results in action only in the context of other mental states, a one to one correlation between mental states and dispositions to act is implausible. Derek's desire to seduce the next attractive woman he meets may be countermanded by the desire not to seduce the wife of his boss if he next meets the wife. But his failure to act does not imply that his desire did not exist after all, as a crude behaviourism would imply. Functionalism avoids this problem because it claims that mental states mediate between perceptions and actions as a network rather than individually. It also differs from behaviourism in that mental states are not merely disguised descriptions of behaviour but are internal states playing a genuinely causal role in the production of behaviour.

- Type-identity physicalism identifies types of mental state with types of physical state. But this identification is implausibly chauvinist because it seems possible that creatures with very different physiology might possess the same mental states. Functionalism escapes this charge because it claims that what matters for the identity of a type of belief is a second-order property rather than the first-order properties of physical states. Nevertheless, it is still consistent with the more modest physicalist claim that each token (of a type of) mental state is a physical state.

A key influence behind functionalism was the development of the computer. The connection at its most general is simply that the distinction between software and hardware provides an analogy for that between mind and body. Two computers can be in the same kind of software state if they are running the same program even if their underlying physical processes are different. But more specifically, the analogy suggests that a computational analysis of mental processes might be possible. Such an analysis would specify the inputs and outputs for each type of mental state.

Very approximately, a functionalist account of pain might define it as something like this (taken from Block 1980: 174). Pain is that type of mental state which is caused by pinpricks and which causes worry and the emission of loud noises. Worry, in turn, is that state which is caused by pain and causes brow, wrinkling. Thus, pain is that property that one has when one has a state that is caused by pin-pricks and causes emission of loud noises, and also causes something else that causes brow-wrinkling. Such a definition – once suitably refined – allows the ascription of pain throughout a population with varying brain chemistry and also across species with fundamentally different physiologies (provided only that they have brows that can be wrinkled). Nevertheless each individual pain which is felt – whether by humans or by other creatures – is simply a physical state or event of one sort or another of the creature involved.

While defining types of mental state by types of functional or causal role may seem attractive for states such as pains, it does not in itself explain mental content. The problem is that there is no clear connection between playing a particular causal role and being *about* something:

> The functionalist thinks of mental states as causal intermediaries between perceptual inputs and behavioural outputs. This is an advance on thinking of them simply as physical states. But, for all that, functionalism still presents mental states as part of a system of causal pushes and pulls inside the head. And there still isn't any obvious place in this picture for any conception of mental states as *representing* anything . . . [O]nce we have specified a set of 'horizontal' relationships between perceptions, mental states and behaviour adequate for our explanatory purposes, why should we need in addition any 'vertical' relationships between mental states and the things we intuitively think of them as standing for. (Papineau 1987: 46–7)

Representationalism recognises that something has to be added to a simple form of functionalism if it is to account for intentional states as well as for sensations. To a first approximation, representationalism adds the claim that the abstract states identified by functionalism *encode* meanings. Thus, the possession of propositional attitudes by people is explained by the postulation of internal states within them which encode those propositional attitudes. Quite how such encoding takes place is an issue on which representationalists disagree. Some answers diverge from functionalism proper. For simplicity I will, however, continue to talk of representationalism as a form of functionalism.

One of the most thorough representationalist theories of mind is provided by Fodor:

> At the heart of the theory is the postulation of a language of thought: an infinite set of 'mental representations' which function both as the immediate objects of propositional attitudes and as the domains of mental processes. More precisely, RTM [the Representationalist Theory of Mind] is the conjunction of the following two claims:
> *Claim 1* (the nature of propositional attitudes):
> For any organism O, and any attitude A toward the proposition P, there is a ('computational'/ 'functional') relation R and a mental representation MP such that MP means that P, and
> O has A iff O bears R to MP . . .
> *Claim 2* (the nature of mental processes):
> Mental processes are causal sequences of tokenings of mental representations. (Fodor 1987: 16–17)

I shall return shortly to the claim that mental representations comprise a *language* of thought. For the moment, what is of central importance about this summary of representationalism is the claim that propositional attitudes are explained via internal mental states or representations that encode meaning and that enter into causal relations.

This account is sometimes described in the following way. Suppose Mij intends to paint Wetherlam in a realist manner but believes (or perhaps fears) that she will paint it in a Cubist style. Then, according to Fodor, there is mental representation in her 'intention box' that encodes the content *I will paint Wetherlam in a realist manner*. At the same time, there is a representation in her 'belief box' (or 'fear box') that encodes the content *I will paint Wetherlam in a Cubist style*. Had her intention and her belief been reversed then the very same mental representations would simply have been located in the opposite boxes. This talk of mental boxes is a metaphorical shorthand for describing the functional role that the mental representations 'placed in them' play. The causal consequences for behaviour and for other mental states are characteristically different for intentions and for beliefs as a whole. Thus, to intend such-and-such is to stand in a functional or computational relation, corresponding to the attitude of intending, towards a specific mental representation that encodes the content *such-and-such*.

Fodor's account is just one example of a representational theory of content. I shall now set out four key claims that characterise representationalism in general. These are:

- Mental states possess underived and natural intentionality.
- The content of mental states can be explained by the possession of *inner* mental representations.
- The systematicity of thought is explained by causal relations between mental representations.
- The intentionality of thought is explained by causal relations between mental representations and the world.

Because representationalism is a family of theories with common underlying assumptions rather than a single rigidly defined philosophical theory, these claims are neither rigidly necessary nor sufficient conditions for representationalism. But they are important characteristic elements of such theories. All are rejected by Wittgenstein.

3.1   Mental states possess underived and natural intentionality

The first general characteristic of representationalism is its commitment to the thesis that mental states possess *underived, natural* or *intrinsic* intentionality. This is a combination of two claims:

- A distinction can be drawn between intrinsic and conventional or derived intentionality.
- The bearers of intrinsic intentionality are mental states.

I shall briefly discuss these two claims in turn.

The claim that there is a distinction between intrinsic and derived intentionality is a substantial claim with significant philosophical consequences. It is widely, though not universally, held. Searle, for example, who does not subscribe to representationalism, still suggests that two genuine kinds of intentionality can be distinguished:

  1. I am now thirsty, really thirsty, because I haven't had anything to drink all day.
  2. My lawn is thirsty, really thirsty, because it has not been watered in a week.
  3. In French, 'j'ai grand soif' means 'I am very thirsty'.
  The first of these sentences is used literally to ascribe a real, intentional state to

oneself . . . Sentence 2 is used only metaphorically, or figuratively, to ascribe thirst to my lawn. My lawn, lacking water, is in a situation in which I would be thirsty, so I figuratively describe it *as if* it were thirsty . . . The third sentence is like the first in that it literally ascribes intentionality, but it is like the second and unlike the first in that the intentionality described is not intrinsic to the system . . . [I]ntrinsic intentionality is a phenomenon that humans and certain other animals have as part of their biological nature. It is not a matter of how they are used or how they think of themselves or how they choose to describe themselves. (Searle 1992: 78–9)

The intentional content of human thirst is the desire that *one should drink*. This is a form of *natural* or *intrinsic* intentionality because the fact that thirst concerns drinking is not the result of any convention governing its interpretation. It is, instead, an essential feature of the state that it has that content. ('Intrinsic' in this context stands in contrast to 'derived' and not to 'relational'. Intrinsic intentionality is still relational in so far as it concerns distinct, perhaps future or non-existent, states of affairs.)

By contrast, according to this view, the meaning of linguistic items results from conventions. The signs that are used to carry meaning in public language are arbitrary and contingent. An unlimited number of sounds or shapes could be used to carry the meanings that are currently carried by standard English words. Equally, the standard words could have been granted completely different meanings. What fixes the meanings of signs are conventions governing their use and interpretation by language users. Signs are used with the purpose of communicating mental contents. The intentionality of words is thus derived from the intrinsic intentionality of the users of the language.

I suggested above that the claim that intentionality can be so divided was a substantial philosophical claim and thus in need of some justification. Aside from whatever intuitive plausibility it has, there is a methodological motivation for adopting it. It fits the first explanatory strategy concerning content that I summarised earlier. That strategy attempts to explain linguistic meaning by showing that it derives from mental content and then 'naturalising' the latter. It presupposes that linguistic meaning possesses derived intentionality and that the meaning of mental states must be basic. This is the explanatory strategy which representationalism adopts.

To say that mental content is intrinsic or basic is not to deny that it can be further explained. It is just to say that it is the most basic form of intentionality. Representationalism does not claim that mental content is intrinsic in the sense of being unexplainable, but it is not derived from any more basic form of intentionality. Representationalism aims to explain mental content by reducing it to non-intentional phenomena. Regress is avoided in this explanation because it steps outside the circle of intentional concepts. The yet more basic underlying processes by which representationalism explains the intentionality of mental states do not themselves presuppose intentionality.

The second claim concerns the bearers of intrinsic intentionality. These are mental states and, as I shall describe in the next subsection, are more precisely *mental representations*:

> I'm not particularly anxious that the theory that naturalises the semantic properties of mental representations should work for smoke, tree rings, or English words. On the contrary, I'm prepared that it should turn out that smoke and tree rings represent only relative to our interests in predicting fires and ascertaining the ages of trees, that thermostats represent only relative to our interest in keeping the room warm, and that English words represent only relative to our intention to use them to communicate our thoughts. I'm prepared, that is, that only mental states (hence, according to RTM, only mental representations) should turn out to have semantic properties *in the first instance*; hence, that a naturalised semantics should apply, strictu dictu, to mental representations only.
>
> But it had better apply to them. (Fodor 1987: 99)

This raises two questions that will guide the rest of the discussion of representationalism below.

- Why assume that *mental* content, rather than *linguistic* meaning, possesses intrinsic intentionality?
- Why assume that the bearers of mental content are *internal* states?

One answer to the first question has already been given. Linguistic meaning requires conventions for the use and interpretation of signs whereas mental content does not. But there is a second reason for this. As will become clear shortly, causal and teleological reductionist explanations of content can work only for mental content. Thus, there is a methodological reason for taking mental content as basic and thus the candidate for reduction.

The second question is why mental content should be explained through *internal* states. I have already described the functionalist origins of modern forms of representationalism. In the next subsection I shall set out three ways in which mental representations count as *internal* states. They are ontologically independent of the external world, are the inner termini of causal chains resulting in action and are known about by hypothesis. But there are two further reasons that I will set out in the third and fourth characteristics of representationalism. Both depend on the causal roles of mental representations. The structure and systematicity of thought is explained through the causal relations between mental representations. And the intentional properties of mental content depend on the external causal relations between mental representations and worldly items. Both explanations require that the same items which encode content stand in causal relations.

3.2   The content of mental states can be explained by the possession of inner mental representations

The central feature of representationalism is its commitment to the explanation of mental content through the postulation of *internal* or *inner* mental representations. Their internal status will become clearer in the last two characteristics of representationalism. But the claim can be provisionally explained as itself involving three aspects. Mental representations are inner states because:

- They are ontologically independent of the external world.
- They are the internal causal origins of action.
- Their existence is a matter of hypothesis.

(In what follows I shall use the phrase 'mental representation' to refer specifically to the philosophical idea of internal states characterised by representationalism. I shall not use it to refer to beliefs with representational content that are not construed on this explanatory model as *internal* states.)

The first claim is that whether or not a mental representation exists depends upon its non-relational intrinsic properties. It is an assumption that modern representationalism holds in common with Cartesian and Lockean theories of mind. Those historical accounts populated the mind with *ideas*: discrete, free-standing, albeit immaterial, particulars inhabiting a mental realm discontinuous with the physical world. Ideas no more depended for their existence on states of affairs in the external world outside the mind than pieces of furniture in a room depend on the world outside the room. Like pieces of furniture, they possessed non-relational intrinsic properties that were all that mattered to whether they existed or not.

No contemporary representationalist need hold that mental representations are immaterial, nor that they exist in an ontologically discrete realm. But they still agree that mental representations are ontologically independent of the world. Instead of relying on immaterial ideas, modern representationalism adopts the (physicalist) claim that mental states are really states of the body, albeit described in second-order functionalist terms. As states of the body, they possess non-relational intrinsic properties which are all that matter to their existence and are thus ontologically independent of the external world. Thus, they are *inner* states because they are not tied to the existence of outer states of affairs.

It is worth noting here an important feature of this ontological independence. Because the mere fact that an idea existed did not depend upon any relation to the external world, this conception of the mind fed directly into Cartesian scepticism. The mind could be populated with exactly the same ideas whether or not the world existed. Ideas might be caused by outside factors, but they were independent of those causal factors. Thus, Descartes faced the question: how can we know that the world is as we take it to be? Scepticism is the most obvious consequence of this picture. But there is another more fundamental problem. What gives ideas their intentional properties in the first place? What makes them about anything? Because it shares the basic assumption that mental representations are internal in the sense of ontological independence from the world, representationalism faces a similar challenge. I shall return shortly to the most common representationalist responses to this problem.

A second sense in which mental representations are *internal* states stems from their causal role. In common with functionalism, representationalism asserts that mental representations play a causal functional role in the production of behaviour. They lie at the inner termini of the causal chains that result in action. They are thus able to play a role in the explanation of action analogous to the role that, in the physical sciences, unobservable microscopic objects play in the explanation of observable macroscopic behaviour. Mental representations cause action only in virtue of their local intrinsic first-order properties. They can possess such properties only if conceived of as concrete states *within* or *of* the body.

Thirdly, given their general causal role as the origins of action, access to mental representations (at least in the case of other people) resembles epistemological access to theoretical unobservables in the physical sciences. Mental representations are never directly observed. They have instead to be *inferred* as the best explanation of behaviour, its *underlying* causes. Behaviour is a visible feature of the outer world but mental representations are hidden from general view. This is the third sense in which mental representations are internal states. They are inner in so far as they are hidden.

3.3 The systematicity of thought is explained by causal relations between mental representations

The third characteristic of representationalism is its explanation of the systematicity and structure of thought. At the start of this chapter I described two respects in which content is structured:

- One is the *rational* structure into which propositional attitudes fit. This is part of the point of saying that content is normative and also that it plays a role in a systematic explanatory framework. In ascribing a propositional attitude to an agent, one is ascribing something with normative consequences for the agent's other attitudes. The ascription of attitudes presupposes their rational inter-connectedness in an overall system.

- The other is the systematicity of thought captured by Evans's Generality Constraint. It concerns the structuring *within* thoughts which has consequences for relations between thoughts. The ability to understand a thought is a structured ability that presupposes the possibility of the exercise of the constituent abilities in understanding other thoughts.

Any attempt to provide a reductionist explanation of mental content has to account for its twofold systematicity. Representationalism attempts to explain it by postulating an isomorphous systematicity in the causal behaviour of internal mental representations. The causal structuring of mental representations explains how the thoughts that they encode are able to stand in their normative and rational relations.

This isomorphism might be invoked to explain two different things:

- It might be part of a full-blooded attempt to explain the demands of rationality in causal terms. Such a project would be thoroughly reductionist. It would aim at a form of *psychologism* in that logical and mathematical norms would be explained by appeal to the causal workings of the mind. Millikan appears to subscribe to this view (Millikan 1984: 11).
- More modestly it might aim merely to explain in mechanical terms how thought processes can follow, or correspond to, rational norms. It might aim to show how the causal relations in which mental states stand mirror their normative and rational relations. This position would not be a form of psychologism because it would not attempt to explain how rational norms derive from causal processes. Fodor appears to have this more modest aim (Fodor 1975, 1987, 1991).

I shall not be concerned with the differences between these representationalist strategies. But it is worth noting that, while the modest strategy may seem more likely to succeed, it is something of a half-way house. If the motivation behind representationalism is to naturalise intentional concepts by reducing them to causal processes, simply helping itself to the conceptual structure of rationality or logic, perhaps backed up by a form of Platonism, is far from naturalistic. If the underlying motivation is to explain how intentional states can be part of the natural world, then simply presupposing the rational structure in which they stand appears question-begging. But, in any case, both options face a similar key problem.

The problem that the optimistic strategy faces is to devise a way of mapping rational relations on to causal relations so as to translate the former concepts into the latter. The more modest strategy, while conceding that the demands of rationality and the demands of causality are conceptually different, faces a related problem. It owes an account of how these disparate systems can coincide. If the causal relations holding between mental representations explain how it is that we can think in accordance with the demands of rationality, what guarantees that the causal mechanisms governing mental representations continue to be faithful to the rational structure of thought that the representations encode?

The most explicit answer to these questions is provided by the language of thought hypothesis. According to this version of representationalism, mental representations are symbols in a language of thought with a compositional syntax and semantics. The most direct motivation for this thesis is a swift response to the explanation of systematicity. One problem is to explain the systematicity of thought. But such systematicity is also apparent in language. A language capable of representing the fact that Simon loves Lesley (in English, by the sentence 'Simon loves Lesley') is also capable of representing the fact that Lesley loves Simon, by reversing the symbols for Simon and Lesley in the representing sentence. So one obvious explanation for the systematicity of thought is to say that thinking comprises the manipulation of inner representational symbols in a language of thought. Thus, as well as granting that the *content* of the thought that Simon loves Lesley is structured, in accordance with Evans's Generality Constraint, the language of thought hypothesis claims that the *internal bearer* of this content is a structured or compositional symbol in an inner language.

Fodor distinguishes the language of thought ('LOT') from a simple functionalism in this way:

> Practically everybody thinks that the *objects* of intentional states are in some way complex: for example, that what you believe when you believe that . . . P & Q is . . . something composite, whose elements are – as it might be – the proposition that P and the proposition that Q. But the (putative) complexity of the *intentional object* of a mental state does not, of course, entail the complexity of the mental state itself. It's here that LOT ventures beyond mere Intentional Realism . . . LOT claims that *mental states* – and not just their propositional objects – *typically have constituent structure.* (Fodor 1987: 136)

Such a claim ensures that those able to think the first thought are able to think the second thought because of the systematic relations between compositionally structured mental representations. So much then for the explanation of the systematicity of thought. But what of the rational structuring of thought? The systematicity of mental representations explains the fact that, if one is able to think 'P and Q' one must also be able to think 'P' but not that one *ought* to think it. The language of thought hypothesis, however, also has an explanation of the rational or normative nature of our thinking.

The computer provides an influential metaphor. Computers are machines that can be programmed to manipulate symbols so as to respect the semantic or rational relations of the contents that they encode. This manipulation, encoded in the lowest levels of computer programming languages, depends on causally relevant properties of the symbols that, by design, correspond to their syntax. Thus, the harmony of the causal properties of symbols and the rational properties of contents is effected by the syntax of the symbols that encode those contents. This suggests that language-of-thought versions of representationalism can make use of a similar account to explain the rational structure of thought.

On this account, mental representations comprise symbols in a language of thought, the syntax of which governs their causal interactions such that the demands of rationality are respected. In other words, the mind is a computer, the computations of which involve the manipulation of internal symbols. Thinking comprises the causal manipulation of internal symbols according to a system of laws that matches the rational structure of the contents of thoughts encoded by the symbols.

While the language-of-thought hypothesis is the most explicit representationalist attempt to explain the systematicity of thought, not all forms of representationalism are committed to it. An alternative explanation relies not on an inner linguistic structure but on a structure based upon inner maps or models (e.g., C. McGinn 1989). Briefly, it has been argued that maps can also explain the systematicity and rational structure of thoughts. The same mapping conventions and symbols which enable a representation of Cambridge as to the east of Oxford could also represent Oxford as to the east of Cambridge. There is a systematicity in such mapping relations. An explanation of the rational structuring of thoughts based on maps is less clear than the language-of-thought explanation. But there is no reason in principle why a similar kind of story might not be developed. The harmony of the causal properties of map symbols and the rational properties of contents could be effected by a kind of spatial syntax of the mapping symbols which, on this account, encode those contents. In what follows I shall ignore the differences between language-of-thought and mental-model versions of representationalism.

The language-of-thought and the mental-models hypotheses attempt to explain the structure of mental content through the structuring of internal states. But, while these attempt to explain the 'syntactic' properties of thought (literally the syntax in the case of the language of thought and an 'internal' structure akin to syntax in the case of mental models), they do not explain the intentional or semantic properties of thought. This is the subject of the fourth characteristic of representationalism.

3.4   The intentionality of thought is explained by causal relations between mental representations and the world

The representationalist picture of mind that I have outlined so far postulates ontologically independent internal mental states standing in systematic causal relations one to another. This omits a central element that can be approached through the question: why think of mental representations as representations *of* anything? Why think that they possess intentionality? Representationalism adds to the elements so far outlined a further claim. In addition to standing in causal relations to one another, mental representations also stand in causal relations to items in the external world. It is in virtue of their external causal relations that mental representations have intentional content:

> Thoughts are inner representations; thinking is the processing of inner, mental representations. These representations have a double aspect . . . [T]heir role within the mind depends on their individualist, perhaps their syntactic, properties . . . [And] they are representations in virtue of relations with the world. Mental states represent in virtue of causal relations of some kind with what they represent. (Sterelny 1990: 39)

The basic idea is that mental representations gain their content by standing in suitable causal relations to items in the outside world. But simply adding additional external causal relations to the internal causal relations between mental representations does not explain how they come to possess intentionality.

Representationalists do not generally attempt to tackle this problem directly. The problem that is generally acknowledged is accounting for the *normativity* of beliefs. The assumption is something like this. If a representationalist theory of content cannot account for false beliefs, there must be something fundamentally wrong with it. If the theory is not so falsified, then that may be some indication that it is indeed a theory of content. The difficulty that false beliefs present for a causal theory is this. A crude causal theory, which simply identifies the content of a belief with what actually causes it, makes false belief impossible. The theory will instead make the content a disjunction of all its possible causes. Thus, the problem is often called the 'disjunction problem'.

I shall examine the strategies available to representationalism in more detail in the next chapter. Briefly however, respresentationalist solutions to the disjunction are either pure or descriptive causal theories or teleological theories. Descriptive causal theories either attempt to define the content of a mental representation by specifying optimal circumstances under which only true beliefs can be formed (e.g., Dretske 1981), or they pick out the tokening of mental representations that correspond to false beliefs as those which asymmetrically depend on the causal connections that correspond to true beliefs (e.g., Fodor 1987, 1991). Thus, a type of mental representation has the content 'cow' if cows cause it to be tokened in the 'belief box' of a thinker and if those occasions on which it is caused by non-cows depend asymmetrically on the connection to cows.

The teleological account, by contrast, adds to the basic causal theory the idea of the proper or biological function of mental representations (e.g., Millikan

1984, 1993). The content of a mental representation is what it is biologically supposed to represent. The connection between mental representations and the world that determines the content is the connection that has been selected for during the selectional history of the thinker's species.

I can now return to the question left hanging a few pages back. Why assume that mental content, rather than linguistic meaning, possesses intrinsic intentionality? One representationalist answer to this question is the claim that linguistic meaning requires conventions for the use and interpretation of signs. But another can now be given. Pure descriptive causal theories and teleological theories of content are much more likely to be successful for mental representations than for words. This is because whether a word is actually used when the thing to which it refers is present depends, not only on the word's meaning, but also on the intentions of speakers. (The complicated intentions required are those specified in Grice's project for reducing linguistic meaning to mental content.) By contrast, entertaining thoughts is not generally a voluntary act. On seeing a cow before one, one automatically thinks 'cow'. Thus the causal connection between worldly elements and mental contents is more reliable than that between worldly elements and the linguistic tokens. The latter causal chain is shorter. Consequently, the project of reducing content to non-intentional concepts is more likely on the assumption that mental states are the possessors of intrinsic intentionality.

Both of these accounts, however, may raise the following doubt. On the assumption that their favoured causal mechanism explains the content of mental representations, the asymmetric dependence theory and the teleological theory aim to draw a principled distinction between correct and incorrect tokenings of mental representations. But what reason is there to think that the antecedent assumption is true? Why think that causal mechanisms explain content in the first place? Why should adding causal relations between mental representations and the world simultaneously add intentional relations. I shall return to this question at the end of the next chapter. But first I shall outline Wittgenstein's rival approach to content.

4 The Wittgensteinian Alternative

Wittgenstein's account of content is diametrically opposed to representationalism. I suggested in the last section that representationalism could be characterised through four interconnected claims or assumptions about mental content:

• Mental states possess underived and natural intentionality.

- The content of mental states can be explained by the possession of *inner* mental representations.
- The systematicity of thought is explained by causal relations between mental representations.
- The intentionality of thought is explained by causal relations between mental representations and the world.

Wittgenstein rejects each of these points. I shall comment on them in reverse order. Because the purpose of the book is to articulate Wittgenstein's account of content, this summary will be brief.

Wittgenstein argues that no substantial explanation of either linguistic meaning or mental content is possible. No account can be given that breaks these down into underlying mechanisms or processes. Any such attempt will either turn out to presuppose the very thing it attempts to explain, or it will fail to sustain the normativity of content. Causal accounts typically fail in the latter respect. No mechanism or process, characterised in purely causal terms, can account for the way in which mental states prescribe or determine what would satisfy or fulfil them. No mechanistic account of understanding can account for the distinction between the correct and incorrect use of words. The normativity, rationality and systematicity of content resist reduction to the realm of laws.

The fact that the normativity of content cannot be reduced to causal relations undermines the attempt to explain the systematicity of thought and its intentionality in causal terms. But Wittgenstein suggests a more fundamental diagnosis of what is wrong with this attempt. The problem is the fact that content-laden mental states, construed broadly to include linguistic understanding, are characterised as internal states. Once mental states are construed as free-standing independent states, the question of what connects them to behaviour and to the world becomes pressing. But, at the same, it becomes unanswerable. No mechanism makes the *right* connection.

This problem undermines the explanatory usefulness of the distinction between intrinsic and derived intentionality. What gives that distinction philosophical significance is the assumption that the derived intentionality of language can be explained as resulting from the natural intentionality of mental states. Dead linguistic signs are injected with meaning by acts of understanding. But, in the picture of mind that representationalism advances, mental states are as independent of what they are supposed to be about as words or sentences. They are as meaningless and dead as the signs the meaning of which they are supposed to explain:

> It is as if we had imagined that the essential thing about a living man was the outward form. Then we made a lump of wood in that form, and were abashed to see the stupid block, which hadn't even any similarity to a living being. (Wittgenstein 1953: §430)

The diagnosis of what is wrong with the attempt to explain linguistic meaning as the result of mental states which are described in non-relational terms suggests that a different response is needed. Wittgenstein defends instead a kind of philosophical minimalism. Consider the question: what connects understanding the meaning of the word 'cube' with subsequent correct use? Or, what connects an intention to read the second chapter with reading the second chapter? Wittgenstein argues that questions such as these cannot be answered by a substantial explanation such as via a causal mechanism. The best response is to deny the assumption that makes a substantial answer seem necessary. That assumption is that content-laden mental states are free-standing internal states independent of the world.

By rejecting this characterisation of mental states, Wittgenstein rejects a sharp distinction between an inner world of mental objects and the outer public world of everyday objects. Once that distinction is rejected, philosophically minimalist answers are quite sufficient for the questions raised above. Understanding the meaning of a word is not a state that requires connection to the practice of using the word correctly by some further process. To understand the meaning is to know how to use it. But it is not that understanding is an internal state that can contingently be described in this relational way. That would still require that the state and the applications could be correctly connected. And that cannot be done. The connection between understanding and use is direct. Likewise, to intend to read the next chapter is just that, to intend to *read the next chapter*. It is not an independent state which requires connection to such an action.

Wittgenstein thus denies the possibility of a substantial and explanatory philosophical theory of content. He denies the need for, and the availability of, further explanation of meaning beyond those given by everyday resources. Philosophical attempts to dig deeper, to explain meaning by postulating hidden underlying processes that *must* also exist if meaning is possible, are doomed to failure. No such explanation of content is possible.

Wittgenstein's minimalist alternative account of content is thus descriptive rather than explanatory. As language-users we have a basic ability to learn how to use words and to self-ascribe the understanding of particular words without evidence. This ability is basic in the sense that it cannot be broken down into constituent components. Likewise, it is also a basic ability of language-users to form and to self-ascribe mental states that have normative consequences for subsequent speech and action. Content-laden mental states fit into a systematic normative and rational structure with which we make sense of ourselves and of others. They are holistically tied into the fabric of our lives through their normative consequences. This shows the grain of truth and also the inadequacy of saying that, according to Wittgenstein, mental states are behavioural states.

In Chapter 2, I shall set out Wittgenstein's destructive arguments directed against explanatory accounts of content such as representationalism. In Chapters

3 and 4, I shall describe Wittgenstein's minimalist positive characterisation. In Chapters 5 and 6, I shall compare Wittgenstein's attack on internal mental objects with Davidson's account of radical interpretation and anomalous monism.

Further Reading

A good general introduction to the philosophy of mind, that takes a contrasting view to this book, is Jackson and Braddon-Mitchell (1996). An historical introduction, that takes a similar perspective to this, is McCulloch (1995).

A good introduction to the representational theory of mind is Sterelny (1990). The clearest exposition of his own position given by Fodor is Fodor (1987). The teleological theory is introduced in a broader context of the philosophy of mind and epistemology in Papineau (1987). But the *locus classicus* is Millikan (1984).

CHAPTER 2

Wittgenstein's Destructive Criticisms of Explanations of Content

Every sign *by itself* seems dead. *What* gives it life? – In use it is *alive*. Is life breathed into it there? – Or is the *use* its life? (Wittgenstein 1953: §432)

This is the central question with which Wittgenstein wrestles in the *Philosophical Investigations*. What gives words their meaning and mental states their content? His response has two elements:

• An attack on all philosophical *explanations* of linguistic content – 'the life of signs' – and mental content. The philosophical explanation of content can go no further than everyday explanations of the meaning of words or what one meant.
• A minimalist positive characterisation of meaning and content based on the suggestion that the life of signs is simply their use.

This chapter will concentrate on the critical or negative element. I shall outline critical arguments drawn from two sections of Wittgenstein's *Investigations* which are destructive of attempts to *explain* thought and language. I shall then set out Wittgenstein's minimalist positive philosophy of content based on positive characterisations advanced in these two sections in the next two chapters.

Wittgenstein summarises (elsewhere) the form of explanation of which he is critical in the following way:

It seems that there are *certain definite* mental processes bound up with the working of language, processes through which alone language can function. I mean the processes of understanding and meaning. The signs of our language seem dead without these mental processes; and it might seem that the only function of the signs is to induce such processes, and that these are the things we ought really to be interested in . . . We are tempted to think that the action of language consists of two parts; an inorganic part, the handling of signs, and an organic part, which we may call understanding these signs, meaning them, interpreting them, thinking. (Wittgenstein 1958: 3)

This is the representationalist view, set out in the previous chapter, that linguistic meaning is derived from mental content. Wittgenstein criticises its assumption of explanatory priority: that language is to be explained through underlying mental states. But he also attacks the conception of mental states and mental processes upon which it relies. These are construed as internal, onto-logically independent, free-standing states of mind or body. This characterisation is supposed to apply to the states of understanding that are supposed to give signs their life and also to all other intentional mental states. As a result, representa-tionalism has to answer the following questions:

- What connects one's understanding of a word with its correct future application?
- What connects an intentional mental state (such as an expectation) with the event that satisfies it?

These questions are two facets of the more general question:

- What is the connection between thought or language and the world?

Wittgenstein argues that, once this explanatory approach to thought and language is adopted, all these questions become pressing but cannot be satisfactorily answered. I shall argue in the next two chapters that Wittgenstein's own philosophical minimalism refuses, by contrast, to treat these as substantial and thus refuses to give any substantial philosophical or explanatory answer.

In the two sections of the *Investigations* that are discussed in this chapter – the lengthy discussion of rules (§§139–239) and the briefer discussion of intentional mental states (§§428–65) – Wittgenstein focuses on the normativity inherent both in linguistic understanding and content-laden mental states. His criticisms of substantial explanations of content turn on the claim that such explanations fail to account for this essential normativity. For this reason, in the first of the two sections, Wittgenstein focuses on understanding *rules*, linguistic and otherwise. Rules are the most basic and most general expressions of normativity. Under-standing rules stands proxy for understanding linguistic content generally. But Wittgenstein's discussion of *mental* content also depends on its normativity. Thus, an important preliminary task here is to begin to clarify the connection between normativity and content generally, because this plays an important role in the discussion that follows.

1 The Connection Between Content and Normativity

Linguistic meaning has a normative dimension in that words can be used correctly and incorrectly. For any particular use of a word that has a meaning, it can be asked whether it has been used correctly or not. It can be asked whether it has been used in accordance with its meaning. If a word has a determinate meaning, then its correct applications are fixed by that meaning. The correct (and incorrect) applications are determined by the rule or rules that prescribe its correct use. This is not to advance an explanatory account of how the applications *flow from* the meaning. They do not. Rather the correct applications are constitutive of the meaning. But to know the meaning of the word is to know how to use it correctly and thus to know the rule or rules that govern its correct application:

> Suppose someone correctly understands the meaning of, say, 'Add 2'. Her understanding must be something with which, if she is aiming to put that understanding into practice and has reached '996, 998, 1000' in writing out the resulting series, only writing '1002' next will *accord.* (McDowell 1992: 40)

There is, however, a more general connection between content (linguistic and mental) and normativity that I will approach first through the role of truth. Consider assertion. One connection between content and truth consists in the fact that the content of an assertion can be given by stating the condition under which it would be true. This connection is the basis of the *disquotational theory of truth* which states that all there is to know about truth is captured by the disquotational schema: 'P' is true if and only if P. Whether or not such a modest conception of truth is satisfactory as a theory of truth, the schema can be used *at least* to show the connection between assertoric linguistic content and truth. This approach can be generalised to include assertoric *mental* content such as belief. The content of a belief can also be captured by stating the condition under which it is true:

> Meaning is normative. That is the starting point to our investigations. The normativity of meaning comes from the fact that the content of our utterance or thought is something to be assessed as true or false. In judgment we aim thoughts at truth and they are evaluated for whether they hit their target or fail. Without adding anything further about the nature of the concept of truth, this basic fact about meaning forces the following constraint. For any utterance or thought to possess meaning its meaning must be such that it demarcates between those conditions that would render the utterance true and those that would render it a failure in aiming for truth. If the meaning attributed to an utterance does not suffice to make this division upon the world, then it simply is not *meaning* that the utterance possesses. (Luntley 1991: 171–72)

In characterising meaning as normative however there is no need, to insist that meanings are *always* determinate. The division between truth and falsity may not be always clear-cut. Wittgenstein casts doubt on the idea that the rules for the use of words must have clear-cut application in every conceivable circumstance: '[A]re we to say that we do not really attach any meaning to this word, because we are not equipped with rules for every possible application of it?' (§80). But Wittgenstein's caution does not undermine the *general* connection between assertions having meaning and their demarcating between circumstances where they would be true and false. (Only where they do not have clear meaning do they not clearly demarcate circumstances.)

Given this general connection between the content of assertions or beliefs and truth, the issue which Wittgenstein focuses on in the *Investigations* is the connection between an assertion or belief and the state of affairs that determines whether it is true or false. (Throughout this book I shall talk of states of affairs, facts and events without presupposing any particular philosophical ontology.) How does a judgement normatively prescribe or determine some state of affairs? As Blackburn says:

> Our topic is the fact that terms of a language are governed by rules that determine what constitutes correct and incorrect application of them. I intend no particular theoretical implications by talking of rules here. The topic is that there is such a thing as the correct and incorrect application of a term, and to say that there is such a thing is no more than to say that there is truth and falsity. I shall talk indifferently of there being correctness and incorrectness, of words being rule-governed, and of their obeying principles of application. Whatever this is, it is the fact that distinguishes the production of terms from mere noise, and turns utterance into assertion – into the making of judgment. It is not seriously open to a philosopher to deny that, in this minimal sense, there is such a thing as correctness and incorrectness. The entire question is the conception of it that we have. (Blackburn 1984: 281–2)

One approach to the issue of normativity is to ask how false belief is possible. But, in fact, the normativity of content applies more broadly than to assertions, beliefs or judgements. The problem is also to account for: 'cognitive errors: misperceptions, false beliefs, confused concepts, bad inferences, unrealised intentions, and so forth . . . the distinction between the facts of cognition and the norms of cognition' (Millikan 1993: 3).

Wittgenstein emphasises the general importance of normativity to content as a whole and not just to assertoric contents. The content of the *wish* that *such-and-such* is *such-and-such*. Likewise, what is intended in the intention that *so-and-so* is *so-and-so*. Wittgenstein groups all these together as instances of the same general problem in §437 of the *Investigations*. There is a *normative* connection between a state and what the state is about or for. The state normatively *prescribes* what would satisfy it in advance. Hunger for an apple is not hunger for a punch in the stomach nor for a pear even if the first might stop one feeling hungry and the latter ease one's craving just as well. The connection between a state and what satisfies it is normative in the way that the connection between a rule and an application of it is normative. Rules and intentional mental states *determine* what accords with them.

In addition to the normativity implicit in assertoric contents and in intentional mental states more generally, contents can stand in normative relations to one another. One belief can justify, count against, be consistent with or contradict another. Contents can thus stand in 'normative liaisons' (Peacocke 1992: 126). I referred to this in the previous chapter as one aspect of the systematicity of content.

It may seem strange, however, to call these *descriptive* features of linguistic and mental content *normative* or *prescriptive*. In part that is merely a terminological objection. The problem of accounting for the condition, which an assertion, belief or an intention imposes on the world, remains however it is referred to. But the connection between this sense of normativity or prescriptivity and normativity more broadly derives from the idea of fidelity to mental or linguistic contents. Forming an intention, for example, imposes constraints on what we must do to satisfy it. Attempting to use words in accord with their meanings imposes constraints on the circumstances in which we should and should not use them:

> Our meaning things with our words requires that there be a right / seems right distinction for our use, else our use is not a meaningful use.
> So, if I utter the words
> (1) Grass is blue
> with their conventional meaning I am *obliged*, on being presented with a grass sample, to withdraw my utterance. For in uttering (1) I am bound by the meaning of the utterance to acknowledge that there are conditions which would render the utterance correct and conditions that would render it incorrect. That is just what meaning something with our words is like. We take on obligations. (Luntley 1991: 172)

I shall simply follow current philosophical usage, however, in referring to these central aspects of content as manifestations of its normativity. Any attempt to explain content – whether linguistic or mental – must thus be consistent with, and sustain, its normativity. Wittgenstein claims that attempts to *explain* content in terms of underlying mental or physical processes fail in just this way. The section on rules attacks the idea that understanding meaning comprises a mental state or process that mediates between the moment of understanding and subsequent use of words. The later section on intentional mental states attacks the idea that such mental states are connected to what satisfy them through internal mental intermediaries. I will discuss these sections in turn concentrating, in this chapter, on the critical arguments only.

2 Wittgenstein on Linguistic Content

What is the connection between understanding a word now and using it correctly later? How can the understanding of a rule that I arrive at at a particular time *determine* the correct responses that I should make over time? §§139–239 of the *Investigations* pursue this question by examining and rejecting explanations that we may be tempted to offer. These explanations attempt to explain the life of signs through mental or other accompaniments. Wittgenstein shows that all substantive accounts of what it is to understand a rule, which offer an explanation in terms of an underlying process, distort the relation between understanding and application. The postulated processes are shown to be neither necessary nor sufficient for making correct applications and, consequently, they cannot be what understanding comprises. The conclusion drawn at §201 is that understanding cannot be further explained other than as an ability to enact a practice and, in a way that will be further explicated below, should not be thought of as a *mental* process at all.

That such a general conclusion is drawn from the rejection of a handful of postulated alternative explanations may seem cause for concern. Might there not be some substantial explanation that Wittgenstein neglects to consider, making his general conclusion premature? I shall argue at the end of this chapter that these conclusions can be given strong support by a dilemma that any constitutive explanation of rule-following must face. While this does not establish that no substantial explanation could possibly be developed, it provides strong grounds for doubting this possibility. Wittgenstein summarises the problem to be explained as follows:

> But we *understand* the meaning of a word when we hear or say it; we grasp it in a flash, and what we grasp in this way is surely something different from the 'use' which is extended in time! (§138)

> [I]sn't the meaning of the word also determined by this use? And can these ways of determining meaning conflict? Can what we grasp *in a flash* accord with a use, fit or fail to fit it? And how can what is present to us in an instant, what comes before our mind in an instant, fit a *use*? (§139)

Having described the problem in this way, Wittgenstein examines, at some length, explanations that attempt to unify what is grasped in a flash with the temporally extended practice by postulating underlying processes. I shall divide the explanations criticised into:

- mental processes
- metaphysical processes
- and causal processes.

Such a taxonomy does not fit exactly the pattern of argument of these sections of the *Investigations*, but it will provide some guidance through considerations which run, now notoriously, 'criss cross in every direction'.

2.1 Mental processes

Wittgenstein begins by examining mental processes that might unite one's sudden understanding of a rule with the subsequent applications that one can make. A favourite candidate from the history of philosophy is to associate the meaning of a word with a mental image. It may seem that a suitably chosen picture, mental or otherwise, could uniquely determine an object. But this depends on applying particular rules of projection or interpretation to the picture. Changing those rules changes what is portrayed from, in Wittgenstein's example, a cube to a triangular prism. Thus, the determination of a particular object depends on presupposing further rules – rules of projection – and thus this model cannot explain the normativity of rules in general. Wittgenstein concedes that it might be the case that '[t]he picture of the cube did indeed *suggest* a certain use to us, but it was possible for me to use it differently' (§139). If the picture merely *suggests* a use, perhaps because I have not thought long enough about possible alternative interpretations, then this mere 'psychological compulsion' will not meet the normative constraint of understanding a meaning. It will not explicate what the correct application of a word *should* be: only the application that I am disposed, possibly erroneously, to make of it.

Given that the failure of mental images to meet the normative constraint is a result of the fact that the correct rules of projection have to be applied to it, a modification of the theory might be that the image should also depict its own projection rules. Wittgenstein suggests that this might take the form of an image of two cubes joined together by lines that denote how the cube in the image depicts a real cube (§141). Clearly, however, this modification provides no improvement on the first account because it depicts something only in virtue of some system of projection that has yet to be specified. Mental imagery provides no explanation of the normative constraint.

Wittgenstein concedes that it is quite natural to say that an application comes to mind, and it may also be the case that one imagines, or perhaps draws for oneself, the picture of two cubes just described. But the decisive test of what application comes to mind is subsequent practice:

> Can there be a collision between picture and application? There can, inasmuch as the picture makes us expect a different use, because people in general apply *this* picture like *this*. I want to say: we have here a *normal* case, and abnormal cases. (§141)

Wittgenstein goes on to suggest that the usefulness of language as a whole depends on our common reactions and our common response to training in, for example, the representational conventions used for pictures. I shall discuss the connection between language and a background of contingencies in the fourth chapter. The point here, however, is that although, as a matter of fact, humans often react to training in the use of pictorial representation in the same way, any diagrams that come to mind *could* be applied differently. Consequently, understanding cannot *consist* in any of these symbols coming before the mind. The correct use of these pictorial symbols stands in the same need of explanation as the rule that they were meant to explain.

From the standpoint of the late twentieth century, as opposed to the seventeenth century, the idea of explaining grasp of the meaning of a word as entertaining an associated mental image may seem a hopeless non-starter and hardly worth criticising. As we shall see shortly, however, Wittgenstein generalises this argument to more plausible theories of understanding. But it is also worth noting here that an imagistic theory is still an attractive account of imagination and one that Wittgenstein attacks for the reasons given here. Perhaps more paradoxically than this attack on the imagistic theory of understanding, Wittgenstein claims that *imagining* something does not consist in having an image of it (§§363–97). Again the imagistic intermediaries sever the normative connection between imagination and its objects.

Wittgenstein generalises his argument against an imagistic theory of understanding to the idea of entertaining symbols before the mind in any way (§§143–55). Consider the case of someone continuing a mathematical series. Wittgenstein argues that understanding what the numbers in the series should be cannot consist in having a formula in the mind, nor in saying to oneself that, for example, *the differences between successive numbers in the series should always be the same*. The mental formula and the sentence could be misapplied or misinterpreted. The *correct* use of such mental signs is in the same need of specification as the correct use of written signs. Thus, one cannot explain understanding the rule which governs the use of a word in the earlier example or the continuation of a written series here by translating the problem into the medium of mental signs and symbols.

This claim presents a prima-facie objection to representationalism. If understanding is identified with an internal state or mental representation, what determines the correct interpretation of that state? I shall consider three answers available to representationalism at the end of this chapter.

Having rejected the idea that understanding could comprise having a mental image or entertaining a mental sign, Wittgenstein goes on to consider invoking other mental phenomena, suggesting, in advance, that one should not think of understanding as a mental process at all (§154). He clarifies this rather startling claim by considering the case of reading and argues (from §156) that the ability to read aloud cannot be defined by any characteristic mental accompaniment but is an unmediated relation of text and speech only. The key argument for this claim is that the ability to read is justified on the grounds of repeated manifestable success. None of the mental phenomena that a learner may experience is relevant to this question because these phenomena are neither necessary nor sufficient for possessing the ability to read.

As a corollary of this claim, Wittgenstein argues that it makes no sense to ask which word exactly was the first word really read by a learner (§157). There is no precise boundary between occasional random error, which is consistent with a general ability to read, and too frequent or systematic error, which undermines the ascription of ability (cf. §143). Furthermore, it is, Wittgenstein argues, simply a prejudice to think that there *must be* a mental difference (conscious or unconscious) between an act of reading and an act of hitting upon the right word as a matter of luck (or, for that matter an act of shamming) (§§158–61). Such talk of a *mental* difference might mean a difference in the underlying *brain* processes or it might mean an *experiential* difference. I shall return to the arguments that Wittgenstein can offer against the former possibility later when considering his criticism of dispositionalism. Wittgenstein extends his argument to the relevance of any experiential difference through examination of the idea that one may 'feel a mechanism' when one reads.

He argues that one cannot define a felt mental mechanism more closely by, for example, invoking the idea of the *derivation* of sounds from symbols (from §162). All we mean by this is that the reader passes from the letters on the page to certain spoken words according to the rules she has been taught. Thus, the grounds for ascribing derivation are of the same standing as those for reading, which is what this epi-cycle was supposed to explicate. Nor can invoking derivation help clarify precisely when a learner has learned to read because there is also no precise boundary between systematic and random errors in derivation. The fact that one is able to justify the way one reads a word by citing its individual letters does not imply that one always feels a causal mechanism linking letters and spoken words. In normal circumstances, one would not consider any feeling of influence: 'Again, our eye passes over printed lines differently from the way it passes over arbitrary pothooks and flourishes . . .The eye passes, one would like to say, with particular ease, without being held up; and yet it doesn't *skid*' (§168).

I can now return to Wittgenstein's initially strange suggestion that we should not think of understanding as a *mental* process at all (§154). As the examination of reading illustrates, even if there were characteristic mental accompaniments to reading, reading itself could not comprise having those experiences because they would be neither necessary nor sufficient for meeting the normative constraint. The justification for the claim that someone has grasped a rule must be based upon their success in applying it. It cannot be based upon any mental experiences that they may have at the moment that light dawns. Such experiences can be indicative of understanding but are subservient to subsequent practical testing.

Before turning from Wittgenstein's examination of the idea of explicating rule-following in terms of accompanying mental experiences to his criticisms of

metaphysical accounts, it is worth mentioning preliminarily one further suggestion that Wittgenstein criticises briefly, and that is *dispositionalism*. Having argued
that grasp of the normative constraints of a rule cannot be explained by a
formula, or anything else, coming before the mind and before considering the
case of reading, Wittgenstein considers and rejects the dispositionalist idea that
understanding is a state, the *source* of correct applications. The arguments against
dispositionalism briefly offered at this stage are not compelling.

Wittgenstein first suggests that the proponent of this idea is really thinking of a
formula coming before the mind. This idea has already been rejected on the
grounds that the formula could be misapplied and the application made is still the
criterion of understanding (§146). In response, the interlocutor argues that, in
his own case, he does not infer from past performance what his understanding of
the formula was. This leads Wittgenstein to give a preliminary outline of his
positive account that understanding a rule is mastering a technique. But, in this
transition, Wittgenstein gives another brief characterisation of, and inconclusive
criticism of, dispositionalism:

> If one says that knowing the ABC is a state of the mind, one is thinking of a state of a
> mental apparatus (perhaps of the brain) by means of which we explain the *manifestations* of
> that knowledge. Such a state is called a disposition. But there are objections to speaking of a
> state of the mind here, inasmuch as there ought to be two different criteria for such a state: a
> knowledge of the construction of the apparatus, quite apart from what it does. (§149)

This rejection of dispositionalism is not, by itself, compelling. Why, it might be
argued, could one not infer the existence of the relevant disposition from the
applications of a rule that a person makes? Such an objection can be reinforced
by considering what other explanations of understanding are available that are
consistent with a rejection of a dualism of mind and matter. If human action is to
be explained in a way consistent with the rest of our description of the physical
world, then it seems that understanding must be explainable in terms of physical
states or properties. Dispositionalism is an apparently uncontentious way of
satisfying this requirement. It simply needs to assert that understanding is a
dispositional state with some physical realisation. Such a state might be realised
in different ways just as solubility can be differently realised. If an argument of this
sort can be given to show that understanding in general must be dispositional,
then the inference from a manifest ability to a corresponding disposition in a
particular case would be no more unfounded than any reasoning from observable
effects to unobservable causes in the physical sciences. If this were so, then
Wittgenstein's claim that one should be able to identify such dispositions by
criteria other than their effects would be an unreasonable condition.

One line of defence of Wittgenstein's position might run as follows. We may
legitimately infer a disposition simply from its manifestations, but using that

disposition to *explain* anything would be a non-explanation akin to notorious pseudo-explanations that invoke dormitive virtue. In other words, the knowledge of the construction of the apparatus required by Wittgenstein might not be required for inference to the disposition but for *explanation* by the disposition. This is not, however, a good defence. For one thing, if the argument that I sketched out above – that understanding must in general consist in a dispositional state – were sound, then there would be some general explanatory power in saying that understanding a particular rule corresponded to some particular dispositional state. This would be better than explanations of the dormitive-virtue type because there we have no general account of virtues at all, nor reason to believe that they may form part of a respectable theory of the world. Thus, this is not a good defence of Wittgenstein's requirement of a second criterion.

Wittgenstein does, however, provide a general argument to show that no such dispositional account of understanding can explain the normative constraint of rules. That argument also casts light on why it matters that the dispositionalist cannot provide an independent specification of the relevant disposition. The argument will become clearer, however, after examination of his criticisms of metaphysical processes.

Wittgenstein summarises the investigation so far in the following way:

> We are trying to get hold of the mental process of understanding which seems to be hidden behind those coarser and therefore more readily visible accompaniments. But we do not succeed; or, rather, it does not get as far as a real attempt. For even supposing I had found something that happened in all those cases of understanding, – why should *it* be the understanding? And how can the process of understanding have been hidden, when I said 'Now I understand' *because* I understood?! And if I say it is hidden – then how do I know what I have to look for? I am in a muddle. (§153)

2.2   Metaphysical processes

Having argued that grasp of a rule cannot be defined in terms of mental processes, Wittgenstein goes on to consider explaining understanding as grasp of a metaphysical standard. The idea explored is that, when a rule is understood, the potentially infinite number of correct applications have in some mysterious sense already been made. These can then be appealed to to define what the correct actual applications are. Actual applications are correct if they track these independent standards.

A Platonist approach may seem unpromising as a general account of meaning (although see below) but does have some intuitive support as a characterisation of mathematics. This is reflected in the general rejection of a Platonist construal of a Fregean theory of sense whilst there is wider acceptance – in some circles at least – of mathematical Platonism. In mathematics, the metaphor of the explorer seems far more apposite than that of the inventor. It seems, after all, that once a mathematical function is defined, subsequent mathematics merely discovers its remote consequences which exist independently of that process of discovery. This may prompt the thought that, when one acts in accord with a mathematical rule, it is as if one is merely repeating, in a bolder pencil, a move which already exists. Nevertheless, there are fundamental objections to Platonism as an explanation of these phenomena.

Wittgenstein deploys three main kinds of consideration against a Platonist conception of rules:

- The act of grasping a Platonic ideal or sense which determines the correct application of a rule or word is itself normative and thus requires explanation.
- No sense can be given to the idea of grasping the whole use of a word in a flash beyond the everyday idea that is just what requires explanation.
- No sense can be given to a formalism fixing its own application.

These criticisms of mathematical Platonism are also directly relevant to the discussion of content. Because they focus on the inability of Platonism to account for the normativity of grasping a rule, they also apply to an intuitive account of natural-kind words. On this picture, words for natural kinds are correctly applied if they track classifications that somehow already exist. They, also, repeat in bolder pencil natural divisions that are independent of human judgment. Because of this underlying similarity with the mathematical case, I will, somewhat unusually, refer to this position also as a form of Platonism.

Wittgenstein begins his exploration of the attraction and difficulties of a Platonist explanation of understanding a rule using the example of continuing a series. Suppose that someone is being taught by example. If, having counted in twos successfully to 1000, the learner continues 1004, 1008, 1012, then this is a failure to continue correctly. The learner is, however, following a rule of sorts, a 'bent' rule that deviates from the rule intended at 1000:

> In such a case we might say, perhaps: It comes natural to this person to understand our order with our explanations as *we* should understand the order: 'Add 2 up to 1000, 4 up to 2000, 6 up to 3000 and so on.'
>   Such a case would present similarities with one in which a person naturally reacted to the gesture of pointing with the hand by looking in the direction of the line from finger-tip to wrist, not from wrist to finger-tip. (§185)

We may find such 'bent' rules unnatural, but this does not preclude the possibility that a learner might respond to our instructions in this way. Given that the series of natural numbers has no limit, it appears that we can never ensure that a learner has grasped the right rule by establishing his competence within any finite range of numbers. Thus it appears that the rule '+2' lies beyond our powers of explanation. It is this that leads to the mistaken idea that the learner has to *guess* what the examples are gesturing towards (§§208–10). This is a picture in which explanation always communicates less than the complete rule – modelled on the complete infinite extension perhaps – which could only be grasped by God. (This example of explanation also presupposes that the examples given cannot simply *manifest* normativity. Instead the norm must be inferred or guessed. This is an important thread to which I shall return in later chapters.)

While the example of the deviant rule-follower helps motivate a metaphysical idea of rules, it also shows why such an explanation cannot work. The challenge to the metaphysical account is to explain how a metaphysical standard containing all the correct numbers in the series '+2' could help explicate the normative constraint of the rule. But the problem is that there is no account of how the Platonist standard is to be used or applied that does not beg the key question.

The problem is that the learner must grasp the *right* mathematical series in the metaphysical realm (or actual worldly extension in the case of empirical concepts). The deviant learner described above, for example, has grasped a rule, but not the right one. One cannot, however, ensure that the learner picks the right rule by specifying further rules – perhaps most tempting is the rule that the units always follow the sequence '0, 2, 4, 6, 8' – because this just pushes the question back to how we can specify that rule rather than one that changes at 1000. Because it is logically possible that the learner could respond to any specifications of the rule of addition, or any examples of the series, in a deviant way, such an account also owes further explanation of what constitutes the right metaphysical standard.

Wittgenstein's criticism is not that there would be something wrong with a Platonist realm. Nor is the argument based upon the epistemological difficulty of filling out how we could be sensitive to such standards at all. It is not concerned with what sensory organ is involved. It is, rather, that such standards – even if they could exist in a special realm – are by themselves insufficient to explicate normativity. Only once there were also an account of normativity could the notion of correctly specifying a standard be analysed and only then could an epistemology be sketched in. But once there were an account of normativity, there would be no need for the Platonist account.

In attacking Platonism, Wittgenstein is not denying that rules *determine* what applications should be made. That would be to deny the central feature of rules: that they are normative and prescriptive. What Wittgenstein objects to is a particular explanatory theory of this normative constraint: that correctness consists in tracking a metaphysical standard. The interface between human practice and Platonic ideal raises all the problems that Platonism was supposed to answer.

Wittgenstein goes on to consider the response that what determines the correct number at a distant point in the series is the linguistic specification of the rule together with *how it was meant*:

> 'But I already knew, at the time when I gave the order, that he ought to write 1002 after 1000.' – Certainly; and you can also say you *meant* it then; only you should not let yourself be misled by the grammar of the words 'know' and 'mean'. For you don't want to say that you thought of the step from 1000 to 1002 at that time – and even if you did think of this step, still you did not think of other ones. When you said 'I already knew at the time . . .' that meant something like: 'If I had been asked what number should be written after 1000, I should have replied "1002" '. And that I don't doubt. This assumption is rather of the same kind as: 'If he had fallen into the water then, I should have jumped in after him'. (§187)

This passage provides no deeper *explanation* of the fact that the instructor should and would have replied '1002' rather than '1008'. It merely repeats the characterisation of rules that has been assumed from the start. They are normative and prescribe what the correct applications should be. It does not, for example, support a dispositional account of understanding (to which I shall return shortly). Because the instructor understands the rule, he knows how to continue the sequence. The test of what the instructor meant is the way he applies the rule in practice and in sincere counter-factual claims. Invoking the way that the formula was meant provides no help in *explicating* normativity. It merely reiterates it.

This example helps reinforce the motivation for treating linguistic meaning and mental content in the same way. It seems that explanations of rules underdetermine what the correct applications are. A tempting way to try to prevent this underdetermination from implying that rules or meanings are indeterminate is to invoke what was *meant* by the teacher or the rule that was *intended*. One invokes, in other words, the determinacy of mental content to explain how linguistic content is determinate. This strategy would be successful if the determinacy of mental content could simply be presupposed. But, in fact, it presents parallel difficulties (cf. §205). How can the intention that a speaker has at a particular time determine how he should use a word in the future? Without a separate answer to that question, mental content stands in the same need of explication as linguistic content.

The attraction of assuming that Platonism must be the explanation of the fact that, when one understands the meaning of a word or the principle behind a mathematical series, one understands the whole use or series is brought out in the following passage:

> 'It is as if we could grasp the whole use of the word in a flash.' Like *what*? – Can't the use – in a certain sense – be grasped in a flash? And in *what* sense can it not? – The point is, that it is as if we could 'grasp it in a flash' in yet another and much more direct sense than that. – But

have you a model for this? No. It is just that this expression suggests itself to us. As the result of the crossing of different pictures. (§191)

You have no model of this superlative fact, but you are seduced into using a super-expression. (It might be called a philosophical superlative.) (§192)

The idea here is that Platonism is supported by our experience. When we suddenly understand the meaning of a word we have a general understanding of how it is used. Thus, it seems as though the whole use of the word must come to mind. There is something right about this claim, but it does not support Platonism. If one could not subsequently use the word correctly, one could not have understood it. So, in one sense, the whole use is grasped in a flash. But this is not because every application flashes before the mind. The test of whether one has grasped the whole use is not what goes on in the moment of under-standing but one's subsequent abilities.

Having rejected this strategy for explicating a metaphysical account, Witt-genstein considers an alternative. This is to replace the idea that the mind has already surveyed the full extent of the rule with the idea that the symbolic expression of a rule determines its applications itself. Such a picture is particularly compelling in the case of arithmetic where it seems that, once a function is defined, the correct results for given arguments are automatically determined.

Wittgenstein compares this idea with the movement of an ideal machine with perfectly rigid parts depicted in a diagram. The freedom of movement of the cogs and wheels of the machine can be derived from the diagram, and the motion appears to be much more determined than any real machine because we can say that, if one cog is turned one way, then another one *must* move in such-and-such a way. It is as if, Wittgenstein suggests, the motion, or the possibility of the particular way of moving, is already queerly present in the symbolism. But what, he asks, is the possibility of motion so represented?

It is not the *movement*, but it does not seem to be the mere physical conditions for moving either – as, that there is play between socket and pin . . .The possibility of a movement is, rather, supposed to be like a shadow of the movement itself. But do you know of such a shadow? (§194)

We have no model for the presence of the motion other than the way we *use* such models and derive how the wheel should turn. What enables us to derive the conclusion that the motion *must* be such-and-such is that we do not consider, or depict the possibility of, the parts melting together or shearing. The correct use of such diagrams employs principles of geometry and motion and not, for example, principles governing adhesion or fragility. This is one important way in which the ideal machine differs from a real machine. What is more important, however, is that, because we use the diagram of a machine to illustrate rules of motion, we distinguish between correct and incorrect derivations in respect of accord, or not, with those rules. If, by contrast, a real machine breaks down, its motion, or lack of it, may be unfortunate but is not *incorrect*. Thus, the diagram of the ideal machine determines its motion only in so far as we use it to illustrate rules of kinematics. It cannot form the basis of an explanation of rules.

2.3   Causal processes

The misunderstanding of the diagram of an ideal machine runs together two things: the causal processes that govern the autonomous motion of actual machines and the rules we employ when deriving possible motion using an idealised schematic representation of a machine. Causal processes cannot, however, form the model for the normative relation between a rule and its applications, and it is to these that I shall now turn.

Wittgenstein returns (§§218–21) to the idea that, when one understands a rule, all the steps have already been taken with the second metaphor of the rule as rails stretching off into the infinite distance. Such a comparison, like that with a machine, confuses causal and logical determination. The rails lead rolling-stock onwards by a causal process that may break down if there is a heavy fall of leaves. Nothing, however, can upset what the correct applications of a rule should be because the rule sets the normative standard against which correctness is measured. Thus, the link between a rule and its correct applications cannot be explained by a causal relation. It is important to stress that this distinction does not depend on questioning the reliability of, for example, real electronic calculators. The central point is that it is the rule that sets the standard of correctness against which we can assess the reliability of a calculator, not the other way round.

I shall now return to Wittgenstein's attack on dispositionalism. The explicit argument against dispositionalism, described earlier, was unconvincing. Wittgenstein claimed that one could not postulate dispositions to explain under-standing if one lacked other criteria by which to individuate them. But one might object that there were good general reasons to believe that understanding must be realised by some physical states and processes which cause successful manifestations under suitable conditions. There might thus be general reasons to believe that understanding is a dispositional state. If so, reasoning from effect to cause to specify a particular disposition would be no more problematical than such reasoning is in the physical sciences. Thus, it seemed that Wittgenstein had not provided an argument against a dispositionalist account of understanding. Having now looked at Wittgenstein's other criticisms, his response to the dispositionalist can now be re-assessed. This will enable conclusions to be drawn more generally about Wittgenstein's attack on explanatory accounts of rule-following.

As an explanation of understanding rules, dispositions face the same dilemma as the ideal machine. Either dispositions are linked to unfolding applications in the way that a formula determines which numbers satisfy it, or in the way that a mechanism causally determines its subsequent motion. If it is the former, then no explication has been offered because, as has been argued earlier, a formula is open to misapplication in the way that any sign is. If it is the latter, then it fails to explain the normative constraint that a rule establishes. If the cogs in an adding machine fuse together, then it no longer gives the correct response when viewed as an adding machine. Similarly, any disposition, which is identified with a particular physical mechanism but provisionally correlated with a rule, could deviate from that rule. If dispositions are linked to applications by causal processes, then they cannot sustain the normative link between a rule an its applications. If, on the other hand, the identity of the disposition is specified by saying that it corresponds to *whatever* mechanisms are needed to track the rule, then no explanation of the content of the rule has been given.

Wittgenstein's negative claims about understanding rules in general and meanings more specifically can now be summarised in the following brief list. Understanding cannot consist in:

- any sign or symbol coming before the mind. That would no more determine the application that is made than the written symbol would. The method of application of the sign or symbol cannot itself be symbolically or pictorially portrayed without vicious regress.
- any experience or feeling. Those are neither necessary nor sufficient for making the correct application.
- the presence of a dispositional state that leads causally to the correct applications of the rule. Causal mediation cannot explain the normative constraint that a rule imposes on its applications.
- the disposition to make the *correct* responses by whatever causal process. Nothing is explained by such a claim because the only available standard of correctness is accord with the rule, and grasp of this is what was supposed to be explained.
- some mysterious process of grasping an abstract standard or an already existing sequence of correct applications. There is no way of specifying the correct sequence nor the correct application of it.

None of these processes or states, according to Wittgenstein, can explain how dead signs can be injected with meaning because none of them can explain the normativity of meaning. Linguistic content cannot be explained as resulting from more basic mental acts or processes. Wittgenstein himself diagnoses the problem that his critical arguments expose as follows:

This was our paradox: no course of action could be determined by a rule, because every course of action can be made out to accord with the rule. The answer was: if everything can be made out to accord with the rule, then it can also be made out to conflict with it. And so there would be neither accord nor conflict here.

It can be seen that there is a misunderstanding here from the mere fact that in the course of our argument we give one interpretation after another; as if each one contented us at least for a moment, until we thought of yet another standing behind it. (§201)

The mistaken first move is to think that signs must derive their meaning from an inner act of interpretation. That inner act is supposed to explain what connects a word to its correct applications. But, once that assumption is made, the original problem resurfaces for the normativity of the interpretation. The mental intermediaries, which were supposed to explain the connection between the meaning of a word or rule and its correct applications, also need interpretation to fix their meaning. This quickly leads to a vicious regress.

The key problem for interpretational explanations of meaning can be expressed as a dilemma:

- An explanation of content cannot merely presuppose the very notion it attempts to explain by, for example, presupposing the content of an interpretation of a mental sign or symbol.
- On the other hand, it must sustain the normativity of content. And there are reasons to be pessimistic about the abilities of imagistic or causal theories to meet that challenge.

I shall return to the issue of the general application of Wittgenstein's negative result at the end of this chapter. But first I shall turn to the arguments that Wittgenstein advances concerning the explanation of mental content more generally. It is worth noting initially that the arguments advanced against an interpretational theory of understanding meaning would also apply to interpretational theories of mental content more generally. Wittgenstein makes an explicit connection between meaning and intention in the middle of the rule-following considerations. It might otherwise be thought that the meaning of a word could be explained as the way it was intended to be used. But Wittgenstein rejects this strategy in the following passage:

'But it is just the queer thing about *intention*, about the mental process, that the existence of a custom, of a technique, is not necessary to it. That, for example, it is imaginable that two people should play chess in a world in which otherwise no games existed; and even that they should begin a game of chess – and then be interrupted.'

But isn't chess defined by its rules? And how are these rules present in the mind of the person who is intending to play chess? (§205)

In accord with this passage, Wittgenstein goes on to devote a later section to arguing that mental content generally cannot be explicated through underlying mental processes. I shall now turn to the critical arguments deployed in that section.

3 Wittgenstein on Mental Content

While §§139–239 criticise any attempt to explain how understanding linguistic meaning is possible by invoking underlying acts of interpretation, §§428–65 attack a similar model of other content-laden mental states. The question that drives the earlier section is: what is the connection between one's, possibly sudden, understanding of a word and its subsequent application? The question here is: what connects an expectation and what subsequently fulfils it? Wittgenstein again argues that no explanation which invokes mental intermediaries can succeed in regaining the essential normative connection between content-laden states and their fulfilment conditions.

The central theme of the 'chapter' of the *Investigations* between §428 and §465, concerned with mental content, is set out at the start:

> 'This queer thing, thought' – but it does not strike us as queer when we are thinking. Thought does not strike us as mysterious while we are thinking, but only when we say, as it were retrospectively: 'How was that possible?' How was it possible for thought to deal with the very object *itself*? We feel as if by means of it we had caught reality in our net. (§428)

The key question is how mental content is possible, how thought can be *about* something. Wittgenstein suggests a comparison and a contrast between the life of thought and the apparent deadness of signs:

> 'Put a ruler against this body; it does not say that the body is of such-and-such a length. Rather is it in itself – I should like to say – dead, and achieves nothing of what thought achieves.' (§430)

> 'There is a gulf between an order and its execution. It has to be filled by the act of understanding.'
> 'Only in the act of understanding is it meant that we are to do THIS. The *order* – why, that is nothing but sounds, ink-marks. –' (§431)

> Every sign *by itself* seems dead. *What* gives it life? – In use it is *alive*. Is life breathed into it there? – Or is the *use* its life? (§432)

The suggestion, put in the mouth of his interlocutor, is that while signs in themselves lack meaning, thoughts have intrinsic content or intentionality. It is this idea that encourages the thought that an order, for example – whether spoken or written – has no meaning, makes no specific command itself. It is the order only *as it is understood* or entertained in thought that has content and that calls for a specific action to be undertaken. The interlocutor's approach is an example of the first approach to explanatory priority of mental and linguistic content described in the first chapter. Linguistic meaning is assumed to be of secondary importance and to be explained as deriving from mental content. It is this picture that encourages the idea, also discussed in the rule-following considerations, that explanations of what one means succeed by encouraging the listener to *guess* the essential content which cannot itself be conveyed in any finite explanation. That misleading thought is reiterated here:

> When we give an order, it can look as if the ultimate thing sought by the order had to remain unexpressed, as there is always a gulf between an order and its execution. Say I want someone to make a particular movement, say to raise his arm. To make it quite clear, I do the movement. This picture seems unambiguous till we ask: how does he know that *he is to make that movement?* – How does he know at all what use he is to make of the signs I give him, whatever they are? – Perhaps I shall now try to supplement the order by means of further signs, by pointing from myself to him, making encouraging gestures, etc. Here it looks as if the order were beginning to stammer.
>
> As if the signs were precariously trying to produce understanding in us . . . (§433)

This is the dismal result of the explanatory strategy that Wittgenstein rejects earlier with the comment that it is a misunderstanding to explain linguistic content by giving one interpretation after another. But that left the question of what the connection between understanding and practice comprises. How can we understand at an earlier time the demands that a practice makes at a later time? Wittgenstein continues here 'But if we now understand [the signs], by what token do we understand?' (§433).

Even if the distinction between dead signs and living thoughts were useful, an account of what gives thought its content, its connection with the world, would still be needed. If signs are given life by acts of understanding, then the question: what gives understanding its content? requires an answer. Explaining linguistic content via mental content is only satisfactory if an independent account can be given of the latter. Because Wittgenstein's discussion emphasises the common problems and leads to the same resolution of both issues, he equates the two issues here:

> A wish seems already to know what will or would satisfy it; a proposition, a thought, what makes it true – even when that thing is not there at all! Whence this *determining* of what is not yet there? This despotic demand? (§437)

Content-laden mental states share with rules an essential normativity. They *prescribe* what would and what would not fulfil them. Wittgenstein tentatively suggests, via his interlocutor, that this might be expressed by saying that they prescribe what would *satisfy* them. Indeed, this is one of the general terms I have used so far to express what might also be called their fulfilment conditions. But adopting this terminology is not in itself a solution to the problem of what the connection is between a state and what satisfies it. We have no general model of what it is for something (whether a mental state or something entirely different) to be satisfied by something. Nor can what would satisfy the state be defined as what would give rise to a *feeling* of satisfaction in the person in that state. One may be satisfied by something other, and perhaps better, than that for which one wished. Equally '[p]erhaps I should not have been satisfied if my wish had been satisfied' (§441). So the question remains: what is the connection between a mental state and what satisfies it?

Wittgenstein takes as an example the connection between an expectation and what is expected. The problem to be resolved is how there can be a connection between a state of mind and an expected but real explosion: 'I see someone pointing a gun and say "I expect a report". The shot is fired. – Well, that was what you expected; so did that report somehow already exist in your expectation?' (§442). There seems to be something intuitively wrong in the suggestion that the noise already existed in one's mind. How can a shot, which is an objective event in the world order, also be a part of my thought processes?

On the other hand, if the shot itself were not contained in the expectation then the connection between the two would be undermined:

> Or is it just that there is some other kind of agreement between your expectation and what occurred; that the noise was not contained in your expectation, and merely accidentally supervened when the expectation was being fulfilled? – But no, if the noise had not occurred, my expectation would not have been fulfilled; the noise fulfilled it; it was not an accompaniment of the fulfilment like a second guest accompanying the one I expected. (§442)

The alternative which is considered and rejected is that the expectation is not directly satisfied by the shot itself – because it is hard to see how the shot can be part of the content of the anticipatory state – but by an experience that simultaneously occurs when the shot occurs. This might be a feeling of satisfaction or relief, for example. But the phenomenon to be explained is that the *shot* was expected and satisfied the expectation. No surrogate, such as a feeling of satisfaction, would have done. But, on this model, it seems merely accidental that the *shot* occurs when the expectation is satisfied. Any explanation of the link between mental states and the worldly events which relies on such an intermediary will not work. This reiterates the negative conclusions of the discussion of rules.

If a real event cannot itself exist in an expectation, and if a purely indirect connection mediated by sensations fails to sustain the normativity of the connection, then can there be third option? Elsewhere he suggests that what we expect is not the actual event, but a shadow of the event, the next best thing to the event. But this leaves the problem of explaining the connection between the shadow and event:

> Was the thing about the event that was not in the expectation too an accident, an extra provided by fate? – But then what was *not* an extra? Did something of the shot already occur in my expectation? – Then what *was* extra? for wasn't I expecting the whole shot? (§442)

The problem is again that, if the content of the expectation is explained by invoking anything less than the real event, this severs the normative connection between event and object of expectation. That relation cannot be mediated by any third thing, any internal object, such as a 'shadow' of a shot.

There is a further difficulty with any account of the contents of mental states which invoke 'internal' objects. Consider the case where an expectation is *not* satisfied:

> 'The report was not so loud as I had expected.' – 'Then was there a louder bang in your expectation?' (§442)

If this is the case, then a frustrated expectation will require a *comparison* of the two noises: the internal and the external. How is such a comparison to be made? Given the central role of normativity for content, what are the standards of correctness in this comparison?

Wittgenstein compares this case with the case of imagination to expose a further difficulty present even when a mental state is satisfied:

> 'The red which you imagine is surely not the same (not the same thing) as the red which you see in front of you; so how can you say that it is what you imagined?' (§443)

The problem that his interlocutor expresses is premised on the idea that the content of imagination is itself an internal object. Given this assumption, it seems that a mental state could never be fulfilled because the internal object cannot be the very same object as the external object and so the latter cannot satisfy the mental state that has the former as its object.

This is a general problem of identifying content-laden mental states with internal states. Once this identification is made, it severs the relation between these states and their fulfilment conditions or grammatical objects. The way Wittgenstein highlights the problem in this case is by granting that the internal object of a mental state has content – it really is an image of redness – but then questioning how this content can match up to the external object which is the state's proper content. While the strategy is different, the moral is the same as that of the discussion of understanding rules. Once understanding is identified with an internal state, its normative connection to future applications cannot be recovered.

4 The Generality of Wittgenstein's Critical Arguments

I began this chapter with a quotation from Wittgenstein in which he suggests that we are tempted to think that the action of language consists of two parts: an inorganic part, the handling of signs; and an organic part, interpreting them. His criticism of that picture can now be summarised as follows. If content or life is injected into otherwise meaningless or dead signs by inner interpretations, those interpretations must themselves sustain the normative relations constitutive of meaning. This form of explanation then faces a dilemma. If the content of the interpretations is simply presupposed, then no explanatory progress is made. If, on the other hand, the interpretations are individuated, not by their contents but as states of mind with imagistic, syntactic or causal intrinsic properties, then their normative relations cannot be reconstructed. An internal state, described in terms of its intrinsic properties, imposes no normative consequences on future states or acts and thus itself stands in need of further interpretation.

This objection is raised against a picture of language. But it also applies to content-laden mental states in general because, as Wittgenstein emphasises, these states are normative. They prescribe what should satisfy or fulfil them. If mental states are identified with *internal* states of the mind or body, characterisable by non-relational intrinsic properties, then the normative relations that these states have to the facts or events that satisfy them cannot be reconstructed. In the later section on intentional states, Wittgenstein makes this point in a slightly different way. He argues that, if intermediaries are postulated to explain the connection between an intentional mental state and what satisfies it, the right relation between these breaks down. If the content of an expectation is explained by reference to any inner object or process, then it will not count as an expectation of a worldly event because the inner object and worldly event are not the same.

These two discussions are reinforcing in this way. The first argues that one cannot explain the life of signs by accompanying mental acts or processes because those acts stand in just the same need of explanation. The second argues more generally that what is at fault is a common picture of content-laden mental states as internal states linked to what they are about by mental processes. Wittgenstein rejects explanations that use mental intermediaries in both cases. Neither the link between a rule and its application (or the meaning of a word and its correct use) nor that between an intentional mental state and its fulfilment can be provided by further mental or physiological processing. Life is not breathed into dead signs by intrinsically meaningful intentional states, themselves connected to the world by underlying mental processes.

Wittgenstein summarises this result with the following bald claim: 'The mistake is to say that there is anything that meaning something consists in'

(Wittgenstein 1981: §16). This stark summary of Wittgenstein's attack on reductionist explanations of content encourages an objection that may be expressed like this. How can a universal negative conclusion be drawn from the rejection of only a handful of explanations? This is a good question. But the first stage in answering it is to clarify what precisely it is that Wittgenstein denies. This will pre-empt discussion in the next chapter.

One interpretation of Wittgenstein's discussion of understanding rules is that he attacks and undermines our pre-philosophical conception of rules and thus, by extension, of mental and linguistic content. This is the claim made explicitly by Kripke and implicitly by Wright. According to such a reading, Wittgenstein's account of rule-following is a sceptical attack on meaning and mental content as we ordinarily understand them. These notions have instead to be given merely a sceptical ersatz reconstruction. The exegesis that I have given so far of the arguments that Wittgenstein deploys provides no support for that reading. Furthermore, I shall argue in the next chapter that, whatever its exegetical fidelity, it is untenable.

Instead, as I have already suggested, what Wittgenstein is really denying is not the reality of rules or content but explanatory philosophical theories of them. He is not denying that I can grasp a rule that determines correct applications, but rather denying all those theories that explain this by saying that that ability can be broken down into underlying processes. Such theories answer the questions raised in §139 by proposing a mechanism underlying the phenomena of rule-following, and Wittgenstein denies that any can be successful. Thus, in saying that it is a mistake to say that there is anything that meaning something consists in, Wittgenstein is denying not that there is such a thing as meaning (as we ordinarily conceive it) but rather that meaning something can be *reduced* to something else. He denies that rules, and thus content, can be given a reductionist analysis or explanation. Thus, the question here to be assessed is not whether Wittgenstein has successfully demolished the very idea of content, which would be a form of philosophical scepticism. But rather, has Wittgenstein successfully shown that no form of reductionism about meaning is possible?

What makes this question pressing is that Wittgenstein bases his conclusion on just a handful of negative arguments. This fact about the structure of the *Investigations* invites the speculation that there might be a way of reducing content that Wittgenstein simply fails to consider. The mere possibility of such a circumstance casts doubt on the strength of Wittgenstein's claim here. Representationalists will say that Wittgenstein simply did not consider their recent proposals for the reduction of content to causal or teleological notions. I shall return to the question of the full scope of the arguments having first looked at their consequences for representationalism.

5 Wittgensteinian Arguments Against Representationalism

Two key representational claims are undermined by Wittgenstein's arguments. These are that:

- There is a distinction between intrinsic and derived intentionality.
- Mental content is explained by the 'possession' of internal mental representations.

I shall examine in turn Wittgenstein's arguments against these claims.

5.1   Objections to the distinction between intrinsic and derived intentionality

Wittgenstein has two kinds of objection to the distinction between intrinsic and derived intentionality:

- Once the distinction has been drawn, the content of items which are supposed to possess merely *derived* intentionality is threatened.
- The content of items with *intrinsic* intentionality cannot be filled out and remains a mystery.

Thus, the consequence of Wittgenstein's criticisms is not that meaning is always intrinsic or always derived but rather that that very distinction has no application.

The intuitive force of the distinction between derived and intrinsic intentionality is this. Signs, utterances and behaviour seem to require convention-governed interpretation. By contrast, thought requires no interpretation. Thus, signs possess merely derived intentionality and thought possesses intrinsic or natural intentionality. This corresponds to the division of language into organic and inorganic parts quoted above.

But the claim that signs have always to be interpreted leads to devastating consequences for the shared status of meaning. The problem is highlighted in §433, quoted earlier:

> When we give an order, it can look as if the ultimate thing sought by the order had to remain unexpressed, as there is always a gulf between an order and its execution. Say I want someone to make a particular movement, say to raise his arm. To make it quite clear, I do the movement. This picture seems unambiguous till we ask: how does he know that *he is to make that movement?* – How does he know at all what use he is to make of the signs I give him, whatever they are? – Perhaps I shall now try to supplement the order by means of

further signs, by pointing from myself to him, making encouraging gestures, etc. Here it looks as if the order were beginning to stammer. (§433)

The problem is that if signs always require interpretation – if meaning has always to be read into them – then the sharing of meaning is at best a lucky guess and at worst impossible. The only resources available for sharing or explaining what one means are more signs, all of which could be interpreted in multiple ways. Each explanation will require further explanation of what it means, leading to an infinite regress. The full meaning of one's words is never, on this picture, available to others and has always to be guessed. What is available – what is actually given in explanations of meaning – is always something less than the full privately understood meaning. (I shall return to what is wrong with this picture in Chapter 4.)

There is a reciprocal difficulty with the other side of this distinction: intrinsic intentionality. The problem is filling out what it is that is understood. The representationalist *explanation* of intrinsic intentionality is discussed below. But there is a preliminary problem in filling out what it is that is supposed to be explained. The other side of the thought that explanations of what one intrinsically means, using the derived intentionality of signs, always fall short, is that one knows oneself something more than one can explain: 'Isn't there a deeper explanation; or mustn't at least the *understanding* of the explanation be deeper? – Well, have I myself a deeper understanding? Have I *got* more than I give in explanation?' (§209).

The problem in substantiating the thought that one does have a deeper understanding than one can explain is precisely the problem with which the discussion of rules began. Understanding the meaning of a word is connected with understanding how to apply it. If the model of private understanding is to be filled out, it will require a way of 'unpacking' one's own understanding in a way that could *not* be given to others because '[e]very explanation which I can give myself I give to him too' (§210). But the result of the discussion of rules is that there is no private token which one could have in mind – perhaps in a flash of understanding – that could determine the correct application of a word in this way. Thus, there is no reason to believe that one can have a deeper understanding of one's own meaning that must be inaccessible to others.

5.2   Objections to internal mental representations

In addition to distinguishing between intrinsic and derived intentionality, representationalism goes on to *explain* the intrinsic intentionality of mental states through the intrinsic intentionality of internal mental representations. It is important to note that this is supposed to be an explanatory strategy. The content of internal mental representations explains the content of mental states which are themselves normally (and more properly) ascribed to whole persons. If it is to be a successful explanatory strategy, representationalism requires some further explanation of what gives mental representations their content. If not, the claim that when someone is in a mental state there is a mental representation in them, will simply exchange one form of words for another.

There are three strategies available to representationalism to explain the intrinsic intentionality of mental representations. It can claim that:

- Mental representations are themselves symbols and thus require interpretation.
- Mental representations do not require interpretation because they are contents rather than symbolic vehicles of content.
- Mental representations do not require interpretation because they are self-interpreting symbols in the manner of hard-wired computer languages.

I will consider Wittgenstein's criticisms of each of these in turn.

5.2.1   Mental representations are symbolic and require interpretation

Wittgenstein's arguments against any explanation of mental content which relies on the interpretation of internal symbolic representation have already been discussed at length above. This is the picture against which much of §§139–239 is directed. Like the criticism of an interpretative account of signs discussed above, the key criticism is that it initiates an infinite regress. If content is encoded in internal symbols which require interpretation, the correct method of interpretation will also somehow have to be encoded. But, on the model that encoded content requires interpretation, this can only be through a further mental representation which, in turn, requires interpretation.

It may seem unlikely that any theory would fall to such an obvious regress. But I will argue below that the teleological theory of representation has elements of an interpretational theory and thus begs the key question.

5.2.2   Mental representations do not require interpretation because they just are contents

Because the strategy of explaining the intrinsic intentionality of mental states using mental representations which require interpretation leads to a vicious regress, representationalism can attempt to escape that regress by denying the need for interpretation. There are two available tactics: to invoke self-interpreting symbols or to claim that mental representations are not symbols in need of interpretation but, what would be the result of interpretation, contents themselves. I shall consider the latter briefly here and the former at greater length below.

In principle, representationalism might claim that mental representations do not require interpretation because they are not themselves signs or symbols but the *contents* of signs or symbols. The internal states postulated are not the vehicles of contents but the content themselves. According to this version of representationalism, the content of beliefs is explained not by the interpretation of internal states but simply by their possession. Consequently, the regress argument about interpretation can be side-stepped.

But this strategy will not do. Representationalism is supposed to be an explanatory strategy that explains the mental states of whole persons through the contents of internal mental representations. Simply invoking internal surrogates for content provides no insight into how mental content is possible. It simply reiterates the Cartesian picture of the mind as a container of ideas without adding anything to it.

The temptation to think that mental contents are internal representations that do not require interpretation is captured by Wittgenstein in a passage that compares internal representations or the internal objects of mental states both to 'shadows of facts' which require no interpretation because they are the 'last interpretations':

> [W]hat we expect is not the fact, but a shadow of the fact; as it were, the next thing to the fact . . .
>
> We imagine the shadow to be a picture the intention of which *cannot be questioned*, that is, a picture which we don't interpret in order to understand it, but which we understand without interpreting it. Now there are pictures of which we should say that we interpret them, that is, translate them into a different kind of picture, in order to understand them; and pictures of which we should say that we understand them immediately, without any further interpretation . . . The shadow, as we think of it, is some sort of a picture; in fact, something very much like an image which comes before our mind's eye; and this again is something not unlike a painted representation in the ordinary sense. A source of the idea of the shadow certainly is the fact that in some cases saying, hearing, or reading a sentence brings images before our mind's eye, images which more or less strictly correspond to the sentence, and which are therefore, in a sense, translations of this sentence into a pictorial language. – But it is absolutely essential for the picture which we imagine the shadow to be that it is what I shall call a 'picture by similarity'. I don't mean by this that it is picture similar to what it is intended to represent, but that it is a picture which is correct only when it is similar to what it represents. One might use for this kind of picture the word 'copy'. Roughly speaking, copies are good pictures when they can easily be mistaken for what they represent. (Wittgenstein 1958: 36–7)

By tacitly assuming that the last interpretation is a picture that represents through similarity, the question of how representation is possible is ignored.

But, in fact, the model of an inner picture is doomed to fail in the face of the regress argument. Without it, however, this version of representationalism would fail to be explanatory and lapse into Cartesian mysticism.

There would also be a further difficulty with this way of escaping the regress of interpretations for representationalism. This follows from one of its central claims about the role of mental representations. They are supposed to play a causal role in the explanation of thought processes. But once the inner states are identified with contents themselves rather than with the vehicles of content, no straightforward account of this causal role remains. The causally relevant properties of inner states are their local physical properties. But these are properties that the bearers of content might possess but not the contents themselves. Contents do not have any physical properties.

5.2.3   Mental representations do not require interpretation because they are self-interpreting

The third option for representationalism is the one that most contemporary forms actually take (see below for references). It escapes the regress of interpretations by deploying self-interpreting mental representations. But these are not merely aspects of Cartesianism. A further account of how meaning is extracted from inner states without interpretation is available. I will argue, however, that it cannot escape Wittgenstein's criticisms.

The computer provides a powerful analogy for representationalism. This is how Fodor responds to the potential threat of interpretative regress by deploying self-interpretation:

> Real computers characteristically use at least two different languages: an input / output language in which they communicate with their environment and a machine language in which they talk to themselves . . . 'Compilers' mediate between the two languages . . . What avoids an infinite regression of compilers is the fact that the machine is *built* to use the machine language. Roughly, the machine language differs from the input / output language in that its formulae correspond directly to computationally relevant physical states and operations of the machine: The physics of the machine thus guarantees that the sequences of states and operations it runs through in the course of its computations respect the semantic constraints on formulae in its internal language. (Fodor 1975: 65–6)

The idea is that machine languages comprise internal tokens (which can be likened to mental representations) bound by rules of syntax. Like higher-level, input/output languages, they are representational but, unlike higher-level languages, they do not require interpretation by a compiler, which would lead to a regress of compilers because compilers are written in machine language. Instead, they are 'understood' by the computer without compilation. This trick is brought off by a piece of engineering design. The causally relevant properties of the symbols are designed to correspond to their syntax. Thus, what does the work of interpretation – at least as far as syntax is concerned – for the lowest-level languages of computers are the causal relations in which their tokens stand.

This, however, is only the beginning of an answer to the problem of explaining the intentionality of inner states. The problem is to explain how inner states can be *about* anything. The computer analogy helps to show how mental representations can be governed by syntax but it does not address the question of their semantics or content. Simply automating the internal states does not touch that issue. (In fact, it is premature to call the causal transactions between states *syntactic*, but I shall focus instead on the issue of semantics.) Adding horizontal causal relations between representations provides a model of how they can have causal consequences, perhaps eventuating in action, but it does not provide the vertical relations of intentionality. The metaphor of the computer leaves the basic intentionality of the symbols unexplained.

As I set out in the first chapter, representationalism ascribes two kinds of causal relations to mental representations. In addition to the internal causal relations supposedly corresponding to the syntax of mental representations, it also postulates external causal relations holding between inner states and external worldly items. Adding in these additional relations goes beyond the basic computer model. But it still resembles that basic picture in the following way. The central claim remains that mental representations do not require interpretation because the system in which they operate is causally self-interpreting. But the system is construed as including causal relations to items in the world.

Adding in just any external causal relations will not, however, explain how the internal states derive their intentionality. As will be described shortly, some causal relations correspond to errors rather than constituting content. Some further qualification has to be added if there is to be any prospect of accounting for the normativity of content. There are two major approaches:

- descriptive causal theories
- teleological causal theories.

Descriptive causal theories of content

The underlying motivation for a causal theory of content is the fact that effects can sometimes carry information about their causes. One can say 'those spots mean measles' or 'smoke means fire'. Grice called examples such as these cases of natural meaning (Grice 1957). But, as I described in the previous chapter, any *simple* causal theory which identifies the content of a mental representation with whatever causes it cannot account for its normativity. It cannot account for those occasions where having a mental representation corresponds to a *false* belief. In such cases, representations are caused by states of affairs that they do not depict or to which they do not refer. (Which of these two possibilities is the case depends on whether the theory is based on the truth conditions of judgements or the reference of component mental terms. Since this distinction will play no role in what follows I will characterise causal theories in either way.) A simple causal theory will, however, include *all* these causes as parts of the content which a mental representation encodes. The mental representation will stand for a *disjunction* of all its possible causes and misrepresentation will be impossible. Hence the label 'disjunction problem'. Thus, one condition of adequacy of causal theories is that they are able to discriminate between two circumstances in which a mental representation is produced in the mind. There must be occasions where the cause and the content coincide, and occasions of 'deviant' causation where the mental representation is caused by something from outside its extension or of which it is not true.

The most obvious strategy for meeting this objection, within the confines of a descriptive causal theory, is to attempt to fix the content of mental representations by specifying conditions under which they can only be caused correctly. (Examples of this include Dretske 1981 and some versions of the teleological theory (e.g., Papineau 1987). I shall consider a different kind of teleological theory below.) If such optimal conditions can be defined in non-question-begging and naturalistic terms, then the content of the representation can be defined as that which causes (or would cause) it under those ideal conditions. This then serves as a bench mark for its occurrence under other conditions. If it is caused by things which did not cause it (or would not have caused it) under optimal conditions, then that is a case of *misrepresentation*. Such theories can either stress actual historical connections or counter-factual connections established under the optimal conditions (hence the parenthetical alternatives). In either case, they attempt to overcome Wittgenstein's criticisms of causal and dispositional accounts by providing the distinction between correctness and incorrectness which he claims they lack.

But as has recently been argued elsewhere, the strategy of specifying optimal conditions cannot succeed (Boghossian 1989). The problem is this. Even beliefs which are prompted by observation are also mediated by a background of other beliefs. If, for example, one has a strong antecedent reason to believe (falsely) that horses have become extinct, then the presence of a horse will not prompt the belief that there is a horse before one now. Conversely, if one (falsely) believes that the only large animals in a particular part of the world are horses that look unusually cow-like, then the presence of a cow there may prompt a horse-thought. There are no principled limits to this mediation. A specification of optimal conditions – those under which mental representations are caused only by the right things – will have to preclude *any* such distorting background beliefs. But the optimal conditions have also to be specified in non-intentional terms. This requires that there is an independent way of specifying in non-intentional terms that no such distorting background beliefs are present. But that requires a reduction of intentional concepts to causal terms which is just what *this* account is supposed to provide. Thus, the appeal to optimal conditions cannot help descriptive causal theories escape the disjunction problem.

Fodor has, however, set out a descriptive causal theory that does not depend on specifying optimal conditions (Fodor 1987, 1991). Instead, he defines the causal relations which constitute the content of mental representations as those upon which the causal relations which correspond to error asymmetrically depend. Thus, he claims that the 'misfiring' link which may exist between athletic cows and horse-thoughts exists only because of the 'proper' connection between horses and horse-thoughts. Had the latter connection not existed then neither would the former, but not vice versa. The content of mental representations is thus determined by *independent* causal relations, and errors correspond to *dependent* causal relations. Genuinely disjunctive contents, by contrast, correspond to two or more equally fundamental and independent causal connections.

At first sight, Fodor's theory appears to solve the disjunction problem. It seems to draw a principled distinction between correctness and incorrectness and thus account for the normativity of content. But I think that it also falls prey to Wittgenstein's objections to dispositional accounts. To show this I shall focus first on a different aspect of the normativity of content: its systematicity.

I outlined two aspects of this in the first chapter. One is that the ascription of a content to a thinker presupposes a more general ability to think related thoughts – the requirement of Evans's Generality Constraint. Fodor addresses this issue through the postulation of a language of thought. The other is that contents stand in rational relations of support, compatibility and contradiction. These provide further normative constraints on contents. Thus, in addition to explaining how false thoughts about observed worldly states of affairs are possible, representationalism owes an account of how one belief, for example, can imply, support or contradict another. One example of the way in which thoughts can be rationally structured is mathematical. If James believes that there is *one* kitten on the left-hand side of the futon and *one* kitten on the right, he is justified in drawing the conclusion that there are *two* kittens on the futon. What account of this rational systematicity can the asymmetric dependence theory give?

As I commented in the previous chapter, it is unclear whether Fodor sets out to be full-bloodedly psychologistic and thus to explain logical and rational norms in causal terms or whether, more modestly, he merely attempts to explain mechanically how human thought can track those norms. In either case, however, his theory needs to guarantee that the distinction between correctness and incorrectness which it underpins is the right one. Thus, in the case of logically or mathematically related beliefs, the postulated mechanism must give the right logical or mathematical answer. But, as Wittgenstein argues against causal and dispositional theories generally, the asymmetric dependence theory does not have the resources to guarantee this.

All that can be used to explicate the derivation of the *correct* result is a distinction between independent and dependent causal connections between mental representations. While this might seem to be sufficient to distinguish random errors from the conclusion that should be drawn, such a thought presupposes that the independent causal relation tracks the right norm. But there is no principled reason to believe that the demands of rationality and independent or fundamental causal dispositions *must* coincide. An individual may be disposed to make systematic errors in drawing conclusions from her beliefs. She may be systematically disposed to affirm the consequent in logic or to neglect the carry in addition. Even when a whole community is taken into account there is no guarantee that causation and rationality will go hand in hand. Even if they do, this seems to be a contingent matter and thus to undermine the necessity of logic and mathematics.

Once this point has been made about the rational systematicity of content, it can be seen that a similar criticism also applies to the rules governing the representation or naming of observable states of affairs. What gives the asymmetric dependence theory its initial plausibility is the attraction of the thought that whatever is the independent (or fundamental) cause of a mental representation is part of its content. But in fact there is no reason to believe that the independent cause of a mental representation is part of its content. There is no guarantee, in other words, that just being the independent causal relation is enough to guarantee correctness.

This point can be brought out by asking a reciprocal question (see Godfrey-Smith 1989). Instead of asking what guarantee there is that the fundamental causal connections governing mental representations will correctly track their content, one can ask what resources a *purely causal* theory has for distinguishing between the independent causal relation which determines the content of a mental representation and those dependent causal relations which correspond to error? Consider again a mental representation that is caused by normal-looking horses, athletic cows, muddy zebras and so forth. One obvious interpretation of this is that the representation encodes horse-thoughts and that the connections between it and some cows and zebras asymmetrically depend on the connection to horses. But there is another interpretation that is equally plausible given only the facts about causal connections. That is that the mental representation encodes a disjunctive content including normal-looking horses, and some cows and zebras. There is, after all, a *reliable* causal connection between those animals and the representation. It is only *given* the content of the mental representation that one can determine which connections are fundamental and which are dependent, which would hold in nearby possible worlds and which would not. Thus, as Wittgenstein argues, the normativity of mental content cannot be reduced to purely causal processes.

Teleological theories of content

One response to the charge that purely causal theories cannot account for the normativity of content is to think that that a further ingredient has to be added. The most plausible explanation of what ensures that the causal connections between mental representations accord with their rational relations is the process of evolution. This is the motivation for a teleological causal theory (e.g., Millikan 1984, 1993).

Teleological theories of content appear to have an important extra resource for explaining the normativity of content. They can employ the notion of a natural, proper or biological function. There is some debate about how precisely to define such a function. Roughly speaking, however, it is that function which a particular trait of an organism exemplifies and which explains the evolutionary success and survival value of that trait. Crucially, biological functions are distinct from dispositions. The biological function of a trait and its dispositions can diverge. Engineering limitations might cause the actual behavioural dispositions of a trait to diverge from the biological function it thus only partially exemplifies. The divergences might themselves be life threatening and play no positive part in explaining the value of the trait. The best explanation of the survival of that organism and those like it cites the *function* that helped propagation or predator evasion, for example, and not those aspects of its behavioural dispositions that diverged unhelpfully from it.

This point is sometimes put by saying that what matters is not what traits or dispositions are selected, but what *function* they are selected *for*. The distinction between 'selection of' and 'selection for' can be illustrated by the example of a child's toy (Sober 1984). A box allows objects of different shapes to be posted into it through differently shaped slots in the lid. The round slot thus allows the insertion of balls, for example. It may be that the actual balls allowed through or 'selected' in one case are all green. But they are *selected for* their round cross-section and not for their green colour. Millikan stresses the fact that the biological function of a trait may be displayed in only a minority of actual cases. It is the function of sperm to fertilise an egg but the great majority of sperm fails in this regard (Millikan 1984: 34).

Because biological functions can diverge from mere dispositions, teleological causal explanations of content have an extra resource to explain normativity. The distinction between correctness and incorrectness in the tokening of a mental representation can be defined by reference to its functioning in accord with its biological function. Its function may be to be caused only by horses, for example. This, supposedly, solves the disjunction problem with respect to the content of mental representations.

It also seems that an appeal to biological function can also explain how mental representations stand in rational relations. Indeed, Millikan goes further by suggesting that, given a teleological account, logic will become the first *natural* science (Millikan 1984: 11). That is, teleology will underpin a psychologistic explanation of logic and rationality. What makes one thought follow logically from another or one number the correct result of a calculation depends, ultimately, on abstract rules that humans apply to experience and that have had survival value.

There are, however, two fundamental flaws with a teleological approach. One is that it presupposes that the requirements of survival and rationality must go hand in hand. It is far from clear that this is actually so or that it must be so. In some circumstances it seems much more likely that quick approximations will contribute more to survival than a slow derivation of the correct answer (Dennett 1987: 97). But even if, by chance, rationality and survival coincided in the evolutionary history of animals on Earth, this would be a contingent matter and thus undermine the necessity of logic.

The second flaw stems from the real source of the teleological theory's apparent ability to account for normativity. As already suggested, this results from the fact that biological functions are not pure dispositions. The extra normative ingredient derives from this difference. Biological functions are defined by reference to what *explains* the selection of a trait. It is this idea of explanation that introduces the extra normative character of biological function. But two points, that pull in different directions, are important here:

- What matters in this explanation is what traits are selected *for* rather than just what the traits are that are actually selected. This follows from the fact that even traits which are favoured by evolutionary selection may have design flaws. Some behavioural dispositions which are the causal consequences of a successful trait might themselves have deleterious effects on survival.
- But nothing should be counted part of the biological function of a trait that has not contributed to the causal explanation of survival of that trait. This follows from the fact that biological teleology is still really the result of normal non-teleological causal processes.

This latter feature forms the basis of a criticism developed by Peacocke (1992: 125–32). Taking the case of a belief-forming mechanism, he argues that the only consequences that can explain the success of such a mechanism are the consequences of beliefs formed which have a causal impact on organisms that have it. But the truth of the causally relevant consequences of a belief can fall short of the truth of the truth of a belief itself. Thus:

> In a nutshell, the problem of reduced content is this: how is the teleological theorist to block an incorrect assignment of content to beliefs, namely one that requires for its truth merely the truth of all the logical consequences of p that have a causal impact on the thinker, rather than the stronger condition of the truth of p itself? (Peacocke 1992: 130)

Millikan's response is to stress again the first of the points above: what matters is not which mechanism is selected but what it is selected *for* (Millikan 1995). She argues that the best explanation of the presence of any such belief-forming mechanism will not ascribe to it a function of the limited form that Peacocke suggests. Its function is to represent p and not merely to select the consequences of p which have causal impact. This response points, however, to a more fundamental problem already prefigured in the discussion of Wittgenstein.

A teleological account of function is a form of *interpretational* theory because the characterisation of the function which explains the survival of a trait is in effect an interpretation of the past behaviour. Past behaviour comprises signs to be interpreted. Like the interpretation of signs, such behaviour is *consistent* with an unlimited number of possible functions or rules. What ensures the determinacy of biological function – that which selects just one of the rules – is an explanation of the presence of a trait couched in intentional terms that interprets what the trait is for. But finite past behaviour can be explained as exemplifying many different, or 'bent', functions or rules, all of which would have been equally successful in the past.

Millikan dismisses these possible alternatives by stressing, this time, the second of the points above. The explanation of a trait turns on what caused it to survive in the past. Taking the case of the rules that govern a hover-fly's mating behaviour she argues:

> [The 'bent' rule] is not a rule the hoverfly has a biological purpose to follow. For it is not because their behaviour coincided with *that* rule that the hoverfly's ancestors managed to catch females, and hence to proliferate. In saying that, I don't have any particular theory of the nature of explanation up my sleeve. But surely, on any reasonable account, a complexity that can simply be dropped from the explanans without affecting the tightness of the relation of explanans to explanandum is not a *functioning* part of the explanation. (Millikan 1993: 221)

The claim is that 'bent' rules introduce additional and unnecessary complexities that can be dispensed with without damaging the explanation of the success of a biological trait. But the claim that bent rules are over-complex and can be rejected either presupposes a particular interpretation of past behaviour for comparison – in which case it is question-begging – or that judgements can be made about the simplicity of rules from an objective Platonist perspective. And that is an idea which Wittgenstein has demolished.

It is worth noting that, in the case of the mental representations of observable states of affairs, the suggestion that their biological function can be specified objectively via the explanation of their survival is more attractive. But this is misleading because such explanation helps itself to natural kinds in the explanation of what it is that mental representations track. In the context of explaining content, such explanation faces a dilemma:

• Either, natural kinds are identified with the extension of mental representations, in which case they cannot be invoked to explain the content of mental representations.
• Or, they are identified with a classification-independent groupings or patterns in the world. The idea here is that thought tracks groupings that already exist independently of human judgement. This resembles the Platonist theory which Wittgenstein criticises (see above) in that it locates the standard of correctness for such judgements outside human practice. Thus, it cannot account for the normativity of judgements about what does and does not belong to the classification. But a teleological theory faces a more specific difficulty. There is no reason to believe that the biological function of a representation will be to track such natural kinds as opposed to functional kinds. The categories which are useful for an organism may not align with natural kinds.

An example which has been used elsewhere helps emphasise this second point from (Brown 1996: 459). Consider a mental representation that encodes the content poison. This seems to be a functional concept in that it denotes any substance that is toxic to the organism in question. But it is possible that, in the circumstances in which it had survival value, all the causes of that representation belonged to the same natural kind, the same biological species. The problem now is what, according to a teleological theory, distinguishes representations that encode what are, pre-philosophically, functional-kind contents from natural-kind contents? It seems on reflection that even, in the case of mental representations which concern detectable states of affairs, the teleological theory is no improvement on the pure descriptive causal theory. Neither can account for the normativity of content.

There is a further general Wittgensteinian objection to descriptive and to teleological causal theories of content. Both attempt to add something to internal mental states to explain their life. But what they add does not make the right sort of difference. The asymmetric dependence of internal states on types of external states of affairs does not explain why those internal states should be thought of as representational. Equally, the fact that internal states – which have the fortuitous causal consequences for movement – lead to natural selective advantage, does not explain why they are representational.

I commented in the first chapter that functionalism alone did not succeed in explaining the intentionality of mental states. Functionalism characterised them as merely a system of causal 'pushes and pulls in the head'. These 'horizontal' causal relationships could be sufficient to explain behaviour without the need to think of additional 'vertical' relationships of representation. Why think of the internal states so characterised by functionalism as about anything?

The teleological theory is supposed to provide an answer to precisely this question. The suggestion is that, once an account has been given of 'vertical' causal relations between internal states and states in the world, the problem of naturalising content will have been solved. But it does not. All it provides is a further specification of which internal causal states have causally advantageous consequences. It does not explain why the 'vertical' causal relations which it provides should, in addition to fulfilling this causal role, fulfil an intentional role.

5.3   The generality of Wittgenstein's critical arguments again

Having examined the consequences of Wittgenstein's critical arguments for representationalism, I shall return to the issue of the generality of these arguments. The worry is that Wittgenstein suggests that no reductionist explanation of content is possible on the basis of a small number of instances. I think that there are some grounds for modesty. Wittgenstein does not prove that reduction is impossible. Nevertheless he provides good reasons to disbelieve this possibility.

Firstly, there are strong prima-facie reasons to believe that the dilemma that Wittgenstein raises for explanations of content is forceful:

- An explanation of content cannot merely presuppose the very notion it attempts to explain by, for example, presupposing the content of an interpretation of a mental sign or symbol.
- On the other hand, it must sustain the normativity of content. And there are reasons to be pessimistic about the abilities of imagistic or causal theories to meet that challenge.

The onus of proof will lie with those who advocate some form of reduction. One of the morals of the examination of representationalism above is that theories of content based on interpretation are more widespread than they might seem. The other is just how difficult it is to construct a theory of content that meets the normative constraint.

The second general consideration stems from asking what could be added to a dead sign to give it life. Again, there are strong prima-facie reasons to believe that, once one begins from a conception of language as comprising dead signs which need to be animated or from a model of mental states as internal states characterised by their intrinsic properties, nothing can animate them. In other words, while Wittgenstein does not establish conclusively that content cannot be given some form of reductionist explanation, he gives very strong arguments to doubt that possibility.

This result, however, leaves several questions unanswered. For example:

- What connects one's understanding of a word with its correct future application?
- What connects an intentional mental state with the event or events that satisfies or satisfy it?
- More generally, what is the relation between thought or language and the world?

The strong negative result of the critical arguments does nothing to make answering these questions any easier. In the next chapter I shall begin to examine Wittgenstein's positive account of content by contrasting the interpretation I favour – a minimalist philosophy of content – with two others: scepticism and constructivism.

Further Reading

M. McGinn (1996) is a slim introduction to the *Philosophical Investigations*. The most thorough interpretative work is Baker and Hacker (1980, 1985) and Hacker (1990, 1996). Glock (1996b) is a useful dictionary of Wittgenstein's thought.

There is a vast literature on Wittgenstein's account of rule-following, but C. McGinn (1984) and McDowell (1984b) provide interesting discussions while Boghossian (1989) is a thorough survey of the debate. Less work has been done on Wittgenstein's account of intentional mental states, but see Arrington (1991) and Shanker (1991).

There has been a number of Wittgenstein-inspired criticisms of the representational theory of mind. Most, however, either presuppose Wittgenstein's positive account of meaning or fail to take seriously the causal theory of intentionality. Nevertheless, the following are worthwhile: Goldberg (1991), Heil (1981) and McDonough (1989, 1991).

CHAPTER 3

Sceptical, Constructivist and Minimalist Interpretations of Wittgenstein

In Chapter 2, I summarised *critical* arguments drawn from two sections of the *Investigations* that undermine attempts at reductionist explanations of content. In this chapter and the next I shall turn to Wittgenstein's *positive* characterisation of linguistic and mental content. As will become clear, Wittgenstein advocates a form of philosophical minimalism. No substantial philosophical account of meaning is possible. Philosophical clarification of content cannot provide resources that go beyond those used for explanation in everyday life. Explanation of *meaning* goes no further than ordinary piecemeal explanations of *meanings*. But the characterisation of philosophical minimalism will be clearer if contrasted first with two other interpretations.

Chapter 2 left several related questions unanswered:

- What connects one's understanding of a word with its correct future application?
- What connects an intentional mental state with the event or events that satisfies or satisfy it?
- More generally, what is the relation between thought or language and the world?

These questions have yet to be answered satisfactorily. All the answers considered so far have failed to survive Wittgenstein's criticisms. Explanations, of these normative connections, which invoke underlying mental or physiological mechanisms cannot sustain their normativity. Explanations which, instead, presuppose the content of mental interpretations or invoke Platonic connections beg the question about how they are selected and followed *correctly*. Thus, it seems that nothing can explain the connections.

The first two of the three responses discussed in this chapter assume that there is no connection to explain. The sceptical reading assumes that this is what Wittgenstein's attack on other explanations establishes. It then attempts to show how this counter-intuitive conclusion can be accepted. The constructivist reading assumes that the connection is not established in advance by linguistic or mental content but is retrospectively constructed piecemeal by subsequent human judgement. In fact, the sceptical and constructivist interpretations differ more in emphasis than substance because both undermine the normativity of content in similar ways. I shall argue that, as a result, neither is a coherent response. The third interpretation – philosophical minimalism – takes Wittgenstein's critical attack to be directed, not at the normativity of content, but purely at philosophical explanations of it.

Kripke says that, properly speaking, there is no connection (Kripke 1982). He assumes that Wittgenstein has uncovered a new form of philosophical scepticism similar to Humean scepticism about causation. The negative arguments (which Kripke sets out in an original form with admirable clarity) show, according to Kripke, precisely that there is no connection between the rule we understand and our applications of it. Because this is so, ordinary usage can be preserved only by deploying a 'sceptical solution' to the question. This relies on *dignifying* applications of a word as correct – and thus in accordance with meaning – if the linguistic community does not explicitly reject them. This sceptical solution severs the essential normative connection constitutive of content and attempts to make do with something weaker. I shall argue below that this weaker position is not sustainable.

Wright argues that Kripke's explicitly sceptical argument is question-begging and can be resisted (Wright 1987a, 1991). But he thinks that the Wittgensteinian question which Kripke reiterates is a substantial question that requires a substantial answer. Wright deploys a form of philosophical constructivism as that answer. The meaning of words and the content of mental states are plastic and shaped by ongoing human judgements. But, as I will argue, Wright's account is untenable because it begs the key question it attempts to answer and fails to sustain the normativity of content.

The minimalist account which I begin to describe in the third and final section of this chapter and develop in the next chapter argues that no substantial answer can be given to any of these questions. Wittgenstein's critique is directed against explanatory and reductionist answers to the questions raised above. The right response to them is to deny that there can be any explanatory intermediaries but also that there is any explanatory need.

1 Scepticism

1.1   Kripke's sceptical argument and sceptical solution

Kripke thinks that the correct answer to the question 'what connects one's understanding of a word with its correct future application?' is nothing (Kripke 1982: 55). That, according to Kripke, is the moral of Wittgenstein's discussion of rules. Kripke presents this answer as the conclusion of a reformulation of Wittgenstein's arguments. He focuses on the question: what justifies the claim that answering '125' is the correct response to the question 'what does 68 + 57 equal?', building in two simplifying assumptions: that 'correct' means simply in accordance with the standards of one's previous usage of the signs involved and that one has never calculated that particular sum before. Kripke then deploys Wittgensteinian arguments to show that no facts about one's past actions, utterances or even dispositions can justify the current calculation (Kripke 1982: 7–54). These arguments are closely related to those discussed in the previous chapter. But Kripke draws from them a further conclusion. Given that no facts about one's past actions or mental states can provide a justification, he concludes that there is no such justificatory fact and thus no facts about meaning.

Kripke's interpretation of Wittgenstein's critical arguments differs from that set out in the preceding chapter in three respects, two of which are minor, but the third of which marks a deep and significant difference:

- Instead of concentrating on the future directed link between the understanding of a rule that I may have in a flash and the applications that I must make subsequently, Kripke questions how I can *now* know what rule I was following in making *previous* applications. But, despite this difference of tense, the focus of the investigation remains normativity. Kripke asks what feature of my previous state could prescribe the responses that I *ought* to make rather than merely did make. This is a contrast between a normative and a merely descriptive relation.
- Kripke's interpretation of Wittgenstein is explicitly sceptical. It may therefore appear to have an epistemological, rather than a constitutive or ontological, focus. That is, it appears that Kripke is concerned with the question of how one can *know* which rule one followed in the past rather than the nature of rules themselves. The emphasis on epistemology rather than metaphysics is, however, more apparent than real. An ontological point is made by epistemological considerations. This will become clear when I outline the analogy that Kripke suggests between his investigation of rule-following and Hume's investigation of causation.
- Most significantly, Kripke interprets Wittgenstein, not as rejecting merely reductionist *explanations* of content, but as rejecting the very idea that rules have determinate content. This claim, which I will call Kripke's non-factualism, will be developed at some length below.

The analogy that Kripke suggests with Hume is threefold:

- Kripke's Wittgenstein, like Hume, deploys epistemological scepticism to raise a constitutive or ontological question.

- They both offer sceptical solutions to their sceptical problems.
- Their sceptical solutions are forms of projectivism.

I shall explain these points in turn.

The first analogy is the use of scepticism to raise a constitutive or ontological question. For Hume, the subject matter is the relation between cause and effect. For Kripke, it is the relation between a rule and its correct applications. After investigating possible sources of knowledge of the link, both conclude (according to Kripke) that there is no factual link. Hume argues, on the basis of an investigation of how we could come to know about such a connection, that there cannot be a necessitating connection between cause and effect. The sorts of considerations deployed by Hume are that we cannot observe any such connection when we observe paradigmatic cases of cause and effect. Neither can we arrive at such an idea from other experiences we have, such as the experience of the workings of the will.

The fact that he draws a metaphysical conclusion from merely epistemological considerations may seem startling. Surely, it is tempting to argue, the most that could justifiably be concluded is that we cannot *know* that any necessitating connection exists. (That justifiable conclusion is not even as strong as the claim that, when we speak of causation, we do not *mean* such a relation. To reach this further claim, we would require additional argument, because the implication from what we cannot know to what we cannot mean is by no means straightforward. Hume deploys an empiricist semantics to ground this move.) Nevertheless, whether or not his reading is exegetically correct, Kripke argues that Hume draws the yet stronger conclusion, that 'even if God were to look at the events, he would discern nothing relating them other than that one succeeds the other'. (Kripke 1982: 67) Kripke draws a similar conclusion for understanding rules. There is, he argues, no fact of the matter as to which rule I followed in previous behaviour. Furthermore, because the same argument could be given for my current behaviour, there is no fact of the matter about which rule I ever follow.

How can Kripke draw such a conclusion about the link between rules and applications from epistemological considerations? The answer is that an important assumption is built into the sceptical approach. If there were some fact that constituted the relation between a rule and its applications, it would be independently identifiable by the idealised subject that Kripke postulates. Kripke supposes, for the purpose of argument, that one may have all possible information about one's past experiences, mental states and inclinations. He then asks whether any of these would be sufficient to determine the rule that one were following. His conclusion, based on his interpretation of Wittgenstein's arguments, is that none would be. Given the idealisations involved, and the assumption that, had any fact constituted the rule one were following, one would have known it, then there is no such fact of the matter.

This sceptical interpretation of Wittgenstein is reinforced by Kripke's reading of §201. Wittgenstein writes there:

> This was our paradox: no course of action could be determined by a rule, because every course of action can be made out to accord with the rule. The answer was: if everything can be made out to accord with the rule, then it can also be made out to conflict with it. And so there would be neither accord nor conflict here. (§201)

Wittgenstein continues that there is a quite different way of grasping a rule which is not an interpretation. Neglecting this different conclusion (to which I will return in outlining a minimalist interpretation later in this chapter), Kripke interprets this as a sceptical problem generated by the arguments that have preceded it. Kripke writes:

> The sceptical argument, then, remains unanswered. There can be no such thing as meaning anything by any word. Each new application we make is a leap in the dark; any present intention could be interpreted so as to accord with anything we may choose to do. So there can be neither accord, nor conflict. This is what Wittgenstein said in §202 [sic]. (Kripke 1982: 55)

In response to this problem, Kripke deploys a sceptical solution to which I shall turn shortly.

The second analogy between Kripke and Hume is their response to the scepticism they generate. Kripke distinguishes between straight and sceptical solutions to sceptical problems (Kripke 1982: 66). *Straight* solutions are those that show that scepticism about a certain matter is, on investigation, unwarranted. Scepticism is, so to speak, disproved. A *sceptical* solution, by contrast, accepts that the sceptic has proved her point and attempts to suggest some other kind of justification for the matter in question. According to Kripke, Hume offers a sceptical solution to the problem of the link between cause and effect. Kripke, likewise, suggests a sceptical solution to the normative link between rule and applications.

Hume's account accepts that there is no necessitating relation between cause and effect, and offers a different kind of explanation of our pre-philosophical beliefs about them. On experiencing the constant conjunction of events of some first type with events of a second, we have a natural propensity to expect the 'effect' having observed the 'cause'. As a result of projecting this natural habit into the fabric of the world, we mistakenly postulate a necessitating relation to explain our expectation. Kripke suggests that a similar solution can be given to his sceptical problem.

The third similarity between Kripke and Hume is thus the use of projectivism in their sceptical solutions. The account that Kripke gives of following a rule is this. Whether one person is 'following a rule' depends on their being so 'dignified' by a community of 'rule-followers'. We speak, however, as though there were an individual factual relation occurring between the individual's understanding and action, but this is not so. Really, for an individual to be considered a rule-follower, she must be considered as part of a community. (This is again akin to Hume's account where individual causal relations depend on general relations of constant conjunction.)

This brief initial description of Kripke's sceptical solution picks out two important elements. Firstly, Kripke denies the factuality of rule-following, and thus linguistic content, and gives instead a projectivist account of an ersatz version of normativity. Secondly, the community plays an important role in explicating this ersatz version. Although it is natural to combine non-factualism with a communitarian construal of rule-following, the latter is neither necessary nor sufficient for the former. One might have an individualistic non-factualist theory. Nothing really connects the meaning of a word to its correct use but an individual can dignify herself as correctly using the word provided that she is retrospectively satisfied with her uses (see Blackburn 1984a). Or one might have a communitarian but factualist theory. The correct application of a word is simply but positively defined by what uses a community makes over time (see Malcolm 1986). Kripke's communitarian non-factualism is marked by the strikingly weak role the community plays. Kripke writes:

> It is essential to our concept of a rule that we maintain some such conditional as 'If Jones means addition by "+", then if he is asked for "68+57", he will reply "125"' . . . [T]he conditional as stated makes it appear that some mental state obtains in Jones that guarantees his performance of particular additions such as '68+57' – just what the sceptical argument denies. Wittgenstein's picture of the true situation concentrates on the contrapositive, and on justification conditions. If Jones does *not* come out with '125' when asked about '68+57', we cannot assert that he means addition by '+'. (Kripke 1982: 94–5)

Kripke's stark picture of rule-following is akin to the Popperian account of science: interpretations can be falsified but there is no room (officially, at least) for confirmation (Popper 1959). This is the result of the underdetermination of rules by applications that Kripke emphasises, following from the interpretational account of understanding. It is of a piece with his neglect of the suggestion that there is another way of grasping a rule other than interpreting it, to which I will return at the end of this chapter.

As a result, the community performs a wholly negative role of precluding certain interpretations of behaviour. The idea of intentional accord with a rule is replaced by merely not having deviated from it. There is, consequently, something misleading in describing the community's function as providing justification conditions because there is never positive evidence for ascribing the intention to accord with a rule as an interpretation of behaviour to anyone, including oneself. While some interpretations are ruled out, this always leaves an infinite number that are consistent with available behavioural data. There should, therefore, never be grounds for ascribing any rule. According to Kripke, this is not just an epistemological problem but, given the idealisations involved, reflects an objective indeterminacy in rules. The idea of the normativity of a rule is thus replaced by something much weaker, and rules lack factuality.

The revisionary consequences of Kripke's account are manifested in two kinds of consideration:

- There are practical consequences for interpreting others. There is no such thing as correctness in the ascription of a rule, no justification for an assertion that a particular rule is being followed. No evidence can be offered in positive support; there is simply elimination of some of the possibilities. But even the notion of *incorrectness* is weakened. Demonstrations of rules on Kripke's picture rule out far fewer interpretations than we ordinarily think because any interpretation which is logically compatible with the growing corpus of actual responses made remains. To establish which rule is being followed on any occasion should, therefore, be an unending process of gradual elimination akin to Popper's official account of scientific testing.
- The idea that the ascription of meaning to an utterance can be correct or incorrect is undercut. There are no such things as meanings to be correctly ascribed. Given that the account has no resources to eliminate rules which are logically possible, and that this is the result of underlying indeterminacy rather than an epistemological difficulty, the ascription of rules lacks factuality. Disagreement about an ascription need not indicate a cognitive failing. Even disagreement with the community does not imply error because there is nothing to be in error about. It is simply that the individual and the community cease to be in step.

Kripke's non-factualism is important because it is one of the two poles towards which an account of linguistic meaning may be drawn. Wittgenstein's negative arguments are made in response to a series of explanations of understanding rules which might be offered. Each explanation is rejected as unsatisfactory. Kripke's conclusion is that because the search for an independent fact in which meaning could be said to consist has failed, there is no such constitutive fact and therefore there is never a fact of the matter about what a speaker means by an utterance. I shall argue below that this in turn leads disastrously to a denial of factuality for all judgements. Resisting this conclusion requires a different response to Wittgenstein's argument that the deployment of any symbol or the undergoing of any process cannot constitute the normative constraint that a rule imposes. Without, however, invoking some sort of Platonism, such as a symbol that imposes its correct interpretation or process that cannot go wrong, it is not yet clear what response can be given that will preserve factuality. That is the task to which I shall return at the end of this chapter. But first I need to establish that Kripke's solution is untenable.

1.2   The problem with Kripke's sceptical solution

The problem with simply denying that anything connects a rule or the meaning of a word with its correct applications is that this infects the factuality of all judgements. No facts survive the denial of the factuality of meaning. While this conclusion is now generally agreed upon, it remains difficult to formulate uncontentiously the exact nature of the problem. I shall outline three basic approaches:

- The account must be wrong because non-factualism about meaning spreads virulently to all facts.
- The account cannot be stated without formal contradiction.
- The account precludes the expression of a distinction upon which it relies.

One attempt to formulate the problem runs as follows (Boghossian 1989: 524). Non-factualism amounts to the claim that, for any sentence S and propositional content p, 'S means that p' is not truth-conditional. Because the truth-condition of a sentence is in part a function of its meaning, this implies that for any S and p 'S has truth-condition p' is not truth-conditional. Because 'S has truth-condition p' is never true, 'S' is not truth-conditional. Thus, assuming that possession of factuality implies the possession of truth-conditions, the denial of factuality concerning rules implies a universal lack of such factuality.

This argument has been criticised by Wright on the grounds that it presupposes that even a substantial concept of truth has disquotational properties. These license the transition from the fact that a mentioned sentence lacks a truth condition to its lack of truth and from that to a denial of the content of the sentence (Wright 1992: 214–20). Wright suggests that, in the context of a debate about realism, this cannot be assumed. If one distinguishes a substantial notion of truth (amounting to normativity and something more such as a correspondence theory) from a more minimal notion of correctness (normativity alone), it is far from clear that these transitions hold good. The fact that a sentence lacks substantial truth need not justify the denial of the mere correctness of its content. A proper assessment of this objection is beyond the scope of this book. But three points can be noted:

- The objection does not yet refute the key claim that the lack of factuality for rules imposes a similar lack on all judgements. If successful merely one argument for that fails.

- On the reading presented above, at least, Kripke's account does not preserve even a minimal notion of truth. Normativity is replaced by something much weaker. Thus, the objection is not relevant.
- The transition from lack of factuality of meaning to a general lack of facts can be set out without recourse to talk of truth conditions.

The third point can be filled out as follows. Empirical judgements can be divided into those that are made directly and those that are made on the basis of inference, whether from inductive evidence or theoretical inference. To take an example of the former category first, one judges that a pillar-box is red, for example, having seen it reasonably close up on a sunny day. If rules are non-factual, then the correctness of such direct applications of colour terms is also non-factual. There is thus no fact of the matter as to whether the pillar-box is red. If a judgement is made on the basis of inference, then, because the rules of inference are non-factual, by Kripke's account, so will the final judgement be. In either case, non-factuality of rules leads to non-factuality of judgements and so to a universal lack of factuality.

Such a result is surely in itself sufficient to show that there is something very wrong with Kripke's sceptical solution. The objection can, however, be refined to derive a formal contradiction. One such argument runs as follows (Boghossian 1989: 525–26). Non-factualism must presuppose a more substantial notion of truth than that described in a redundancy theory of truth because that theory enables truth to be ascribed whenever a declarative sentence can be asserted. Because non-factualism denies that certain classes of declarative sentences are truth-conditional, it must presuppose a substantial notion of truth. But the judgement as to whether something possesses a substantial property is itself (surely) a factual matter. Thus, the denial that any judgements are factual must itself be a factual judgement and thus be self-contradictory.

There are two possible problems with this criticism. The kind of objection considered above might also be applied here. Perhaps some sense could be made of the idea that it is merely a matter of minimal correctness that judgements do not possess a substantial truth-condition. Alternatively, the denial of factuality, which apparently itself presupposes factuality, may serve as a move towards a philosophical understanding from the perspective of which the good sense of the claim is denied. In other words, the denial may have the status that Wittgenstein accords within the *Tractatus* to the claims made there: a ladder that must be discarded once climbed. I do not wish to suggest that such a defence would be fully satisfactory, but to show only that the contradiction derived may not be decisive. A more decisive though less elegant, objection can be given however .

On the assumption that non-factualism about meaning spreads to non-factualism about the content of all assertions, what a statement of Kripke's sceptical solution – that meaning is projective rather than factual – expresses is itself projective rather than factual (cf. Wright 1984). But this means, in other words, that it cannot express a *truth* about meaning. It is not *true* that meaning is projective. Thus Kripke saws off the branch upon which his account sits.

Now some defences are available against this objection. It might be objected that the criticism depends on an illicit presupposition which Kripke denies. An analogy with relativism may help explicate what this presupposition is and how the defence might go. It has long been claimed that relativism is self defeating because it faces an unacceptable dilemma. Either the truth of the assertion that all truth is relative is itself absolute or it is relative. The problem with this objection as it stands is that, while relativists cannot accept the first horn without contradicting the universality of their thesis, there is no reason why they cannot 'bite the bullet' and accept that the truth of relativism is relative. In a similar manner, it might be claimed on Kripke's behalf that the 'fact' that rule-following should be given a projectivist account should itself be given a projectivist account.

But even if this defence could be made good for the *status* of the claim that meaning is projective, the *content* of the projectivist sceptical solution faces a second related difficulty. No account can be given of what Kripke's sceptical solution amounts to here without appeal to a contrast with genuinely factual statements. Projectivism about some judgements requires a set of facts that are not subject to such an account and that can form the basis of the projection. Projectivism in a delimited field, such as ethics, explains ethical judgements as the result of a projection of an affective response on to the state of affairs that evokes it. A projectivist account of ethical judgements thus depends on a factual account of human affective responses. These are what the subject 'really' has and ground the further projected judgment. While the making of ethical judgements does not require that further judgements are first made about one's affective state, the philosophical account of ethical judgement must be able to pick out such a class. The problem in Kripke's case is to explain what it is that is projected in the case of rule-following. The universality of the claim undermines a necessary contrast. Thus, Kripke's claim about meaning fails.

The outcome of these various objections is that non-factualism about linguistic meaning cannot be a coherent response to Wittgenstein's critical arguments. The answer to the question 'what connects one's understanding of a word with its correct future application?' cannot be nothing. The sceptical solution is no solution. Given the distinction between sceptical and straight solutions to sceptical arguments, and given that a sceptical solution to scepticism about content is untenable, a straight solution is needed instead. Fortunately, one is available.

The argument for scepticism about content can be defused with the following diagnosis. The sceptic assumes that knowledge of the rule that one followed in the past or the meaning that guided one's behaviour is based on an *inference* from other (past) mental or behavioural phenomena. Investigation shows that no such phenomena could possibly determine a rule or a meaning. The sceptic then concludes that there are no such things as rules or meanings as normally conceived. But that conclusion is premature. One could instead conclude merely that rules cannot be *reduced* to other phenomena. In other words, the fact that facts about one's current linguistic (or mental) content cannot be reduced to other – non-normative – facts does not show that content is any the less a matter of fact (Wright 1987a). Kripke's underlying assumption is, on this diagnosis, the same as the representationalist assumption exemplified by Fodor that content or intentionality is real only if it is really something else.

The only argument that Kripke has against non-reductionism about content is an argument from 'queerness' similar to that of Fodor:

> Perhaps we may try to recoup, by arguing that meaning addition by 'plus' is a state even more *sui generis* than we have argued before. Perhaps it is simply a primitive state, not to be assimilated to sensations or headaches or any 'qualitative' states, nor to be assimilated to dispositions, but a state of a unique kind of its own . . . Such a state would have to be a finite object, contained in our finite minds. It does not consist in my explicitly thinking of each case of the addition table, nor even of my encoding each separate case in the brain: we lack the capacity for that. Yet (§195) 'in a *queer* way' each such case already is 'in some sense present'. . . What can that sense be? Can we conceive of a finite state which *could* not be interpreted in a quus-like [deviant] way? How could that be? (Kripke 1982: 51–2)

Kripke argues that any *sui generis* conception of meaning is too strange to be real. But, in the passage just quoted, he builds an important qualification into his description. A *sui generis* meaning would be a finite *object* contained in our finite minds. If this were the only model – meaning as an inner object – then Kripke would be right to reject a *sui generis* non-reducible conception of meaning. No object before the mind's eye could fix the normative consequences of meaning. But to assume that meaning must be conceived this way is already to be partially committed to the representationalist model. Effectively, Kripke assumes that either a representationalist explanation of meaning is possible or, properly speaking, there is no such thing as meaning.

I shall return to the other options in the final section of this chapter when setting out Wittgenstein's minimalist position. But it is worth remembering here that the problem of normativity applies to mental content as well as understanding linguistic meaning. Thus, another model for that which Kripke sees as the genuinely strange idea of understanding meaning is everyday mental states with intentional content: intentions, expectations, hopes and fears. These are also states that *prescribe* what would satisfy them. Thus, the argument from queerness can be disarmed and there remains no reason to be sceptical about meaning.

2 Constructivism

2.1   Constructivism and the order of determination test

If scepticism about content is incoherent, what other answer is there to the questions with which this chapter began?

- What connects one's understanding of a word with its correct future application?
- What connects an intentional mental state with the event or events that satisfies or satisfy it?
- More generally, what is the relation between thought or language and the world?

In this section I shall consider and reject a constructivist response in which the correct application of a word – and thus its meaning – is constructed over time. By constructivism I mean the thesis that content is constructed by ongoing human practice.

Setting representationalism and scepticism aside for the moment, it can seem that Platonism and constructivism exhaust the possible responses to these questions. Scepticism, I have argued, is incoherent while representationalism itself tends to oscillate between Platonism and constructivism. If it invokes internal states which need no interpretation, or worldly natural kinds, then it implicitly embraces a form of Platonism about meaning. If, on the other hand, it attempts to explain the normativity of content through causal processes, it implicitly embraces a form of constructivism. Normative determination is replaced by ongoing causal determination. Thus, it seems that, if anything connects the meaning of a word and its use or mental states and what satisfies them, then either Platonism or constructivism must be true.

Platonism claims that a rule itself autonomously determines its applications independently of human action. Similarly, the content of a judgement in conjunction with the state of the world determines whether or not it is true by a kind of linguistic action at a distance. We simply latch on to pre-existing connections. But, as I described in Chapter 2, Wittgenstein has powerful arguments against this picture. Hence the motivation for constructivism.

Constructivism is a radical theory of meaning. To get a preliminary understanding of this, consider the rule governing the application of a descriptive classificatory predicate such as 'red'. On a Platonist picture of meaning, a convention is required to connect the arbitrary symbol 'red' to its meaning, sense or form, but, once that connection is made, the meaning autonomously determines the extension of 'red'. Constructivism denies that any such autonomous linguistic action at a distance is possible. Instead it claims that the extension of 'red' is slowly fixed by unfolding human agreement in judgement. Independent of such agreement, the issue of what belongs to the extension is indeterminate. The same considerations apply to determining the truth of the sentence 'my cup is red'. Its truth depends on whether the cup belongs to the extension of 'red' and thus depends on human agreement. It is not just that human agreement decides which completed extension the word 'red' picks out from a range of already determined alternatives. The extension itself has to be determined by human agreement. Thus, the truth of sentences stating empirical facts is not fixed simply by the conventions involved in the definitions of components because the correct applications of these definitions has itself to be unfolded. As Wright says, meaning is 'plastic in response to speakers' continuing performance' (Wright 1986: 289).

Despite the attractions of constructivism, I shall argue that it fails as a coherent interpretation of Wittgenstein. To do this I shall articulate some of the most sophisticated arguments offered in support of constructivism in a number of papers by Wright. Wright initially contrasts his position with Kripkean scepticism by showing how the argument for scepticism is question-begging, as argued above (Wright 1987a: 395). In addition to that diagnosis, he points out in some detail how intentions share many of the features of understanding in order to disarm the argument from queerness. That much is consistent with the philosophical minimalism that I will defend later in this chapter. But Wright does not then rest content with that philosophical counter-move.

The problem that Wright sees is this. The fact that intending serves as a good analogy for understanding rules or meanings cuts in two directions. The analogy can be used to block Kripke's sceptic but it invites a closely related question to that which motivates the rule-following considerations. How does an intention which can be arrived at in a flash normatively constrain those actions that would accord with it in the future? As I have emphasised, the normative connection between an intention and that which accords with it seems as mysterious as that between understanding a rule and its correct applications. Wright, in other words, re-emphasises the fundamental connection between the problem of linguistic meaning and mental content that Wittgenstein sets out. Wright deploys constructivism to explicate both.

According to Wright:

One of the most basic philosophical puzzles about intentional states is that they seem to straddle two conflicting paradigms: on the one hand, they are avowable, so to that extent conform to the paradigm of sensation and other 'observable' phenomena of consciousness; on the other, they answer constitutively to the ways in which the subject manifests them, and to that extent conform to the paradigm of psychological characteristics which, like irritability or modesty, are properly conceived as dispositional . . . It appears that neither an epistemology of observation – of pure introspection – nor one of inference can be harmonised with all aspects of the intentional. (Wright 1991: 142)

Intention is only one example of a general phenomenon that also includes understanding, remembering and deciding. In each case, the subject has a special non-inferential authority in ascribing these to herself which is, nevertheless, defeasible in the light of subsequent performance. Wittgenstein's attack on reductionist explanations of such states shows that they cannot be modelled on a Cartesian picture of observation of private experiences. But, if understanding, intending and the like are to be modelled on abilities instead, as Wittgenstein seems to suggest, how can the subject have special authority in ascribing these to herself in the light of the attack on reductionist explanation?

Constructivism appears to provide a solution to this problem. The basic idea is to deny that there is any inner *epistemology* and to devise a constructivist account of intention instead:

> The authority which our self-ascriptions of meaning, intention, and decision assume is not based on any kind of cognitive advantage, expertise or achievement. Rather it is, as it were, a *concession*, unofficially granted to anyone whom one takes seriously as a rational subject. It is, so to speak, such a subject's right to declare what he intends, what he intended, and what satisfies his intentions; and his possession of this right consists in the conferral upon such declarations, other things being equal, of a *constitutive* rather than descriptive role. (Wright 1987a: 400–)

All other things being equal, a speaker's sincere judgements constitute the content of the intention, understanding or decision. They determine, rather than reflect, the content of the state concerned. If this is to work as a general response to the Wittgensteinian questions set out at the start of this chapter – and thus as an explication of content – the contrast between constructive and tracking or detecting judgements has to be substantiated. Wright's constructivism depends on deploying what he calls the 'order of determination test' to carry this burden. This is most easily understood as an analogical development of a method of distinguishing between primary and secondary qualities. The order-of-determination test serves there to distinguish between primary qualities that inhere in the world independently of judgement and secondary qualities the extensions of which are fixed by judgement.

The idea is as follows. There is a biconditional that holds between the instantiation of secondary quality concepts and judgements that they obtain: x is R iff x would be seen as R by normally functioning observers in normal circumstances. Like the Euthyphro paradox, this can be read in two contrasting ways. Read 'right to left', it states that the judgements track or reflect the fact that the concept applies. Read the other way, it states that it is in virtue of the judgements being made that the concept applies. That that is the case does not undermine the *truth* of the application of the concept. But the explanation of that truth is different. The concept applies because of the practice of judgement rather than the fundamental constitution of the world.

The test requires that four conditions are met. These are individually necessary for a judgement to be constructive and, according to Wright, jointly sufficient (Wright 1989b: 247–9). While it is not necessary here to spell these out in detail, they are in brief:

- a priority: the truth of the biconditional must allow a-priori knowledge;
- non-triviality: the background conditions must avoid trivial 'whatever-it-takes' specification;
- independence: the satisfaction of the background conditions must be logically independent of facts about the extension of the concept judged to apply;
- and extremal: there must be no better explanation of the biconditional than extension determination.

If these are satisfied, then the conditional is extension-determining. The reason is this. If one can spell out, a priori, substantial conditions under which judgements of a certain kind will turn out to be true, then, if there is no better explanation, the best explanation of this is that these judgements themselves serve as the standard of correctness. The extensions of the concepts judged are determined or constructed by the judgements.

Applied to secondary qualities, the idea is that one can state a priori substantial conditions for making judgements of colour, for example. Normal observers with normal visual systems under normal afternoon lighting will make correct judgements about colours. The best explanation for this general a-priori truth is that judgements of this sort serve to fix the colours. This is all there is to being a particular colour. But the test is also applied to underpin constructivism about content. Here the idea is that a similar biconditional (with some important differences) can be devised to link the judgement of agents about their own intentions to those intentions. The best explanation of this relation between the content of mental states and first-person judgements about them is that their contents are constructed by such judgements.

The application of the order-of-determination test to intention varies from its application to colour because of the problem of self-deception. In the colour case, it is more plausible that substantial conditions for successful colour judgement can be specified that meet the four provisos for extension determination. In the case of intention, however, the conditions for successfully judging the content of an intention have to include the condition that one is not self-deceived. Because absence of self-deception cannot be described non-intentionally, this introduces a circularity that Wright attempts to avoid via the claim that it is a 'positive presumptive' condition which can be assumed to hold and thus be deleted. Once it is deleted, the biconditional left no longer falls foul of the provisos on triviality and independence but remains non-trivial. That we can form such a non-trivial biconditional stands in need of explanation according to this view. The constructivist explanation is that first-person judgements of intentions generally determine their extensions. Thus, it provides a substantial explanation of mental content.

In summary, the strategic context of the order-of-determination test is this. Wright argues that Kripkean scepticism about rules can be blocked by proposing we have direct, rather than inferential, knowledge of a *sui generis* state. Kripke's only argument against this, the argument that it is too strange to be true, is then disarmed through analogy with intentions. This analogy raises a further question corresponding to the one at the start of Wittgenstein's discussion of rule-following. How can I be in a state now that can be satisfied or frustrated by an unimagined set of future acts? Wright attempts to give a substantial answer to this question through constructivism. This is explicated by the order-of-determination test.

Setting out the strategic role of the test helps reveal a surprising tension. Intentions are deployed to disarm an argument against a *non-reductionist* account of rule-following. But they are in turn explicated through a *reductionist* account via construction by the subject's avowal. The motivation for this is twofold. Firstly, Wright assumes that the appropriate response to Wittgenstein's question is to devise a substantial explanation. Secondly, he rejects what I will call the autonomy of meaning: the claim that rules determine their correct application independently of ongoing human use. Wright rejects this as a form of Platonism and claims that meaning is instead plastic to ongoing use. The deployment of the order-of-determination test for intentions and rules can be seen as a further development of this constructivist theme in Wright's response to Wittgenstein.

2.2   Objections to a constructivist account of content

There are two fundamental objections to this account:

- It fails to substantiate the distinction between constructive and detective judgements.
- It fails to sustain the normativity of content.

The first objection runs as follows. Constructivism cannot substantiate the contrast between extension determining and extension tracking which is central to this account. This problem can be highlighted by asking what determines the extension of a group of concepts when one method of judging them is tracking rather than determining? If such judgements are tracking, then there must be independent extensions to be tracked. There are two explanations of how this can be possible:

- Either the extensions are determined autonomously of any judgement.
- Or they are determined by some other judgements.

If the latter holds, then for every concept there is some corresponding extension determining judgement for which an appropriate biconditional could be derived. But it is unlikely that it will generally be possible to set out conditions for successful judgement that do not employ the concepts in question and thus unlikely that the independence condition can be met (as Wright concedes in 1989b: 256). Thus, it is unlikely that the order-of-determination test will deliver the right results in these cases without the general use, and justification for that use, case by case, of positive presumptive conditions. Such a general project seems very unlikely to succeed. In that case it cannot be used to draw the kind of distinction that is presupposed by the test.

The only alternative explanation, however, is not available to constructivism because constructivism denies the autonomy of meaning. Independent extensions cannot be explicated by recourse to the effects of linguistic action at a distance established when the concepts are first devised. The central point of deploying a constructivist response to Wittgenstein is that any form of linguistic action at a distance appears to be a form of Platonism and refuted by Wittgenstein. (It is here being assumed that constructivism and Platonism exhaust the possibilities of answers to the question of what links rules and applications. I will argue that in fact they do not.) The alternative account, in which meaning is plastic to ongoing use, is precisely that which the order-of-determination test is supposed to explicate. The rejection of the autonomy of meaning and the application of constructivism to rule-following undermine the idea that the extension of any concept might be independent of all judgements. Thus, both ways in which contrast between extension determination and tracking might be explicated fail. Applying the order-of-determination test to rules undermines its application in other cases – such as primary and secondary qualities – because its effects in the former case ramify in such a way that the contrast that is presupposed in all these cases is evacuated of content.

The second objection recapitulates Wittgenstein's discussion outlined in the previous chapter. There are two related charges. A constructivist account presupposes an answer to the general question of how there can be mental content and also fails to sustain the normativity that is a necessary feature of such content. One critic sets out the first aspect of the difficulty thus:

[I]t is inconceivable, given what *judgement-dependence* amounts to, that the biconditionals in the case of mental content should satisfy the requirement that their left-hand-sides be free of any assumptions about mental content. For, at a minimum, the *content of the judgements* said to fix the facts about mental content have to be presupposed. (Boghossian 1989: 547)

To unpack this a little, the problem is that the application of the order-of-determination test to intentions is significantly different from its application to secondary qualities. This stems from the fact that the issue is one of explaining the construction of mental content (intentions rather than colours) by invoking contentful judgements. Because content is simply assumed in the latter case it seems that no progress is made in explaining intentions.

By itself this criticism may not seem telling. Constructivism has been defended against this argument by the following counter-claim:

[M]y judging that I intend P is constituted trivially and obviously by my judging that I intend P. We should note that intending P was problematic, because it was subject to first-person epistemic authority, and yet seemingly gave hostages to fortune in the shape of requirements on future behaviour, if one did not change one's mind in the interim. But *judging* that one intends P is not in this way problematic, because it is an *act* and as such is complete in that it implies nothing about future behaviour. (Edwards 1992: 27)

The idea is that the judgement that I have a particular intention is a single mental act that happens at a particular time and the content of which can be completely captured without reference to anything that happens on any other occasion. Its content is constituted by the act of judgement there and then, and this content can be used via the biconditional to explicate the more problematic content of the intention. This optimism is misplaced, however. Given the strategic burden that the account is supposed to bear, the content of the judgement that a particular case is an instance of a general rule cannot be presupposed if a substantial answer is to be given to the Wittgensteinian question that constructivism assumes is pressing.

The question of how I can judge whether this instance is the same kind as a set of others is the central question of Wittgenstein's rule-following considerations. How can I grasp the rule that governs what counts as the same and different in indefinitely many cases without anticipating all these cases in advance? When I judge that a state is an intention that P, I classify it as the same kind of thing as the set of instances that comprise the extension of the concept of the intention that P. The content of the judgement links this state with those others. It is a normative 'one-to-many' relation and is thus akin in this respect to intention. While an intention establishes a normative relation to the unlimited set of acts what would satisfy it, a classificatory judgement establishes a normative relation between the item judged and the unlimited set of other items of the same kind. Thus, if what accords with an intention is supposed to be constructed by an act of judgement, the theory needs to be augmented by a further account of what is in accord with that judgement. Judgements resemble intentions in that no feature of sensuous consciousness is necessary or sufficient to determine their content. The normative constraint which they impose on what can satisfy them thus stands in just the same need of explication as that of intentions, alongside expectations, hopes, orders and the like. Consequently, constructivism fails.

In addition to begging the key question, it also fails in a second respect. It fails to sustain the normativity necessary for intentions and for rules. The content of both is claimed to depend on piecemeal construction in subsequent acts of judgement. Because these judgements *determine* content they cannot be said to *accord* with any normative standard, nor to be, in any substantial sense, *correct* representations of the intention or the rule. But it is part of our everyday understanding of an intention and rules that acts are or are not in accord with them. Intentions and rules are normative and determine which acts accord with them, and this feature is missing from constructivist accounts.

It is apparent that this form of constructivism shares both of the defects of the philosophical theories that Wittgenstein considers in order to answer his central question of how one can grasp something in a flash which normatively constrains applications over time. Either the theories propose mechanisms that are insufficient for the normative constraint (typically by postulating causal mechanisms but also by invoking communal ratification) or they presuppose the sort of link that they were supposed to explicate (by postulating self-interpreting signs, for instance). Wright's constructivist account falls prey to both objections together. Some insight can be gained into why this account is so flawed by, again, considering it in its broader context.

Constructivism is deployed as a substantial answer to the question that re-echoes Wittgenstein's question: how can something I grasp in a flash determine future events? Constructivism has the virtue that it eschews explanatory metaphysical mechanisms – such as Platonism – and says that, instead, all there is is human practice. But, as we have seen, it fails to provide a satisfactory answer to the Wittgensteinian question and, furthermore, it fails in a way very similar to the substantial answers that Wittgenstein considers and rejects. Wittgenstein famously summarises their failure:

> It can be seen that there is a misunderstanding here from the mere fact that in the course of our argument we give one interpretation after another; as if each one contented us at least for a moment, until we thought of yet another standing behind it. What this shews is that there is a way of grasping a rule which is *not* an *interpretation*, but which is exhibited in what we call 'obeying the rule' and 'going against it' in actual cases. (1953: §201)

We can now see that the constructivist account of intention is importantly similar to this failed strategy in that it offers something akin to a series of interpretations of the intention in the form of subsequent judgements of its content.

Like the interpretative theory of understanding rules or meanings, Wright assumes that Wittgenstein's question needs, and can be given, a substantial answer. He attempts to explain the problematic content of intentions by postulating contentful intermediaries. The tactic is as flawed as the interpretative theory of rules because it initiates a regress of similar questions about the content of the intermediaries while simultaneously threatening to undermine the normativity of intentions. This latter threat – Wittgenstein's first objection – is realised if the theory does not require that the intermediaries are the *correct* interpretations of the content of the original state. The versions of the interpretative theory of rules that Wittgenstein considers attempt to avoid this problem by requiring the interpretations to be correct and consequently fall prey to his second objection: begging the question. Wright's novelty consists in abandoning the requirement that the intermediaries are correct and thus he succumbs to the first objection. Nevertheless, he also falls prey to the second objection because the intermediaries have content even if they are not required to track the content of the original contentful state.

The moral that I shall draw from this latest constitutive theory is that Wittgenstein's rejection of interpretations should be construed broadly. No explanation via intermediate mechanisms can work. The mechanistic urge to explain mental content by inventive philosophical tinkering to decompose mental states into component parts should be abandoned. The substantial question that Wittgenstein, and later Wright, ask has to be turned aside as Wittgenstein does rather than answered directly as Wright attempts and fails. Wright fails in his account of intention not because he stumbles in the execution of something that Wittgenstein fails even to attempt out of metaphilosophical scruple. Rather his account shares the defect that Wittgenstein exposes in all interpretative accounts. One might say that Wittgenstein and Wright ask the question with different intents. Wittgenstein uses it to focus a critique of a range of different approaches to meaning and mind and then proposes no substantial theory to replace them. Instead he gestures towards more broadly anthropological facts about the context of the practice of rule-following, about our abilities to deploy and comprehend samples and such like. The moral of the rule-following considerations is precisely that no substantial answer can be given to the question and that the phenomenon must simply be presupposed and described. This is the central tenet of the third response to Wittgenstein I shall consider in this chapter: philosophical minimalism.

3 Minimalism

In Chapter 2, I examined the consequences of Wittgenstein's critical arguments about content for representationalist theories. I argued that representationalism faces a dilemma that can be extracted from Wittgenstein's criticism of inter-pretational theories of meaning. Either it presupposes the very thing it was supposed to explain, or it fails to sustain the normativity of content. In either case, it fails as an account of content.

In this chapter I have considered two responses to the question of what connects a rule with its applications – or understanding the meaning of a word with its use – which have been put forward as interpretations of Wittgenstein's positive account. Both take for granted that Wittgenstein refutes Platonism and suggest that he advocates a radical alternative. The sceptical interpretation denies that there is any real connection. The constructivist interpretation argues instead that the consequences of a rule are retrospectively constructed from applications subsequently made. But neither of these interpretations can satisfactorily account for the normativity of content.

In the rest of this chapter I shall begin to sketch out another answer to this question: philosophical minimalism. (Chapter 4 will then fill out a minimalist account of content more generally.) According to this response, the opposition of Platonism to scepticism or constructivism is a false dichotomy. What makes those seem the only available positions is the shared assumption that Wittgenstein's question requires, and can be given, a substantial explanatory answer if content is to be possible. Minimalism asserts that this question has to be turned aside.

3.1   Minimalism and linguistic content

Representationalism, scepticism and constructivism have one assumption in common. They all assume that the meaning of linguistic signs should be explained as resulting from prior mental acts or processes and that those acts can be characterised independently of the content that they are supposed to explain. But, once understanding is identified with a free-standing mental state or process, nothing can reconnect that state to future acts. Any *interpretation* which might bind an independent mental state or act to future linguistic usage will itself have to be explained. Once a state is characterised independently of the normative connections which constitute content, those connections cannot be recovered.

Having summarised the unsuccessful strategy for explaining the normative connections a rule has with its correct applications, Wittgenstein comments:

What this shews is that there is a way of grasping a rule which is *not* an *interpretation*, but which is exhibited in what we call 'obeying the rule' and 'going against it' in actual cases. (§201)

And hence also 'obeying a rule' is a practice. And to *think* one is obeying a rule is not to obey a rule. (§202)

At first sight, invoking practice may seem neither radical nor helpful. The whole of the practice of correctly using a word can no more flash before the mind than can the whole of a mathematical series (cf. §187). But the invocation of practices is not a move made in the context of the failed strategy but marks a change of strategy.

On a minimalist interpretation, Wittgenstein rejects the assumption that understanding a rule is an independent mental state that has to be connected to its applications via some mediating process. Instead, he claims that nothing mediates understanding and its applications. There are no explanatory intermediaries between understanding a word and making the correct use of it. When one comes to understand the meaning of a word, one acquires an ability to use it correctly which cannot be further explained. One simply masters a practice or technique.

This practical reorientation is coupled with Wittgenstein's rejection of the idea that signs are injected with meaning through acts of understanding. He rejects the division of language into 'inorganic' signs and 'organic' understanding. Practices are not deployed within the context of the two-component picture of language but as a replacement for it. The problem with that picture springs from the distinction it draws between the mental state of understanding and the subsequent use of a word. Once that gap is opened up, nothing can close it. (Platonism looks the best solution, but even it leaves the normativity involved in latching on to the *right* standard unexplained.)

The minimalist response is instead to conclude that the 'mental state' of understanding the meaning of a word cannot be characterised independently of the practice of using the word. Understanding a meaning is a piece of 'know-how', a practical ability. One way of putting this is to say that meanings and rules are individuated by practices and that understanding a meaning or a rule is thus individuated by the practice over which one has mastery. But it is important to distinguish Wittgenstein's position from any which concede that understanding has to picked out relationally, via the use of words, but identify it with an internal state which causes those uses. Given the failure of attempts to connect any independent mental item with temporally extended practices, and the suggestion that understanding is more like an ability, Wittgenstein cautions against calling it a mental 'state' or 'process' at all (§§154, 308). Thus, one reason for characterising this as a form of philosophical minimalism is that it abandons the attempt to *explain* the connection between a free-standing mental state of understanding a word and its use. Understanding cannot be identified with any such free-standing state.

This position is different from a sceptical response to the discussion of linguistic content. According to a minimalist interpretation, Wittgenstein does not claim that there are no facts of the matter about meaning. He does not assert that there is no connection between a rule and its applications – and thus between one's understanding of a rule and its applications – as scepticism does. Rather, he denies that this connection can be *explained* through the mediation of other mental or physical processes. Wittgenstein's scepticism is not directed against the reality of content but against philosophical and reductionist explanations of it.

A second respect in which Wittgenstein's account of meaning is minimalist and anti-reductionist concerns the description not of understanding but of the corresponding practice. Just as the state of understanding cannot be described in non-normative terms if its normative connection to practice is to be preserved, neither can practice be reductively described. Tying understanding to practice is not the first stage of a reductionist account of meaning in which practice is then characterised in non-normative, non-intentional terms. That is what Kripkean scepticism and constructivism attempt to do. But once practices are described in norm-free terms, their normativity cannot be recovered. Kripke attempts to derive normativity from the communal criticism, and Wright attempts to derive it from ongoing judgements. But neither attempt at reconstruction arrives back at the everyday normativity of meaning.

This leads Wittgenstein to a modest and minimalist conception of the philosophy of content. Because no form of reduction of meaning is possible – neither by reducing the 'state' of understanding nor the practices of using signs to something non-normative – philosophy cannot provide insight by exploring the hidden underlying structures of meaning. All that there is to meaning is, according to Wittgenstein, open to view (§§121–33). The philosophical resources for explaining meaning cannot exceed the everyday resources for explaining meanings, including description, example and ostensive definition. Philosophy achieves the insight it does here not by digging below the surface of human abilities and practices but by describing them clearly.

Such an account, however, leaves unanswered the question raised at the start of the discussion of rules in §139. How can one understand the meaning of a word in a flash? The moral Wittgenstein draws looks at first to be pessimistic. There is no possibility of a philosophical answer to this question which goes beyond everyday resources. No mental mechanisms or speculative machinery can help. But, in fact, by denying that understanding is a free-standing mental state, Wittgenstein undercuts the need for explanation. The ability to understand meaning is a *primitive* ability that cannot be broken down into constitutive parts. As language users, we have a primitive ability to self-ascribe understanding. Such self-ascriptions are, however, defeasible in the light of subsequent performance. One can sometimes think that one has understood a rule only to discover, when one attempts to apply it, that one has not. This may be more likely in the case of complex rules, such as the rules governing long division, than simply rules governing the use of words. Nevertheless, the self-ascription of understanding a meaning is a fallible glad start underpinned by a general ability and not justified by introspection of an inner state.

Minimalism about linguistic meaning thus comprises the following points:

- The meanings of words are individuated by practices or techniques of use.
- There are no explanatory intermediaries between understanding and use.
- Instead, understanding the meaning of a word is direct unmediated mastery of its use.
- This appeal to practices is part of an alternative to the two-aspect theory of language and not a version of it.
- Neither understanding nor practice can be reductively explained in independent norm-free terms.
- No substantial or constitutive explanation can be given of understanding which is a primitive ability.

Points closely related to these also comprise the minimalist account of mental content.

3.2   Minimalism and mental content

The question that drives the discussion of intentional mental states from §§428–65 is: what connects an intentional mental state (such as an expectation) with the event that satisfies it? The clue which Wittgenstein provides for a minimalist response to it comes from considering a related question at one semantic level higher:

> One may have the feeling that in the sentence 'I expect he is coming' one is using the words 'he is coming' in a different sense from the one they have in the assertion 'He is coming'. But if it were so how could I say that my expectation had been fulfilled? If I wanted to explain the words 'he' and 'is coming', say by means of ostensive definitions, the same definitions of these words would go for both sentences. (§444)

The problem raised at the start of this passage is a linguistic symptom of the 'internal object' theory discussed in the previous chapter. If that theory were true then the words characterising the content of an expectation would designate an internal object (or event), a mere shadow of an external event, and those characterising its fulfilment would designate a different external object (or event). As a result they would have different senses. The description of the fulfilment condition would have nothing to do with the description of the content of the expectation. That the same words were used would be merely a grammatical coincidence. But, as Wittgenstein points out, the words do have the same senses. This is shown by the fact that we can give the same (ostensive) definitions of them. They are not given their meaning by two distinct methods of definition but by one. Thus the internal object theory is false.

Wittgenstein then proposes to approach the general problem of the content of intentional states from the different perspective suggested by this response. Instead of seeing linguistic representation as secondary, he proposes that we see it as of primary importance. The *representation* of expectations and their fulfilment can provide an answer to what links the two:

> But it might now be asked: what's it like for him to come? – The door opens, someone walks in, and so on. – What's it like for me to expect him to come? – I walk up and down the room, look at the clock now and then, and so on. – But the one set of events has not the smallest similarity to the other! So how can one use the same words in describing them? – But perhaps I say as I walk up and down: 'I expect he'll come in.' – Now there is a similarity somewhere. But of what kind?! (§444)

> It is in language that an expectation and its fulfilment make contact. (§445)

This idea is the key to Wittgenstein's explanation of how mental content can normatively determine its fulfilment. But it needs careful interpretation.

Three reinforcing positive suggestions can be derived from the assertion that the relation between an expectation and its satisfaction is revealed by the characteristic expression of the expectation:

- The words which comprise the characteristic *expression* of a mental state can be converted into a *description* of its fulfilment condition.
- Mental states are *individuated* by their fulfilment conditions.
- The connection between a mental state and its fulfilment *depends* (in some way yet to be articulated) on the *linguistic* connection between the characteristic expression of a state, the description of the state and the description of its fulfilment condition.

The claim that states are individuated by their fulfilment conditions suggests some similarity with some of the conclusions of the discussion of rules. In that context there were two related claims:

- The meaning of words are individuated by practices or techniques of use.
- There are no explanatory intermediaries between understanding and use.

Parallel claims can now be made for mental content. Content-laden mental states are individuated by what fulfils them and not by internal mental processes or causal mechanisms underlying them. They are not free-standing internal states. Thus, there is no need to postulate explanatory intermediaries between mental states and their fulfilment conditions. Nor is there any question of first identifying the state – via internal mental processes – and then asking what would satisfy it. *The state just is the state it is in virtue of its having the fulfilment condition it has.*

> 'An order orders its own execution.' So it knows its execution, then, even before it is there? – But that was a grammatical proposition and it means: If an order runs 'Do such-and-such' then executing the order is called 'doing such-and-such'. (§458)

Denying that mental states are free-standing internal states or that their content is given by internal objects suggests one connection to language. If a state is an expectation that *such-and-such* then, nothing will be correctly *described* as fulfilling it which cannot also be described as *such-and-such*. The connection between the two is mirrored by a linguistic or grammatical relationship. A similar discussion of expectation in *Zettel* makes a related claim: 'Like everything metaphysical the harmony between thought and reality is to be found in the grammar of language' (Wittgenstein 1981: §55). This suggests that the philosophical enterprise of attempting to explain the relation between items of thought and items in the world is misguided. The only account that can be given marks the connection, internal to language, between a hope that *such-and-such*, and *such-and-such*. This same minimalist thought is suggested for an account of false thought. While it is tempting to identify the content of true thoughts with corresponding worldly facts, false thoughts cannot be so identified. This is one of the motivations for an internal object theory. Wittgenstein suggests, however, that there is continuity rather than discontinuity between accounts of true and false thoughts:

> The agreement, the harmony, of thought and reality consists in this: if I say falsely that something is *red*, then, for all that, it isn't *red*. And if I want to explain the word 'red' to someone, in the sentence 'That is not red', I do it by pointing to something red. (Wittgenstein 1953: §429)

According to Wittgenstein, the content of true and false beliefs is specified using language that can also be used to describe worldly facts. Given how mental states are individuated, the grammatical platitudes outlined above follow. If a belief that something is red is false then it is not the case that that something is red. If the belief is true then that something is red. The content of the true belief is indeed the fact that the something is red. But this does not require that the content of false beliefs is given in a different way from that of true beliefs. They do not depend on shadows of facts or internal objects.

Commenting on Wittgenstein's remark that thought can capture reality in its net, McDowell says:

> We can formulate the point in a style Wittgenstein would have been uncomfortable with: there is no ontological gap between the sort of thing one can mean, or generally the sort of

thing one can think, and the sort of thing that can be the case. When one thinks truly, what one thinks *is* what is the case. So since the world is everything that is the case (as he himself once wrote), there is no gap between thought, as such, and the world. *Of course thought can be distanced from the world by being false*, but there is no distance from the world implicit in the very idea of thought. (McDowell 1994: 27) [italics added]

The positive side of McDowell's account captures Wittgenstein's remark. There is no gap between true thoughts and the world because the way thoughts are individuated by their contents reuses the same language used to describe facts. This is what we mean by content-laden mental states. But the suggestion that thought can be distanced from the world by being false may suggest the wrong explanation of this. It may suggest that, while the content of true beliefs can be explained by direct appeal to the facts – and thus that there is a direct connection between true thoughts and facts – false thoughts have to be explained in a more round-about way. In other words, the picture may suggest that false thoughts are distanced from the world not just be being false but by being connected to the world in a less direct way. But Wittgenstein's comment about the harmony of thought and the world in §429 suggests that this is not so. The contents of true and of false thoughts can be explained in the same way which will include pointing to samples of redness in the example above. There is no difference in distance from the world of true and false thoughts. But if the thought that *such-and-such* is false then it is not the case that *such-and-such*.

Nevertheless, saying that the connection between state and fulfilment is a matter *internal* to language leaves the following doubt. How can thought ever break out of language to catch reality in its net? Similarly, the claim that there are no explanatory intermediaries between a state and what satisfies it leaves the question: *how* do states determine what would satisfy them? Talk of the individuation of mental states could be construed as merely epistemological. It would be consistent with the idea that mental states are free-standing internal states that we sometimes pick out relationally. The fact that we label mental states by their effects does not explain *how* they have those effects. I think that the connection Wittgenstein makes to language can, however, play a second role in turning these questions aside.

The connection with language might be interpreted as supporting a constructivist account of mental content. Constructivism asserts that the act of self-ascribing a mental state, using the phrase which describes its fulfilment, *determines* or *constructs* the connection between the state and its fulfilment. Such an interpretation would here have the advantage of explaining Wittgenstein's claim about the role of language. But, as I argued in the second part of this chapter, it fails as a coherent interpretation in two ways. It fails to account for the normativity of mental content and, at the same time, presupposes the content of judgements in its attempt to explain the content of mental states.

The alternative to the dichotomy of Platonist or constructivist accounts of the link between a state and its fulfilment is, again, a form of philosophical minimalism. The key negative claim for minimalism about linguistic content was that the connection between understanding a sign and using it correctly cannot be given further explanation. A parallel negative claim has already been made for mental content. No explanation can be given of how it is that mental states determine their fulfilment conditions. The corresponding positive claim for linguistic meaning was that understanding the meaning of a word is, instead, direct unmediated mastery of its use. The positive claim here can be made, with some risk of misunderstanding, by saying that mental states themselves determine their fulfilment conditions directly.

What is misleading about asserting minimalism using this claim is that it may be taken to imply the existence of graspable mental entities or signs that guide people to the fulfilment conditions of their mental states. This is not so. In forming a mental state, one orients or directs oneself directly towards the state of affairs or event that would satisfy it. Just as understanding the meaning of a word is a direct unmediated ability to use it, so having a mental state is a direct orientation towards a possible state of affairs. Thus, mental states are closer to norm-laden behavioural dispositions than inner representations. Quite how close they are to behavioural dispositions is the subject of Chapter 4. Such a characterisation, however, leaves two questions untouched. Firstly, if content-laden mental states are credited with the ability to determine their fulfilments themselves by being behavioral orientations towards them, the substantial question is pushed back one stage. How are we able to form or entertain such states? Secondly, what is the role of language? Answering the second question will, however, shed light on the former.

According to a minimalist interpretation of Wittgenstein, the connection between mental states and the possession of language is less direct than the one proposed by constructivism. It is not that the content of mental states is constructed by their linguistic expression and is thus directly dependent on linguistic content case by case. Rather, the ability to form content-laden mental states depends on a prior ability to discriminate their fulfilment conditions. One cannot intend to avoid the cracks in the pavement, for example, unless one has some way of discriminating what this would amount to. For all but the most rudimentary mental contents, the only method of doing this is via representation in language. Thus, if one were not able to represent in language the fact that *such-and-such*, one could not entertain the intention to bring about the fact that *such-and-such*.

One learns the ability to *form* content-laden mental states as a result of learning the language that describes their fulfilment. These two abilities are distinct and it is conceivable that one might learn the latter without learning the former. One might learn the language to describe the state of affairs that *such-*

and-such without learning the ability to form the expectation that *such-and-such* will come about, or the intention to bring it about. But, as a matter of fact, we do learn the latter having learnt the former.

The connection with practice in the case of understanding linguistic meaning helps fill out how this comes about. First-person avowals of mental states are an extension of natural responses based upon a prior grasp of the language used to describe their fulfilment conditions. Language is grafted on to a background of both linguistic and natural practices (cf. Malcolm 1982). The language of intentions, wishes and the like is grafted on to the everyday descriptive language used to describe what would satisfy them and also on to prior primitive intentional behaviour such as reaching out for desired objects. In learning the language used to self-ascribe mental states one extends the range of one's mental life and behaviour. Without language the range of intentional behaviour is limited to that which can be given non-linguistic behavioural expression. One can only discriminate fulfilment conditions behaviourally. Language radically extends the range of one's discrimination and thus the range of states that one can form:

> Why can a dog feel fear but not remorse? Would it be right to say 'Because he can't talk'? (Wittgenstein 1981: §518)

> Only someone who can reflect on the past can repent. But that does not mean that as a matter of empirical fact only such a one is capable of the feeling of remorse. (§519)

> There is nothing astonishing about certain concepts' only being applicable to a being that e.g. possesses a language. (§520)

One way one might put this account of the relation between mental states and language is to say that one cannot form an intention unless one can *represent to oneself* its fulfilment condition and one has this ability only if one can speak a language. There is something right about this but it may also encourage a misunderstanding of the key idea. While one could not expect something to happen which one could not represent to oneself, this does not indicate an explanation of the inner processes of expectation. Wittgenstein's discussion of rules shows that representation cannot be explained as the result of inner speaking, or entertaining any mental sign or symbol. So the suggestion that one cannot form an expectation unless one can represent its fulfilment condition to oneself should not be construed as offering a partial explanation of what happens internally when one can form such a state. Instead, if one were not capable of discriminating that state of affairs, one could not be oriented towards it. Mental states, such as intentions and expectations, are possible only as part of a more general representational practice.

Minimalism about mental content can now be summarised through the following points:

- The contents of mental states are individuated by their fulfilment conditions.
- There are no explanatory intermediaries between mental state and fulfilment condition.
- Instead, possession of a mental state is direct unmediated orientation towards its fulfilment condition.
- Neither possession of a mental state nor its fulfilment condition can be reductively explained in independent norm-free terms.
- The philosophy of content is thus minimalist and eschews explanation.
- No substantial or constitutive explanation can be given of the possession of mental states which is a primitive ability, albeit one that depends on language.

This characterisation of Wittgenstein's response to the question of what connects meaning and use, mental states and their fulfilment, leaves much about the nature of content unanswered. Chapter 4 will examine in more detail the connection between Wittgenstein's account and other theories of content. It will also examine the consequences of Wittgenstein's account for the distinction between sense and reference and externalism. But there are two final points to note in this chapter. One concerns explanatory priority. The other concerns the reason why a minimalist response is apt to go unnoticed.

Wittgenstein argues that the possession of at least some mental content requires the possession of language. This suggests that he is best characterised as subscribing to the second approach to explanatory priority outlined in the first chapter: explaining mental content through linguistic content. But the accounts of linguistic meaning and mental content are basically the same. Both depend not on internal processes but on normative practices governing the use of signs. This suggests he is best characterised as pursuing the third strategy: assigning no priority. What is important is that Wittgenstein rejects the strategy of explaining the meaning of words through acts of understanding and the two-component view of language.

What makes a minimalist interpretation of Wittgenstein a difficult inter-pretative possibility to spot is that Platonism and either scepticism or con-structivism seem to exhaust the possible answers to the question of what links a rule and its applications. Consider again the biconditional relation between judgement and extension explored in the discussion of constructivism. It was suggested that this could be read in two ways. Either the antecedent extension determines correct judgement or correct judgement determines the extension. The latter reading corresponds to constructivism, and I argued that the former option depends on a form of Platonism. A minimalist interpretation of Wittgenstein provides a third way of responding to the biconditional. This is to deny that the original distinction can be drawn. A minimalist interpretation of Wittgenstein's account of rules denies that the practice of judging can be characterised except by reference to what is judged and that an extension can be specified except by appeal to human practice. That distinction, embodied by the two component view of language is precisely what has to be abandoned if a coherent account of content is to be provided. In Chapter 5, I shall show how this Wittgensteinian conclusion relates to Davidson's attack on the dualism of scheme and content.

Further Reading

Further criticisms of Kripke's interpretation of Wittgenstein can be found, among many others, in Baker and Hacker (1984b), C. McGinn (1984) and in the collection by Puhl (1991). Wright's interpretation is criticised in McDowell (1984, 1991) and Diamond (1991: 205–23).

The minimalist interpretation defended in this chapter and the next owes much to McDowell's work on Wittgenstein, for example McDowell (1984b, 1991, 1992, 1994) as well as Diamond (1991: 39–72) and Luntley (1991).

CHAPTER 4

Wittgenstein and the Theory of Content

Chapter 3 examined three interpretations of Wittgenstein's discussion of linguistic meaning and mental content by focusing on the questions:

- What connects one's understanding of a word with its correct future application?
- What connects an intentional mental state with the event or events that satisfies or satisfy it?
- What is the relation between language or thought and the world?

I argued that sceptical and constructivist interpretations of Wittgenstein failed to give a satisfactory answer to any of these questions. Instead, Wittgenstein is best interpreted as promoting a form of philosophical minimalism in which his key target is philosophical *explanation* of language and mind rather than our everyday concepts. I applied this interpretation to the first two questions.

This chapter will extend and develop that interpretation to examine the kind of overall theory of content that can be derived from Wittgenstein. It will show how Wittgenstein provides materials for meeting key criteria for any plausible theory of mental and linguistic content. These include accounting for the six *pre-philosophical* characteristics of content identified in Chapter 1:

- Content possesses 'aboutness' or intentionality.
- Content can be specified by a 'that-clause'.
- Content is normative.
- Content is asymmetrically accessible from first and third person.
- Content is structured.
- Content plays a role in the explanation of speech and action.

By organising Wittgenstein's account around these points, I shall present the *theory* of content that is implicit in Wittgenstein's later work. Aside from showing systematically how these characteristics relate, marshalling Wittgenstein's thoughts into a theory will help assess two *philosophical* questions. These concern at a deep level the way in which the mind and world are related in mental content. One concerns the debate between internalism and externalism. This concerns the independence or otherwise of mental contents. Could the facts about a person's content-laden mental states be just the same even if there really were no external world, as Descartes considers in the First Meditation? Or does mental content depend not just for its truth but for its very constitution on connections with the world? I shall argue that Wittgenstein supports a minimal version of externalism.

The second philosophical issue is whether Wittgenstein's account of content is consistent with a theory of sense as opposed to a referential theory of meaning. The underlying worry is whether an externalist account of content can be sensitive to the fact that one can think about the same object in different ways, or with different senses. I shall argue that this does not present a problem for Wittgenstein's account.

But there is a preliminary objection that has to be overcome before proceeding in this way. The objection is that any interpretation which ascribes an implicit *theory* to Wittgenstein cannot be right because of his notorious metaphilosophical objections to theorising in philosophy. The objection does not have to suppose that Wittgenstein's actual method *always* lives up to his methodological claims. But because the discussion of content is the central theme of the *Investigations*, it is unlikely that method and methodology would diverge in this case.

One way of responding to this objection might simply be to concede the point and refer instead to Wittgenstein's *philosophy* of content. But there is a reason, in this chapter at least, for confronting the objection explicitly and attempting to regiment Wittgenstein's account into a theory of sorts. Such a structure helps to demonstrate that Wittgensteinian philosophy is relevant to contemporary work on the theory of content. Chapter 5 will compare Wittgenstein's work with that of Davidson and McDowell. And, by responding explicitly to the claim that Wittgenstein cannot be seen as putting forward any sort of systematic theory, I hope to clarify the kind of insight that Wittgenstein provides into this area of philosophy.

1 Wittgenstein and Theories

Wittgenstein's objections to theorising are presented in a short series of methodological remarks as well as in methodological interruptions throughout the body of the *Investigations*:

> And we may not advance any kind of theory. There must not be anything hypothetical in our considerations. We must do away with all *explanation*, and description alone must take its place. (§109)

If one tried to advance *theses* in philosophy, it would never be possible to debate them, because everyone would agree to them. (§128)

The rejection of explanation in favour of description stems from Wittgenstein's conception of philosophical problems:

> And this description gets its light, that is to say its purpose, from the philosophical problems. These are, of course, not empirical problems; they are solved, rather, by looking into the workings of our language, and that in such a way as to make us recognize those workings: in *despite of* an urge to misunderstand them. The problems are solved, not by giving new information, but by arranging what we have always known. Philosophy is a battle against the bewitchment of our intelligence by means of language. (§109)

Philosophical problems are, according to Wittgenstein, conceptual problems. They result from misunderstanding the workings of language. Wittgenstein suggests a variety of sources for this confusion. One example, among many, is a craving for generality. We think, for example, that the relation between the first person and third person that holds for one verb will hold for all verbs, or that the connection between names and what they designate is the same in all cases. But, in fact, closer examination of how we use these words shows that that is not the case. Despite knowing how to speak our language, and thus knowing the rules that govern it, we sometimes misdescribe them. This, in turn, leads us to philosophical confusion.

> A main source of our failure to understand is that we do not *command a clear view* of the use of our words. – Our grammar is lacking in this sort of perspicuity. (§122)

> The fundamental fact here is that we lay down rules, a technique, for a game, and that then when we follow the rules, things do not turn out as we had assumed. That we are therefore as it were entangled in our own rules.
>   This entanglement in our rules is what we want to understand (i.e. get a clear view of). (§125)

One problem with this post-linguistic turn conception of philosophy is that few, if any, philosophers in previous centuries would have recognised this picture of their own activities. A linguistic construal of philosophy seems to require massive past error on behalf of those philosophers. But Wittgenstein's approach to philosophy minimises the implausibility of the error involved. The key source of philosophical error is the drive for explanation. We attempt to explain and to justify the rules that govern language by postulating hidden structures or mechanisms. Take, for example, the claim that only I can feel my pain. The metaphysical approach to philosophy, which Wittgenstein rejects, regards such a truth as an important clue inviting an explanatory account of how pains, unlike most possessions, are private. The truth serves as a starting point for a substantial explanation of the underlying inner realm that leads to the mythology of the Cartesian view of the mind or of representationalism.

According to a minimalist interpretation, Wittgenstein rejects all such explanations but does not deny the claims that inspired them. He does not deny, for example, that only I can feel my pain. But he does deny that it requires substantial explanation through the metaphysical characterisation of the special subjective status of pains. It is, instead, a rule that governs the concept of pain. Thus, it is partly constitutive of what we mean by pain that the subject of the pain is the one who feels it. But this need be no more significant than the claim that only I can have my hiccups.

Because philosophical problems are really conceptual confusions, philosophy, according to Wittgenstein, should aim at achieving a clear view of the workings of language. Once this is attained, then the confusion which might otherwise lead to speculative metaphysical explanation is dissolved rather than answered:

> It is the business of philosophy, not to resolve a contradiction by means of a mathematical or logico-mathematical discovery, but to make it possible for us to get a clear view of the state of mathematics that troubles us . . . (§125)

Wittgenstein argues that, once one has attained a clear view of the workings of an area of language, the confusions and bogus explanations to which it had previously given rise are dissolved. It is not that philosophical questions are answered. Instead, the need to ask, and thus answer, them falls away. For this reason, Wittgenstein argues that explanation has no place in philosophy and should be replaced by description:

> Philosophy simply puts everything before us, and neither explains nor deduces anything. – Since everything lies open to view there is nothing to explain. For what is hidden, for example, is of no interest to us. (§126)

> Philosophy may in no way interfere with the actual use of language; it can in the end only describe it.
>   For it cannot give it any foundation either. (§124)

Although these are meta-philosophical remarks, they can be given some support by Wittgenstein's ground-level account of linguistic rules. One result of that discussion is that the rules which govern language *cannot* be given Platonic foundations nor be explained via underlying causal processes. Thus, if Wittgenstein's view that philosophical problems are always only conceptual problems were true – though this is a substantial and contentious claim – then his prescription for their correction would be correct. The rules which govern linguistic representation cannot be explained in deeper non-normative terms.

Analysis has instead to begin and end with the description of the rules given using normative and intentional concepts. Any attempt to dig deeper and explain the rules using underlying mechanisms will fail to capture their normativity.

This brief characterisation of Wittgenstein's view of philosophy places his rejection of philosophical theorising in context. The target is not all theory, but only explanatory theory. Furthermore, the positive claim that philosophy should aim at a clear overview of language suggests that there might be a role for a descriptive, as opposed to explanatory, theory. Such a theory could clarify and summarise an area of language, on the model of a grammatical theory. It could present an overview of how some of our concepts interrelate and represent their rational and normative connections.

The aims of descriptive theories could be modest while still providing clarification in a limited area. Wittgenstein expresses scepticism that language as a whole could be regimented into a formal deductive structure. Instead he compares it to a sprawling city:

> Our language can be seen as an ancient city: a maze of little streets and squares, of old and new houses, and of houses with additions from various periods; and this surrounded by a multitude of new boroughs with straight regular streets and uniform houses. (§18)

> But how many kinds of sentence are there? Say assertion, question, and command? – There are *countless* kinds: countless different kinds of use of what we call 'symbols', 'words', 'sentences'. And this multiplicity is not something fixed, given once for all; but new types of language, new language-games, as we may say, come into existence, and others become obsolete and get forgotten. (§23)

But Wittgenstein's principled motivation for attacking philosophical theories is not that their subject matter is too complex, unstructured or open ended (although that is true of language as a whole). It is rather that theoretical *explanation* is an inappropriate response to philosophical confusion that can be treated only by clarifying the rules of representation. Given this characterisation of Wittgenstein's view of philosophy and theories, it is entirely consistent to ascribe to him an implicit theory of content. But constraints are placed on the kind of theory it can be.

Before giving an illustration of the kind of theory that is consistent with Wittgenstein's view of philosophy, it will be useful to mark a potential ambiguity. The phrase 'theory of content' can be used in two ways. It can be used to refer to the body of largely implicit knowledge or lore that we use to make sense of, or interpret, one another's actions. In this sense it is synonymous with folk psychology. But it can also be used to refer to a philosophical or reflective account of that ground-level 'theory'. There are some connections between these two levels. It is, for example, a matter of some debate whether folk psychology can properly be called a *theory* at all. Whether or not it can turns on considerations at the reflective level, at the level of a philosophical theory of content.

In ascribing an implicit theory of content to Wittgenstein, I do not mean that he supports the characterisation of folk psychology as a body of theoretical knowledge. Later in this chapter I shall argue to the contrary that, although folk psychology can explain action, it is not an empirical theory of human behaviour. But Wittgenstein supports an implicit theory of content in the second sense. His remarks can be framed as a reflective, philosophical, meta-theory of folk psychology. But they must be characterised as a descriptive, and not an explanatory, theory. They aim at a perspicuous view of the interconnections of the concepts employed and not an explanation of the underlying structures or processes that make them true.

The contrast between descriptive and explanatory theories can be illustrated by contrasting representationalism with a contemporary form of behaviourism. Representationalism attempts to explain the success of folk psychology by postulating an underlying machinery of mental representations. Fodor, for example, argues at some length that interpretative platitudes of folk psychology are generally successful in the explanation of behaviour and have no serious rivals in this task (Fodor 1987: 1–26). He goes on to argue that the only way to explain their success is to conclude that there *really are* underlying, causally active mental representations in a language of thought that mirrors, and explains the success of, the principles of rational explanation. The inference to the existence of a language of thought is a form of inference to the best explanation: a form favoured in much philosophy of science.

Representationalism attempts to provide a justificatory and explanatory meta-theory for the ground level theory of folk psychology. The truth of the ground-level theory is explained – in the higher theory of representationalism – through the postulation of hidden causal mechanisms. It is this that justifies or provides foundations for the platitudes that comprise our everyday interpretative stance. This approach runs counter to Wittgenstein's meta-philosophical prescriptions. The attempt to *explain* the interpretative platitudes of folk psychology and the postulation of a *hidden* mechanism to do this are anathema to Wittgenstein.

A philosophical account of folk psychology, however, need not be explanatory in this way. Dennett, for example, develops a modern non-reductive form of behaviourism that avoids this. Dennett employs two key distinctions (Dennett 1987: 43–68). The first concerns the nature of philosophical reflective understanding of folk psychology. Philosophy aims at a reflective understanding of folk psychology. But this can be provided in two different ways. One can provide an explanatory theory as representationalism does. Or one can provide what

Dennett terms a 'definition' or what might be put more broadly as conceptual analysis. Dennett invokes Ryle's *Concept of Mind* as an example of the latter approach (Ryle 1949). As should be clear from this example, conceptual clarification can be systematic and detailed rather than a simple definition. This is even clearer in the second example he gives which is valence theory in chemistry independent of, or prior to, a detailed atomic theory of atoms. The valence theory is a systematic description of the behaviour of chemical elements. It is a piece of 'logical chemical behaviourism' (Dennett 1987: 45) – a form of conceptual clarification for the practices of chemistry, a meta-theory of the practice. Reflective understanding can thus take the form of the articulation of a systematic theory without postulating underlying mechanisms to explain the rules of the theory. This is not to say that the practices of interpreting and making sense of each other can be formalised as a strict deductive theory like valence theory. That remains an issue to be resolved by philosophical reflection.

Dennett's second distinction concerns theoretical entities. Dennett borrows Reichenbach's distinction between two sorts of theoretical entity: illata and abstracta. *Illata* are posited theoretical and causally interactive entities. *Abstracta* are calculation-bound entities or logical constructs (ibid.: 53). Dennett rejects Fodor's 'industrial strength realism' concerning mental states with the suggestion that Fodor has mistaken the nature of folk psychology's ontological commitment. Although it is committed to the existence of content-laden mental states, these should be construed as abstracta that are specified in an interpretative theory of human behaviour and not as illata that underlie and explain the success of such a theory. Folk psychology is, according to Dennett, abstract in the sense that the states it postulates need not causally interact with one another or exist as physically distinguishable states. All that is needed is that they perform a role in a systematic interpretation and explanation of behaviour. Dennett's meta-theory of folk psychology takes mental states to be abstracta the nature of which is codified by the principles of folk psychology. They are manifest in the surface of folk psychology, not hypothesised to explain it.

In contrasting Dennett's position with representationalism, I am not claiming that Wittgenstein's theory of content is the same as Dennett's. My claim is merely that Dennett provides an already familiar model of a theory of content that avoids the two central meta-philosophical objections that might be thought to rule out articulating Wittgenstein's account of content as a theory. Provided it does not hypothesise underlying and explanatory mechanisms, there are no principled objections to ascribing a theory of content to Wittgenstein.

2 Wittgenstein's Account of the Pre-philosophical Characteristics of Content

2.1 Mental states are content-laden

The first stage of presenting Wittgenstein's remarks as a theory of content, in this reflective sense, is to show how he accommodates the six pre-philosophical characteristics of content articulated in Chapter 1. Given Wittgenstein's hostility to philosophical explanation, these characteristics are not *explained*. But they are placed in a broader descriptive context. In this section I shall briefly and provisionally examine the first three:

- Content possesses 'aboutness' or intentionality.
- Content can be specified by a 'that-clause'.
- Content is normative.

Wittgenstein presupposes the normativity and intentionality of mental states. These are the features that make mental states and language philosophically puzzling. The linguistic practices he investigates are those concerned with understanding and explaining speech and action by ascribing states with an intentional and normative role rather than, for example, brain states with a causal role. These mark out the territory for investigation. But even this preliminary claim – that content has a role to play in making sense of humans – has come under fire from two directions:

- One argument is that there is something wrong with the very notion of content. Kripke and Quine provide arguments of this sort. Kripke's misinterpretation of Wittgenstein, discussed in the previous chapter, centres on an argument that the very notion of content, at least as we have previously understood it, is incoherent. Kripke's argument turns on the fact that content cannot be reduced to any other non-normative mental or physical facts. Quine deploys a similar argument but one based on the claim that content cannot be reduced to specifically *scientifically* respectable properties (Quine 1960). He goes on to claim that the scientifically respectable evidence for fixing the meaning of utterances is insufficient to determine meaning uniquely and thus that meaning is indeterminate.
- A second source of criticism also derives from a view of science. Starting with the assumption that folk psychology is a theory of behaviour susceptible to the same sort of criticism as a scientific theory, it is argued that folk psychology is a bad theory that should be replaced either by neurophysiology or by a scientific psychology the categories of which are informed by neurophysiology

(e.g., Churchland 1989). This argument is typically based on the enumeration of folk psychology's supposed areas of inadequacy as a general scientific theory of behaviour. One such is its inability to explain sleep. The conclusion drawn is that content-laden mental states should be eliminated from a scientifically respectable account of the world.

I argued in the previous chapter that, by contrast with Kripke's interpretation, Wittgenstein is best understood as *defending* content against the sceptical consequences of bad philosophical theories. The fact that, in virtue of its normativity, it cannot be reduced to non-normative, non-intentional notions provides no argument to doubt its reality, merely its reducibility. A similar response is appropriate to Quine's sceptical argument. The fact that meaning is not uniquely fixed by the non-normative facts or evidence which Quine considers scientifically respectable, does not show that meaning is indeterminate. Instead it shows that Quine has an impoverished conception of the appropriate facts or evidence. Quine's attempt to reduce meaning to causal dispositions to respond to stimuli is one of the pictures of meaning that Wittgenstein attacks.

By contrast, Wittgenstein provides no explicit arguments against the second line of criticism of content. That is an argument he simply does not consider, partly because it is premised on a conception of folk psychology that runs counter to Wittgenstein's view: the view that folk psychology is an empirical theory of human behaviour. Because folk psychology is not a theory in that sense – although it is systematic – it is not a candidate for revision or refutation in the light of contemporary findings. For this reason, I shall ignore this threat here. (I shall return to the question of its theoretical status later in the chapter.)

Thus, Wittgenstein simply takes for granted that we make sense of one another, explain and predict behaviour by ascribing content-laden, intentional mental states. He does not provide further foundations to justify this practice. That would run counter both to meta-philosophical proscriptions and also to the minimalist account of linguistic meaning. But he does defend meaning or content against philosophical misconceptions that would have sceptical consequences.

As well as assuming that mental states have content, Wittgenstein stresses their normativity and connects this to the fact that their content can be specified using a 'that-clause'. As I set out in the second chapter, Wittgenstein's arguments for the irreducibility of linguistic and mental of content presuppose their normativity. This is the key premise of the discussion. The meaning of a word *determines* right and wrong uses of it. A mental state *prescribes* what would satisfy it. Wittgenstein argues that all attempts to explain or reduce this connection fail to sustain its normativity.

Having shown that the normativity of linguistic meaning and of mental content cannot be explained through mental intermediaries or underlying processes, Wittgenstein instead claims that normativity is an irreducible feature of content. Taking mental content first, there is no question of first specifying a state and then questioning what its fulfilment condition would be. It is the state it is in virtue of prescribing or being directed towards that condition. It is not just that mental states are internal free-standing states that are picked out relationally. They are themselves relational states. Similarly, linguistic rules and meanings are linked directly and without mediation to appropriate practices or applications. Understanding meanings or rules is individuated by practices. But, again, this is not just a matter of an internal state with intrinsic properties with a merely relational epistemology. Such a free-standing state would somehow have to be connected to the right practice. But any intermediary would undermine the normative connection which (understanding) a rule imposes on its correct application. The rule is constituted by the practice, and one understands that practice directly.

The essential connection between a mental state and what would fulfil it is reflected by the fact that it is individuated by its fulfilment condition. The same language which is used to describe the fulfilment condition is used to describe the mental. The condition that would fulfil an intention that *such-and-such* is the condition that *such-and-such*. I can satisfy the order that *so-and-so* by bringing *so-and-so* about. This reuse of language ensures that the content of mental states can be given by a 'that-clause'. Normativity, intentionality and the use of that-clauses are linked in the individuation of mental states.

It seems, however, that these remarks simply fail to address the question: *how* does thought latch onto things, *how* can mental state be about things? I shall return to the question of what, if any, positive account of intentionality Wittgenstein offers towards the end of this chapter. But, at the risk of repetition, it is worth re-emphasising here that Wittgenstein rejects one of the assumptions that makes those questions pressing. *If* one thinks of mental states as free-standing internal states – whether brain states or mental tokens – then the question of how they can be connected to things in the world is substantial and unanswerable. But Wittgenstein denies the antecedent assumption. If, however, mental states are not internal states, what sort of states are they? This will become clearer throughout this chapter.

2.2   Content is asymmetrically accessible from first and third person

It is the normativity of linguistic meaning and of mental content that makes first- and-third person access philosophically puzzling. Because understanding the meaning of a word or forming a content-laden mental state has normative consequences for one's future access, what connects prior understanding or mental state to the future? But there is also a problem for third-person access. How can the whole meaning of a word be explained? Paraphrase postpones the problem to explaining the substituted words. But explanation by example could be interpreted in various ways.

2.2.1   First-person access

The minimalist account of first-person access, outlined in the previous two chapters, is largely negative. There can be no substantial explanation of what connects one's understanding of meaning with use over time, or a mental state with what would fulfil it. There is no inner state from which the correct use of a word, for example, is inferred or read off. Nor can understanding or another content-laden mental state consist in any mental signs or representations that have to be interpreted. Any such theory which attempts to decompose under-standing into component processes will fail in one of two ways. It will beg the question by, for example, presupposing the content of the interpretation of inner symbols. Or, it will fail to sustain the normativity of linguistic or mental content if it invokes a merely causal connection or a form of constructivism.

In the place of mechanistic explanation, Wittgenstein offers merely a descriptive claim. Understanding the meaning of a word is a practical mastery of the technique of using it correctly. This ability is basic in that it cannot (generally) be explained as resulting from further, underlying mental processes. (I say *generally* because one can imagine exceptional cases where one's under-standing the meaning of one word requires that one takes active steps to avoid confusing it with another, perhaps using a mental mnemonic. I shall take this qualification for granted in what follows.) There are no mental intermediaries that can explain how one's understanding connects to the use one makes. One simply understands that use.

The rejection of explanatory intermediaries seems most radical and un-realistic in the case of sudden understanding with which Wittgenstein begins the discussion of rules. In such cases, it seems that there must be a further explanation because otherwise it is quite mysterious how one knows, in a flash, that one has the ability to use a word in the right way. But Wittgenstein argues that the characteristic experience of sudden understanding is really a fallible glad start. It is subject to, and can be overturned by, future testing. One may not, after all, be able to use correctly the word that one thought one had mastered. Although there may be characteristic experiences which occur when one suddenly understands something, none of these experiences *constitutes* understanding in a flash. None *explains* how one is able to use a word correctly afterwards.

Wittgenstein's account of first-person access to mental states is similarly austere. The ability to form mental states with intentional content cannot be explained through decomposition into non-normative constituent processes. One simply learns to form and to self-ascribe states which must be characterised in normative terms that prescribe what would satisfy them. While this ability cannot be broken down into underlying non-normative processes, Wittgenstein does connect it to linguistic competence. Being able to form all but the most rudimentary mental states depends upon, and is an extension of, being able to describe what would satisfy them. Having learned the latter ability, one learns also to orient oneself towards future states of affairs, to guide one's behaviour by consideration of them, and to form mental states about them. The acquisition of language extends a person's behaviour and his or her mental life (Wittgenstein 1981 §§518–20).

In addition to this austere and critical account of what first-person access does *not* comprise, there are two further positive characterisations discussed in the *Investigations*. One occurs in the final section of the first part (§§661–93):

'You said, "It'll stop soon". – Were you thinking of the noise or of your pain?' If he answers 'I was thinking of the piano-tuning' – is he observing that the connexion existed, or is he making it by means of these words? – Can't I say *both*? If what he said was true, didn't the connexion exist – and is he not for all that making one which did not exist? (§682)

I draw a head. You ask 'Whom is that supposed to represent?' – I: 'It's supposed to be N.' – You: 'But it doesn't look like him; if anything, it's rather like M.' – When I said it represented N. – was I establishing a connexion or reporting one? And what connexion did exist? (§683)

What is there in favour of saying that my words describe an existing connexion? Well, they relate to various things which didn't simply make their appearance with the words. They say, for example, that I *should have* given a particular answer then, if I had been asked. And even if this is only conditional, still it does say something about the past. (§684)

These passages could be interpreted as advocating a form of constructivism. First-person access would then be construed as *making* connections that did not previously exist between thoughts and their objects. But, if so, they would be susceptible to the criticisms set out in Chapter 3. The motivation suggested in these passages for a constructivist account of first person access is the failure of the only obvious alternative. There does not appear to be the sort of connection between thought and its objects that might be perceived by introspection (cf. §666). Again, however, the need for that sort of connection is based on a conception of thoughts as internal free-standing states. Wittgenstein continues: 'Certainly such a connexion exists. Only not as you imagine it: namely by means of a mental *mechanism*' (§689).

Wittgenstein also suggests a different model of first-person access to mental states in the case of sensations. First-person reports of sensations are not judgements but *expressions* of being in those states (e.g., §§244, 256). The verbal report that one has a throbbing toothache replaces, and stands in the place of, natural expressions of that pain such as crying out and holding one's mouth. One way of interpreting this claim is as a denial that first-person reports of sensations are judgements, capable of truth or falsity. This is not an altogether convincing account of the first-person access to sensations. It seems even less promising for complex content-laden mental states. The problem is that first-person reports can enter into the rational structure of reasons in ways that suggest that they are statements.

But what is important about Wittgenstein's connection between first-person reports and expressions is that it serves as an alternative to the Cartesian picture in which first-person reports are the result of inner perception. That is the picture that Wittgenstein wishes to overthrow. Natural expressions of sensations provide an alternative to an inner epistemology of private objects. But they are not an obligatory alternative. The best strategy here is again minimalist. It is to recognise the force of the critical arguments and to abandon the Cartesian model. But one should also resist the temptation to assimilate all first-person access to the model of the expression of sensation, and then propose no further model. The key claim is negative: we have a primitive fallible ability to report our mental states without mediation. But this does not imply that first-person reports are not statements capable of truth and falsity.

Wittgenstein's position can also be contrasted with the representationalist explanation of first-person access. According to representationalism, the relation between first-person reports and the states they report is causal. Representationalism populates the mind with inner states standing in causal relations. A causal model has even been suggested by one Wittgensteinian commentator to explain reports of sensations (Hopkins 1975). But Wittgenstein cannot subscribe to that model of access to intentional states (nor sensations, although I will present no arguments for this claim here). Firstly, it presupposes that one can stand in causal relations to inner states which runs counter to Wittgenstein's attack on the inner. Secondly, mere causal relations cannot accommodate the normativity of first-person reports.

2.2.2 Third-person access

Third-person access receives less attention than first-person access in the *Investigations*. But there is an important parallel in their treatment. Just as Wittgenstein attacks inferential or interpretative models of the latter, he also attacks an inferential account of the former. The explanation of first-person access which he attacks inserts interpretations between the state of understanding a word and using it or a mental state and its fulfilment. The faulty explanation of third-person access inserts them between others' use of words or behaviour and the meaning or content of the words or actions. Wittgenstein argues that there is no role for such epistemic intermediaries in either case.

The motivation for inserting interpretations in this third-person case is the thought that explanations of meaning can never contain the whole of the meaning, and behaviour can never fully demonstrate one's mental state. Explanation cannot contain the whole of the correct use of a word because that use is open ended. Explanation by paraphrase simply postpones the problem to that of explaining the correct use of the substituted phrase. Explanation by example covers only a vanishingly small fraction of the possible correct applications of the word. Instead, it seems that successful explanation consists in getting the person to *guess* the correct interpretation of the examples (§210). If all goes well and a pupil correctly guesses what is meant by the teacher, then he or she has a deeper understanding than that which was actually conveyed. The same kind of argument can also be applied to the interpretation of behaviour because behaviour is consistent with an unlimited number of different mental states, and a particular mental state is consistent with an unlimited number of different kinds of behaviour.

Interposing interpretations has, however, the same disastrous consequences as the interpretational theory of first-person access. One problem is this. If an interpretation is needed to convert what is communicated into a fully fledged meaning or rule then, if normativity is to be preserved, there has to be a standard for the *correct* interpretation. But no such standard can be set because it would also have to be communicated and its consequences explained and this fact starts a vicious regress. The problem is not that explanations might be widely misunderstood, or not understood correctly. The problem is that, on this model, there is no such thing as understanding an explanation correctly. All explanations necessarily underdetermine what they seek to fix. There is not really any third-person access.

McDowell raises a second related epistemological objection (McDowell 1981: 244). Suppose there were Martians who looked and sounded like humans but in general, their words carried different meanings. Short bursts of Martian speech might sound like intelligible human speech. But, after longer encounters, we would, generally, realise that we had not really understood the Martian at all. We had merely thought that we had. The problem McDowell raises is how we can ever know that we understand a stranger:

> For one would need to be able to exclude, purely in terms of what is available to one at the putatively foundational level, the possibility that he is just such a Martian; and has one enough, at that level, to exclude that possibility? Once one has this worry, extending to any

finite length the periods during which things seem to go smoothly cannot make any difference of principle. So it comes to seem that any claim to understand someone's utterances goes beyond what we have any genuine epistemic right to. (ibid.: 244)

In addition to these problems, Wittgenstein also points out the absurdity of thinking that there is something missing from a third-person explanation. The problem is to fill out what it is that can be privately added to the public explanation to arrive at the understanding that the teacher has and is trying to convey. Any further explanation that she might give to herself *sotto voce* as to how the examples are to be taken, she could say aloud. So if explanation aloud underdetermines meaning, then private explanations should also fail to fix content (§§209–11). If an argument of this sort is not to undermine private understanding, there has to be a form of private understanding that cannot be made public. But, as Wittgenstein demonstrates, there are no candidates for such private explanation – because inner signs or templates fail to sustain normativity – and thus the picture of a deeper private understanding cannot be filled out.

What drives this mistaken picture of third person access is an impoverished conception of what is shared in an explanation:

If I give anyone an order I feel it to be *quite enough* to give him signs. And I should never say: this is only words, and I have got to get behind the words. Equally, when I have asked someone something and he gives me an answer (i.e. a sign) I am content – that was what I expected – and I don't raise the objection: but that's a mere answer. (§503)

But if you say: 'How am I to know what he means, when I see nothing but the signs he gives?' then I say: 'How is *he* to know what he means, when he has nothing but the signs either?'(§504)

It is tacitly assumed that the *pattern* of use of a word cannot be manifested in an explanation. The same assumption is made about linguistic practice in general. And it is this assumption that also drives one version of the problem of other minds: that the mental states of others have to be *inferred* from intrinsically meaningless behaviour. The correct conclusion to be drawn from the discussion of explanation is that, if the examples which are given are shorn of the norm that they exemplify, then normativity cannot be reconstructed (cf. Luntley 1991). Explanation, linguistic utterances and behaviour are all ineliminably norm-laden. Any satisfactory philosophical account of them must build in their norm-ladenness in their initial characterisation. Third-person access to linguistic and mental content is not a matter of inference from lifeless signs but the direct experience of irreducible norms present in linguistic and other behaviour.

This is the picture of third-person access that McDowell proposes (McDowell 1982). Put roughly, we can have direct access to what other people mean when they speak, and to their mental states more generally.

What is given in third-person access does not fall short of the facts about meanings or mental states themselves. They are not inferred from some thinner version of communication. In fact, this claim has to be toned down to take account of a plausible pre-philosophical distinction between those cases where the full fact is directly available – such as the meaning of words – and those where a state is *expressed* in speech and action:

> The idea of a fact [about others' meanings or mental states] being disclosed to experience is in itself purely negative: a rejection of the thesis that what is accessible to experience falls short of the fact in the sense I explained, namely that of being consistent with there being no such fact. In the most straightforward application of the idea, the thought would indeed be – as in [direct] realism – that the fact itself is directly presented to view, so that it is true in a stronger sense that the object of experience does not fall short of the fact. But a less straightforward application of the idea is possible also, and seems appropriate in at least some cases of knowledge that someone else is in an 'inner' state, on the basis of experience of what he says and does. Here we might think of what is directly available to experience in some such terms as 'his giving expression to his being in that "inner" state': this is something that, while not itself actually being the 'inner' state of affairs in question, nevertheless does not fall short of it in the sense I explained. (ibid.: 472–3)

For simplicity I shall talk in what follows of direct access to others' mental states.

However, the rejection of an inferential or interpretative theory of third-person access to linguistic and mental content, however, risks inviting two related criticisms:

- If meaning could be communicated directly – including explanations by example – then it would not be in any sense a theoretical notion. But meaning is theoretical. So this account of direct access must be wrong.
- If mental content is visible in the surface of behaviour, then it is not independent of behaviour. Thus, folk psychology cannot be explanatory. (But it is explanatory. So the account of direct perception must be wrong.)

The answer to both these questions turns on the normative structure of content. I shall consider them in turn while setting out the role of the last two pre-philosophical characteristics of content in Wittgenstein's account.

2.3   Content is structured

The first objection to Wittgenstein's attack on interpretational theories of content is that any alternative undermines the necessarily *theoretical* character of meaning. Bilgrami raises this objection against McDowell's Wittgensteinian account (McDowell 1981):

> [McDowell] argues that we must think of understanding others as a form of *direct* perception of their meanings and he intends that analogy to be taken quite literally. By it, he means

that we must think of understanding as simply perceiving *in* the bodily motions and sounds of others, their meaning and their thoughts . . . which, I believe does make the mistake of denying all theoretical status to "meaning". I . . . take meaning to be a theoretical notion . . . constructed partly out of the relations in which their possessors' sounds and bodily motions stand to their environments. (I contrast theoretical posit not with common sense posit, but with the idea that there is something directly perceived and which is not to be viewed as a construction out of a theoretical procedure which involves an essential appeal to an external element in the constitution of what is constructed.) (Bilgrami 1992: 202–3)

[M]eaning and content are not a matter of direct perception. They are theoretical notions. (ibid.: 207)

The objection is, that if meaning can be directly perceived, it cannot be theoretical. The passage offers three characterisations of a theoretical account of meaning:

- Meaning is not directly observable and must instead be a matter of theoretical inference.
- It thus involves construction from non-meaningful, norm-free items: mere sounds and motions.
- It depends on relations between speakers and their environments.

The first two claims are false. The third claim is true. But it can be made without concluding that meaning is theoretical.

Taking the third claim first, if meaning is essentially relational, it cannot be based on internal objects or mental representations. Signs and utterances possess intentionality. They can refer to distant or non-existent states of affairs. Mental states prescribe the facts or events that would satisfy them. If the claim that meaning is directly observational were inconsistent with these comments, then it would be right to say, instead, that it must instead be a matter of theoretical inference. Thus, one (fallacious) motive for saying that meaning is theoretical is the assumption that nothing which has the normative and relational consequences of meaning could be directly observable. But that turns on the idea that what is directly perceivable must be norm-free. And that is just the claim that I have argued is incoherent.

The second characterisation of meaning provides evidence that this is the presupposition of the objection. If the claim that meaning is theoretical means that it results from theoretical construction from norm-free input, then it must be false. As Wittgenstein demonstrates, such a characterisation makes sharing meaning impossible while the alternative – private meanings – requires just the substantial explanation of meaning that Wittgenstein's discussion of understanding rules out. But this characterisation can be rejected without threatening the correct point that content is normative.

It is not necessary to regard meaning as theoretical in the sense of requiring construction from meaningless items, such as bare sounds and bodily motions, to accept that it is theoretical in the sense that the ascription of meaning to utterances and content-laden mental states to people is always subject to correction. This point is, however, better put simply by saying that content is structured.

In the first chapter I distinguished two ways in which content is structured. One is the *rational* structure into which propositional attitudes fit. The ascription of attitudes presupposes their rational interconnectedness in an overall system. The other is the systematicity of thought captured by Evans's Generality Constraint. The ability to understand one thought presupposes the ability to understand other thoughts because all turn on constituent abilities.

Wittgenstein's account helps explicate Evans's Generality Constraint. The ability to use language to describe or to represent states of affairs depends on ability to use words and to combine them in grammatical sentences. It depends, in other words, on mastery of linguistic rules. But, according to Wittgenstein, these are essentially general abilities. To know the meaning of a word is not to be in an internal state but to have mastered a *general* technique or practice. One would not count as understanding meaning without being able to make more than one application. Thus, the ability to represent one thing presupposes an ability to represent others.

Because, according to Wittgenstein, the ability to form and entertain more than primitive mental states depend upon, and is an extension of, mastery of linguistic representation, the explanation of the Generality Constraint for language carries over to mental content as well. To be able to form a mental state presupposes an ability to discriminate what would fulfil it. Because that ability is necessarily general, then so is the ability to form content-laden mental states. Wittgenstein does not attempt to explain the Generality Constraint by postulating an inner vehicle of representation that is also governed by it. Rather, the constraint follows from the nature of the abilities which are criterial of understanding meaning or having mental states.

Similarly, there is no need to explain the rational and normative structure of content by appeal to underlying mental or physical mechanisms. Spoken or written symbols and sentences stand in rational relations because of the normative connections fixed by linguistic rules. Mental states inherit these rational relations through their description using that-clauses. Because content is normative, being in one content-laden state has consequences for other states and behaviour. If one has a particular belief then one ought not to believe other things that contradict it. If one desires something, one ought to avoid behaviour that will frustrate that desire. These are normative relations fixed by the identity of the states. They stand in need of no further explanation through underlying causal mechanisms.

Because content is relational, normative and systematically structured, there is something right about saying that it is theoretical. But this does not imply that meanings and mental states cannot be directly perceived and must instead be constructed from brute and meaningless data, bare sounds and motion. This claim may invite the following response. How can something which is normative and relational be present in the surface of behaviour? I shall return to this question in Chapter 5 when I discuss Davidson's account of radical interpretation (which is the account that underpins Bilgrami's criticism). But the short answer is this. While meaning can be directly perceived once one has mastered language, such perception is fallible. It stands open to correction by appeal to a broader context. Individual perceptions are subject to correction in the light of subsequent (or prior) behaviour in much the way that first-person access is also subject to broader context. But more light will be shed on this by looking at how folk psychology can be explanatory.

2.4   Content plays a role in the explanation of speech and action

The second objection to Wittgenstein's account of third-person access is related to this point. If mental content is visible in the surface of behaviour, then it is not independent of behaviour. Thus, folk psychology cannot be explanatory. But again, the response to this is that folk psychology can be explanatory because of its structure and systematicity. Explanation using content puts actions in context and explains their meaning and purpose. (I shall return to the question of whether it is also *causal* in Chapter 6.) Ascribing content-laden mental states reveals the pattern into which individual actions fit, shows what they have in common and what they are directed towards. Content-laden mental states play an explanatory role through the rational pattern they impose on action:

> An expectation is imbedded in a situation, from which it arises. The expectation of an explosion may, for example, arise from a situation in which an explosion *is to be expected.* (§581)

> 'But you talk as if I weren't really expecting, hoping, *now* – as I thought I was. As if what were happening *now* had no deep significance.' – What does it mean to say 'What is happening now has significance' or 'has deep significance'? What is a *deep* feeling? Could someone have a feeling of ardent love or hope for the space of one second – *no matter what* preceded or followed this second? – What is happening now has significance – in these surroundings. The surroundings give it its importance. And the word 'hope' refers to a phenomenon of human life. (§583)

The response that folk psychology can be explanatory because it places actions, or speech, in a context or pattern which reveals their point does not imply that it forms an *empirical* theory of human action. It is not, as a whole, a true or false characterisation of human behaviour. Firstly, the abilities involved in learning to form states and to express, report or describe them are interdependent. The concepts employed do not reflect completely independent states. This is not to say that *constructivism* is true. It is not that *each* state is constructed by reporting it. But the general abilities to form mental states and to report them are interconnected.

Secondly, the systematic connections between states on which folk psychology relies do not generally depend on contingent empirical generalisations. There may be some empirical generalisations such as that absence makes the heart grow fonder. But the general framework of folk psychology is not contingent. The connection between understanding a word and subsequently using it correctly is not contingent. The rational structure which governs mental content is not a matter of empirical discovery but rather reflects normative connections between the descriptions that are used to individuate mental states. In learning to form such states one learns to orient oneself and one's actions within a rational 'space' of reasons that is distinct from causal connections (cf. McDowell 1994). But the fact that folk psychology is not generally an empirical science of behaviour does not undermine its explanatory status. While the categories it comprises are not empirical postulates which characterise an independent ontology, one can still explain speech and behaviour by describing the mental states of its author. But there are two objections to Wittgenstein's account of mental content that might be thought to undermine the explanatory role of folk psychology.

Wittgenstein sometimes argues that explanation should be replaced by description. Thus, it might be objected that the claim that mental states explain action therefore runs counter to Wittgenstein's general philosophy. This is not, however, a serious objection and I suggest it merely to prevent a misunderstanding. Wittgenstein's attack on explanation is a metaphilosophical proscription and not a general philosophical distrust. It is one of Wittgenstein's methodological claims about the form that philosophical insight should take. It rules out theoretical or hypothetical explanations of linguistic practices and mental abilities via the postulation of underlying or hidden processes. But it is not intended as a criticism of everyday explanatory practices. To the contrary, Wittgenstein urges that philosophy should leave everything outside philosophy unchanged. Wittgenstein's anti-revisionism leaves folk psychological explanation as it is.

There is a second and more serious objection which is that Wittgenstein supports a form of behaviourism. The objection runs as follows. If mental states are defined as dispositions to behave in certain characteristic ways, then mental-states cannot *explain* action because they are not sufficiently independent of it. According to behaviourism, mental state descriptions are really disguised or shorthand versions of behavioural descriptions. Thus, they cannot be invoked to explain the same chunks of behaviour.

One response to this objection is to deny that Wittgenstein advocates any form of behaviourism. Aside from providing a rich description of mental phenomena throughout the *Investigations*, Wittgenstein himself explicitly rejects the accusation:

'But you will surely admit that there is a difference between pain-behaviour accompanied by pain and pain-behaviour without any pain?' – Admit it? What greater difference could there be? – 'And yet you again and again reach the conclusion that the sensation itself is a *nothing*.' – Not at all. It is not a *something*, but not a *nothing* either. (§304)

'But you surely cannot deny that, for example, in remembering, an inner process takes place.' – What gives the impression that we want to deny anything? When one says 'Still, an inner process does take place here' – one wants to go on: 'After all, you *see* it.' And it is this inner process that one means by the word 'remembering'. – The impression that we wanted to deny something arises from our setting our faces against the picture of the 'inner process'. (§305)

Why should I deny that there is a mental process? But 'There has just taken place in me the mental process of remembering . . .' means nothing more than: 'I have just remembered . . .'. To deny the mental process would mean to deny the remembering; to deny that anyone ever remembers anything. (§306)

'Are you not really a behaviourist in disguise? Aren't you at bottom really saying that everything except human behaviour is a fiction?' – If I do speak of a fiction, then it is of a *grammatical* fiction. (§307)

In these passages Wittgenstein carefully distinguishes between mental states and behaviour and thus should not be interpreted as attempting to obliterate that distinction.

Nevertheless, there are close ties between mental states and behaviour. Because mental content depends on linguistic content, being able to form mental states requires underlying practical abilities to use and explain signs. These practical abilities play a constitutive role in the formation of mental states. Thus, there is an a-priori and analytic connection between mental states and behaviour. Whether or not that connection is sufficient to warrant the account being called behaviourist, it might be thought enough to support the objection to the explanatory role of mental states.

But, I think, the objection relies on an overly narrow interpretation of Wittgenstein's claim that an inner process stands in need of outward criteria (§580). The argument for a connection between behaviour and mental states does not imply a one-to-one correlation between content and characteristic behaviour. Wittgenstein does not support a reductive form of behaviourism in which being in a mental state implies and is implied by a particular piece of behaviour or disposition. Early arguments in favour of functionalism and against behaviourism were right to emphasise that a mental state leads to action only in the context of other mental states (Block 1980: 175). My thirst will not dispose me to drink water that I also believe to be poisoned. But the link between mental states and actions which Wittgenstein claims is not a one-to-one correlation susceptible to this argument. The rational structure of mental content mediates between any one mental state and the action that it justifies.

Some light is shed on the connection between behaviour and mental states by considering the analogy that has been made between linguistic content and character (Wright 1986). Consider two opposing ways of thinking about a person's character. One might think of it as a template, fixed at birth and modified only as a result of traumatic experiences, which guides or determines a person's actions throughout his or her life. In the broad sense in which I have used the term, this would be a form of Platonism about character. Alternatively, a constructivist might argue – as Wright does – that a person's character is a logical construct from the totality of a person's actions. On such a picture, it is possible to act out of character on occasion if one's action fails to fit the best overall pattern. But it is not (logically) possible for all one's actions to be out of character. These two positions thus stand as analogues of the possible relation between the meaning of a word and its use.

I argued in Chapters 2 and 3, however, that neither Platonism nor constructivism could successfully accommodate the normativity of meaning. Thus, the correct analogy rejects the Platonist explanation of a fixed template, but adds to the constructivist account the further claim that actions can be described characterfully. The account of character is not a *reductionist* behaviourism that explains what a character is using non-character-related language. Thus, actions which constitute one's character might be described as, for example, brave or cowardly actions. (Some, however, will not be appropriately described as manifesting any particular character in themselves.) Nevertheless, an assessment of a person's character does depend on a broader pattern of actions. (Unlike a constructivist account, minimalism does not have to depend on the totality of actions because character – normativity – is built into the description of at least some of the actions, and thus the character can be determined by a subset of all the actions ever undertaken. Other actions can be of the same sort, following the same pattern.) An action which would usually indicate bravery would not be a sign of brave character if the context suggested it was undertaken when drugged. And one-off brave acts would not outweigh a lifetime of cowardice. The correct connection between actions and character is thus more flexible than the one to one correlation that reductive forms of behaviourism take. It is this that enables some distance between character and individual actions and that in turn, enables the characterful explanation of action. Actions can be non-vacuously contextualised in a broader pattern.

This analogy with character is intended to shed light on how the ascription of propositional attitudes can be explanatory. Description using intentional concepts places actions in context. The systematicity of content is what underpins its explanatory capacity. (The causality of such explanation is another issue and the subject of Chapter 6.) But it also sheds light on the connection between content-laden mental states and behaviour. The possession of mental states depends upon a complex of abilities and norm-laden behavioural dispositions. But this does not obliterate the distinction between possession of mental states and behaviour.

Firstly, the connection is not reductionist. By learning to form mental states of increasing sophistication one's behavioural repertoire also increases. One learns, for example, to make assertions or promises, or to express hopes or fears. These actions could not be fully described in non-intentional terms, however. Secondly, although mental states presuppose practical and behavioural manifestations, this does not imply that to have a mental state is merely to act as though one has. One might act with the characteristic behaviour of someone intending to get married while secretly intending to abandon proceedings at the altar. Nevertheless, the ability either to intend to get married or to intend merely to pretend to, depends on prior practical abilities to discriminate the actions of getting married. The formation of content-laden mental states presupposes practical abilities.

Context is apparent in explanation in another way. Even behaviour which serves as the typical expression of a mental state may depend on a broader context:

> Now suppose I sit in my room and hope N.N. will come and bring me some money, and suppose one minute of this state could be isolated, cut out of its context; would what happened in it then not be hope? – Think, for example, of the words which you perhaps utter in this space of time. They are no longer part of this language. And in different surroundings the institution of money doesn't exist either.
>
> A coronation is the picture of pomp and dignity. Cut one minute of this proceeding out of its surroundings: the crown is being placed on the head of the king in his coronation robes. – But in different surroundings gold is the cheapest of metals, its gleam is thought vulgar. There the fabric of the robe is cheap to produce. A crown is a parody of a respectable hat. And so on. (§584)

Any ascription of mental content on the basis of behaviour is defeasible in the light of further context. And even what is normally characteristic of a kind of mental state depends on context. Thus, again, the charge that Wittgenstein undermines the explanatory role of content can be rejected. Explanation using content puts actions in context and explains their meaning and purpose.

3   Wittgenstein's Theory of Content and Externalism

Having now organised Wittgenstein's account of content around the six pre-philosophical characteristics of content outlined in the first chapter, I can now return to two *philosophical* issues. I suggested in Chapter 3 that interpretations of Wittgenstein could be assessed by their responses to two questions:

- What connects one's understanding of a word with its correct future application?
- What connects an intentional mental state with the event or events that satisfies or satisfy it?

and then suggested that these could be generalised as:

- What is the relation between language or thought and the world?

Chapter 3 argued that the best interpretation of Wittgenstein was a form of philosophical minimalism. According to this interpretation, Wittgenstein rejects explanatory or reductionist answers to these questions and returns pleonastic answers. Understanding the meaning of a word connects directly with its correct applications. Mental states connect directly with what would satisfy them. I think that the best answer to the third question is also minimalist. Language and mind themselves connect directly to the world without need of mediation. What makes this answer difficult to spot is the prior assumption that a distinction can be drawn between language or mind and the world. Once that distinction has been made then a substantial answer is needed as to how the two sides can be connected. Wittgenstein, however, rejects that dualism. In Chapter 5 I shall compare Wittgenstein's position with Davidson's rejection of the dualism of conceptual scheme and empirical content. In this chapter I shall examine this issue via the question of whether Wittgenstein supports a form of philosophical externalism.

The debate between internalist and externalist theories of content concerns its world-independence. Internalism is the view that linguistic or mental content is essentially independent of the world. The content of one's thoughts could be just as they are even of the external world did not exist. This is a presupposition of Descartes, discussion in the First Meditation. Of course, many of one's thoughts would be false if there were no external world. But, according to an internalist account of content, the content of one's thoughts – by contrast with their truth values – does not depend for its existence on the nature of the world.

Externalism, by contrast, claims that mental (and linguistic) content depends upon, or is constituted by, states of the non-mental world. This might be a general claim that all thoughts are so dependent (Bilgrami 1992). Or it might be the claim that singular thoughts depend on the world (e.g., Evans 1982,

McDowell 1986). Singular thoughts are thoughts that latch on to objects not by satisfying descriptions – 'the tallest boy in the class' – but through demonstratives – 'that boy!'. Whatever its form, externalism claims, however, that at least some intentional states of mind are not 'self-standing configuration[s] in the inner realm, whose intrinsic nature should be knowable through and through' (McDowell 1986: 151). Instead, they depend upon and are constituted by, connections to the world. The nature of the connections postulated varies but all forms of externalism are united by the claim that there must be some for thoughts to exist.

The difference between externalism and internalism is best regarded as a difference of *explanatory* thesis. Consider my belief that my copy of the *Investigations* is battered. What is the connection between this thought and the world? One answer is simply that it concerns my copy of the *Investigations* and its battered state. So it obviously concerns that part of the world. This much can be read off the description of the belief. Internalism and externalism can agree with this pre-philosophical claim. Where they disagree is how to explain *how* the belief can have that content, *how* it can connect with the world.

In what follows, I shall assume that the question of what connects mind and world asks for an explanation of the intentionality of thought. So, for example, what connects me to my copy of the *Investigations* such that I *can* think the thought that it is battered? This question is made more difficult by false thoughts and thoughts about non-existent objects. But in broad outline, externalism suggests that I must stand in some further relation – whether causal, interpretative or practical – to the world, and in some circumstances to the book itself, while internalism denies that this need be so. Evans, for example, argues that I must stand in a *causal* relation to a book if I am to think the singular thought: *that book is battered* (Evans 1982: 121–204). If I do not, then I do not think a false singular thought but a different kind of thought altogether with a different content.

Given the description of internalism as postulating self-standing configurations in the inner realm, it might seem obvious that Wittgenstein must support some form of externalism. I shall examine three arguments in Wittgenstein. My conclusion, however, is that, although Wittgenstein does support externalism, the *explanatory* connection he postulates between mind and world is minimal. The arguments concern:

• Wittgenstein's use of the anthropological stance.
• Agreement in judgement.
• The role of samples.

3.1   Wittgenstein and the anthropological stance

The first way in which Wittgenstein might be thought to support externalism runs as follows. Wittgenstein establishes a connection between possession of mental states and possession of a language. If the account of the latter supports externalism then content in general will be externalist. But attention to the conditions of possibility of communication implies that the meaning of elements in communal language, at least, depend on external constituents. Before considering the other stages of this argument in more detail I shall first look at the arguments that might be extracted from Wittgenstein to say that the conditions of possibility of communication demonstrate the truth of externalism.

Following the work on the philosophy of language of Quine and Davidson, the most influential thought experiment concerning the interpretation of language is the interpretation of an alien language from scratch by an anthropologist (e.g., Davidson, 1984: 125–39; Quine 1960). The idea of such radical translation or radical interpretation is used to reveal the conditions of possibility of interpretation and the methodological claim is that this is revelatory of meaning in general. I shall return to Davidson's use of radical interpretation in Chapter 5. But the fact that Quine and Davidson draw externalist conclusions from this thought experiment suggests that similar conclusions might follow from Wittgenstein's invocation of radical interpretation.

Wittgenstein says:

> Suppose you came as an explorer into an unknown country with a language quite strange to you. In what circumstances would you say that the people there gave orders, understood them, obeyed them, rebelled against them, and so on?
> The common behaviour of mankind is the system of reference by means of which we interpret an unknown language. (§206)

> Let us imagine that the people in that country carried on the usual human activities and in the course of them employed, apparently, an articulate language. If we watch their behaviour we find it intelligible, it seems 'logical'. But when we try to learn their language we find it impossible to do so. For there is no regular connexion between what they say, the sounds they make, and their actions . . . There is not enough regularity for us to call it 'language'. (§207)

Two related preconditions for interpretation are suggested in this passage. Interpretation requires a common framework of behaviour and, more specifically, there must be a regular connection between utterances and that behaviour. The first claim, that there must be behaviour, reiterates Wittgenstein's emphasis on the general context of behaviour for the explanation of speech and action. The second applies to this case a general moral (§142) that our language would lose its point if there were not the regularities that there are; if exceptions became the rule. But neither claim makes explicit a commitment to externalism for two reasons.

Firstly, there is no indication of the modal status of the first condition. It is not clear whether regularity is necessary for interpretation in all possible worlds or just in this one. More pressingly, although the second condition unpacks the role of behaviour, its precise role remains unclear. Although Wittgenstein suggests that it is a necessary condition for interpretation that there exists a regular connection between utterances and actions, this alone is insufficient to imply that such a regularity enters into the specification of meaning. The difference between these two possibilities is made clear elsewhere when Wittgenstein argues explicitly that 'red' in English does not *mean* 'what most people would call "red"' despite the fact that such agreement is necessary for red to have the meaning that it does (Wittgenstein 1981: §430). Without such agreement this fragment would not have the use it does. Thus, agreement is a precondition of meaning. But that agreement is not part of the meaning.

3.2   Agreement in judgement

The role of agreement is made more explicit in three passages, also concerned with communication, that follow the discussion of rules and precede the discussion of private language in the *Investigations*. These passages introduce the community and communication as a further premiss in addition to those established for rule-following *simpliciter*. Wittgenstein then explores the preconditions for this premiss to hold.

He claims: 'If language is to be a means of communication there must be agreement not only in definitions but also (queer as this may sound) in judgments' (§242). To communicate judgements, it is necessary to have agreement about the concepts used. Agreement about concepts, however, requires agreement among judgements made using or exemplifying those concepts. This agreement is not just, however, an intellectual agreement in reporting the results of some judgements. For that agreement to be possible it is first necessary for there to be agreement in the content of judgements expressed. That in turn requires a harmony in the practice of judging: 'This is not agreement in opinions but in form of life' (§241). Whatever further significance can be attached to the idea of a form of life elsewhere, here it expresses the final grounding of concepts in practices. This role is revealed in the claim: 'It is one thing to describe methods of measurement, and another to obtain and state results of measurement. But what we call "measuring" is partly determined by a certain constancy in results of measurement' (§242).

The grounds for ascribing a shared understanding of a rule is a convergence of practices. This is not to say that it is always necessary, in order to establish another's understanding of a particular rule, to test their applications of it. There may be reason to ascribe an understanding of related rules and of the relations between those and the rule in question. But for this to be the case, there has to be a convergence of practice somewhere. An argument for externalism can be constructed from these remarks. Given human senses and abilities – including, for example, our lack of telepathy – the only way in which a harmony of practice can be established to underpin agreement in judgement is if some judgements concern a shared external world. The objects of judgement must be features of the publicly available world. Thus, communication presupposes a shared world.

As an argument for externalism, the argument I have extracted from these remarks is indirect in two ways:

- The world plays an indirect role in the individuation of content by satisfying a precondition on communication. The world comprises a realm of shared objects about which there can be the agreement in judgement which is necessary for agreement in concepts. But, as I have described it, the objects do not play a constitutive role in linguistic content.
- These passages assume that language is being used as a means of communication. Only if language *must* be communal will these passages – once added to the claim that mental content depends on linguistic content – provide a general argument for externalism about mental content. If there could be solitary language users, then no general conclusion would follow. This is not a question I have addressed in detail, but I see no reason to interpret Wittgenstein's discussion of rules as denying this latter possibility.

Rather than examining the latter point in detail, however, having seen the role that practices play here, I think that it is now clear that the detour via communal language was unnecessary for pin-pointing Wittgenstein's commitment to externalism. In what follows I shall dispense with the idea that representational content requires a community and examine a more direct argument for a minimalist construal of externalism.

3.3   The role of samples

Wittgenstein discusses the dependence of the content of colour judgements on samples immediately before his discussion of the relation between content-laden mental states and their fulfilment conditions:

> The agreement, the harmony, of thought and reality consists in this: if I say falsely that something is *red*, then, for all that, it isn't *red*. And if I want to explain 'red' to someone, in the sentence 'That is not red', I do it by pointing to something red. (§429)

The concentration on false judgement marks a continuing interest of Wittgenstein. A general moral of the possibility of false but meaningful judgements is that whatever links are necessary for content between the world and words cannot be the same as those necessary for correctness. More specifically here, Wittgenstein points out that 'red' has the same meaning in true and in false judgements that something is red as well as in judgements that something is not red. Furthermore, the meaning of 'red' in all these cases is typically given in a demonstration using a red sample. Of course, it is sometimes possible to explain the meaning of one word by using a prior understanding of other words. But at least in the case of words used in the framing of representational contents, such secondary explanations presuppose explanations using samples.

That samples should play such a key role in the constitution of content follows from the emphasis on practice in Wittgenstein's discussion of rules and understanding. Because understanding 'red' comprises the ability to use the word correctly including, centrally, in direct judgements, then red samples play a role in teaching the concept and in normatively determining the correct application of the concept. Likewise, to be able to entertain the expectation that someone is coming, one must be able to discriminate the outcome correctly. This again links content to samples:

> One may have the feeling that in the sentence 'I expect he is coming' one is using the words 'he is coming' in a different sense from the one they have in the assertion 'He is coming'. But if it were so how could one say that my expectation had been fulfilled? If I wanted to explain the words 'he' and 'is coming', say by means of ostensive definitions, the same definitions of these words would go for both sentences. (§444)

The role that samples play in representational practice varies from case to case. While samples of colour are rarely appealed to in judgements, length measurement relies on direct comparison with standard rules (although the Paris metre itself is not often used). Nevertheless, samples can be appealed to in the justification of a judgement even in cases where such direct comparison is not normal. Nor is there uniformity in what counts as a sample. Some contents depend on specific formal samples such as the standard metre, while for others the number of samples is a potential infinity. Virtually any red object could be used as a sample, of redness. What matters is the use that is made rather than intrinsic features of the object in question.

This widespread use of samples indicates Wittgenstein's support for externalism. Because samples are used for the explanation of meaning, the world plays a role in individuating content. The world itself enters into the specification of content. It is not merely that it satisfies a precondition for the possibility of content. As we have seen, that can be the case without the condition directly forming part of the content. Instead, samples play a direct role in the constitution of content.

Although this argument for externalism depends on considerations of normativity, it is nevertheless of modest scope. It is not that normativity in general requires reference to the world – that may or may not be the case but I can find no argument for it in Wittgenstein – but that the normativity of representational content requires reference to the world. The existence of the world is essential for the content of mental states because it plays a role in individuating their content.

The support which this argument provides for externalism is also minimalist in two important respects. In the next section I will argue that the *explanatory* connection it establishes between thought and its object is minimal. It does not require the presence of any connecting mechanism, for example. But it is also minimalist in another respect that will be the subject of the final section of this chapter. That point can be put by saying that it is precisely *not* the case that samples play a role in bridging a gap between mind or language and the world. Because samples play a role in representing rather than being represented, that distinction between language and the world cannot be drawn. Consequently, there is no gap to be bridged. I shall also return to this claim in the discussion of scheme-content dualism in Chapter 5.

3.4   Minimal externalism

I suggested above that externalism is best understood as an explanatory thesis. Wittgenstein's emphasis on the role of samples in the individuation of linguistic meaning and thus, mental content thereby, suggests qualified support for externalism. Independently of the question of their truth or falsity, one could not entertain the contents one can without standing in some relation to parts of the world that can be used as samples in the explanation of meaning. This follows from the practical explication of meaning that Wittgenstein gives together with the use of samples in the definition of representational concepts (§49–51). That is enough to show that Wittgenstein rejects internalism. But his support for an externalist explanation of content is qualified. The external relations invoked do not comprise hidden explanatory mechanisms. They are part of the practice of language use and representation. And the 'explanatory' link which Wittgenstein makes is strikingly weak. This is most clearly brought out in passages in the *Blue Book*:

> Our difficulty could be put this way: We think about things, – but how do these things enter into our thoughts? We think about Mr Smith; but Mr Smith need not be present. A picture of him won't do; for how are we to know whom it represents? In fact no substitute for him will do. Then how can he himself be an object of our thoughts? (I am here using the expression 'object of our thought' in a way different from that in which I have used it before. I mean now a thing I am thinking *about*, not 'that which I am thinking'.)

We said the connection between our thinking, or speaking, about a man and the man himself was made when, in order to explain the meaning of the word 'Mr Smith' we pointed to him, saying 'this is Mr Smith'. And there is nothing mysterious about this connection. I mean, there is no queer mental act which somehow conjures up Mr Smith in our minds when he really isn't here. What makes it difficult to see that this is the connection is a peculiar form of expression of ordinary language, which makes it appear that the connection between our thought (or the expression of our thought) and the thing we think about must have subsisted *during* the act of thinking.

Someone says, 'Mr N will come to see me this afternoon'; I ask 'Do you mean him?' pointing to someone present, and he answers 'Yes'. In this conversation a connection was established between the word 'Mr N' and Mr N. But we are tempted to think that while my friend said, 'Mr N will come to see me?', and meant what he said, his mind must have made the connection.

What we said of thinking can also be applied to imagining. Someóne says, he imagines King's College on fire. We ask him: 'How do you know that it's King's College you imagine on fire? Couldn't it be a different building, very much like it? In fact, is your imagination so absolutely exact that there might not be a dozen buildings whose representation your image could be?' – And still you say: 'There's no doubt I imagine King's College and no other building'. But can't saying this be making the very connection we want? For saying it is like writing the words 'Portrait of Mr So-and-so' under a picture. It might have been that *while* you imagined King's College on fire you said the words 'King's College is on fire'. But in very many cases you certainly don't speak explanatory words in your mind while you have the image. And consider, even if you do, you are not going the whole way from your image to King's College, but only to the words 'King's College'. The connection between these words and King's College was, perhaps, made at another time. (Wittgenstein 1958: 38–9)

Like *Investigations* §§682–4 (quoted earlier), these passages might suggest that Wittgenstein subscribes to a form of constructivism. The suggestion that subsequent reports of one's mental state might 'make the very connection we want' suggests just such an interpretation. But because constructivism about meaning is not a satisfactory philosophical position – as I argued in the previous chapter – a constructivist interpretation should be resisted if possible for these passages like the paragraphs from the *Investigations*. Fortunately another reading is possible.

Consider again the question: what further connection between me and my copy of the *Investigations* explains the connection that is achieved in a thought about it? Wittgenstein here makes the negative point that, at the time of thinking, there need be no such *further* explanatory connection. No additional simultaneous connection is needed to explain the thought. This negative claim mirrors Wittgenstein's general rejection of philosophical explanations. We may think that there *must* be some further underlying connection, but Wittgenstein argues that we should reject this temptation. No intermediaries or underlying processes are apparent or could explain the normativity of the connection between mind and world.

But, although there need be no further simultaneous connections, there must, according to Wittgenstein, be some further connection between the thinker and the object of thought. His positive suggestion here relies on the account of samples. The connection between thought and its object is made by explanations of what one thinks which include practical demonstrations. Names, for example, can be connected to people through ostensive demonstrations. Such explanations need not be as directly world-involving as the examples given in the passages above. The connections can be indirect in the same way that the connection between understanding rules and practical abilities can be indirect. But there must be some practical connection somewhere.

The section in the *Investigations* continues:

> Instead of 'I meant him' one can, of course, sometimes say 'I thought of him'; sometimes even 'Yes, we were speaking of him.' Ask yourself what 'speaking of him' consists in. (§687)

> In certain circumstances one can say 'As I was speaking, I felt I was saying it *to you*'. But I should not say this if I were in any case talking with you. (§688)

> 'I am thinking of N.' 'I am speaking of N.'
> How do I speak *of* him? I say, for instance, 'I must go and see N today' – But surely that is not enough! After all, when I say 'N' I might mean various people of this name. – 'Then there must surely be a further, different connexion between my talk and N, for otherwise I should *still* not have meant HIM.'
> Certainly such a connexion exists. Only not as you imagine it: namely by means of a mental *mechanism*.
> (One compares 'meaning him' with 'aiming at him'.) (§689)

> Is it correct for someone to say: 'When I gave you this rule, I meant you to . . . in this case'? Even if he did not think of this case at all as he gave the rule? Of course it is correct. For 'to mean it' did not mean: to think of it. But now the problem is: how are we to judge whether someone meant such-and-such? – The fact that he has, for example, mastered a particular technique in arithmetic and algebra, and that he taught someone else the expansion of a series in the usual way, is such a criterion. (§692)

In the *Blue Book* passage it is the suggestion that the connection between a thought and its object might be made *after the fact* that seems to support constructivism. I suggest, however, that the best interpretation of these remarks is not constructivist but again reflects the connection between both linguistic and mental content and abilities. Thus, there is something that makes it possible to think about a copy of the *Investigations*, for example. It is a general ability possessed at the time and which is demonstrated in practical explanations. But such practical explanations might themselves come after the particular act of thinking. If one were not able to make such an explanation, one could not think such thoughts. But this does not amount to a retrospective construction of content.

On this account the connection between the ability to think about an object and the ability to explain the object of one's thought is counter-factual. It is like the connection between understanding a mathematical series and the applications of it that one can make.

> 'But I already knew, at the time when I gave the order, that he ought to write 1002 after 1000.' – Certainly; and you can also say you *meant* it then . . . When you said 'If I already knew at the time . . .' that meant something like: 'If I had been asked what number should be written after 1000, I should have replied "1002".' And that I don't doubt. This assumption is rather of the kind as: 'If he had fallen into the water then, I should have jumped in after him'. (§187)

> 'When I teach someone the formation of the series . . . I surely mean him to write . . . at the hundredth place.' – Quite right; you mean it. And evidently without necessarily even thinking of it. This shews you how different the grammar of the verb 'to mean' is from that of 'to think'. And nothing is more wrong-headed than calling meaning a mental activity! Unless, that is, one is setting out to promote confusion. (It would be possible to speak of an activity of butter when it rises in price, and if no problems are produced by this it is harmless.) (§693)

Thus, although Wittgenstein supports a form of externalism, this does not amount to a substantial mechanical explanation of how intentionality is possible. The general connections which make content possible do not support each act of thinking. They are not called upon to connect free-standing mental items to things in the world but are instead partially constitutive of the abilities that underpin ascribing and forming mental states. But there is also a second respect in which Wittgenstein's commitment to externalism is minimalist to which I shall now turn.

3.5   Minimal externalism and sense

The second respect in which Wittgenstein's support for externalism is minimalist is that it does not presuppose that a distinction can be drawn between language or thought and the world. It does not presuppose a distinction between scheme and content. Consequently, samples are not called upon to bridge the gap between language or thought and the world. It is this feature that makes a minimalist externalism consistent with a theory of sense. In this final section I shall make some general comments about the relation between Wittgenstein's view of language, the role of samples and the theory of sense.

I have argued that Wittgenstein's externalism follows from the central use that samples play in the explanation of linguistic meaning and thus of mental content. This externalism can be summarised in the claim that, in such explanation, parts of the world play an essential role in the constitution of content. There may seem to be, however, some risk in putting the matter in that bald manner. The (apparent) problem is that, if the world plays a direct role in the constitution of content, then it cannot account for the phenomena of understanding for which a distinction between sense and reference is sometimes invoked. In other words, it can seem that externalism implies that content is a matter of reference rather than sense. But there are good reasons for saying that content properly belongs to a theory of sense if a theory of sense is construed – as it generally now is – as a way of *making sense* of speech and action rather than as theory of Platonic senses.

(McDowell provides such a general characterisation of a theory of sense in (McDowell 1976). He goes on there, however, to attempt to define a distinction between sense and reference which turns on epistemological notions. Elsewhere, he argues that there is no difficulty in accommodating even singular thoughts into a neo-Fregean theory of sense (e.g., McDowell 1984a). While what follows below is broadly consistent with his later claims, the problem is addressed at a more general level.)

To begin, consider the thought that explanations using samples *bridge a gap* between language on one side and the world on the other. This sort of picture of the connection between language and the world would have something in common with that found in Wittgenstein's earlier writing, although the emphasis is on explanation. In the *Tractatus*, simple names latch on to worldly atoms while combinations of simple names represent facts in virtue of a shared pictorial form (Wittgenstein 1922). Words mean that to which they refer. But, as the arguments in the second chapter demonstrated, no such account of representation is coherent. In addition to the discussion of rules already discussed, however, Wittgenstein provided different criticisms of the picture of word-thing links presupposed here in *Investigations* §§1–64.

One of the points made in this section of the *Investigations* is that ostensive definition cannot provide the kind of theoretical and explanatory link between language and the world that his earlier account presupposed. Ostensive definitions are like any explanations of linguistic rules in that they could be misinterpreted. Only in the context of a great deal of stage setting is the content of the definition determined. This point is not made to undermine the pre-philosophical role of ostensive definition using samples. A general moral of the *Investigations* is that any explanation of meaning can be misunderstood. But the key point here is that ostensive definition cannot provide a reductionist foundation for meaning because the necessary stage setting cannot be described except in intentional terms.

As a correction to that picture, Wittgenstein suggests instead that, in ostensive definition using samples, the connection made is *within* language. The samples themselves function as parts of language not parts of the world. They play a role *within* linguistic representation:

> What about the colour samples that A shews to B: are they part of the *language*? Well, it is as you please. They do not belong among the words; yet when I say to someone: 'Pronounce the word "the"', you will count the second 'the' as part of the sentence. Yet it has a role just like that of a colour-sample . . . that is, it is a sample of what the other is meant to say.
>   It is most natural, and causes least confusion, to reckon the samples among the instruments of the language. (§16)

> We define: 'sepia' means the colour of the standard sepia . . . This sample is an instrument of the language used in ascriptions of colour. In this language-game it is not something that is represented, but is a means of representation. (§50)

Wittgenstein suggests here that it is better to count samples as part of language than part of the world. He makes a similar judgement about the rules concerning colour combinations:

> We have a colour system as we have a number system.
>   Do the systems reside in *our* nature or in the nature of things? How are we to put it? – *Not* in the nature of numbers or colours. (Wittgenstein 1981 §357)

> Then is there something arbitrary about this system? Yes and no. It is akin both to what is arbitrary and to what is non-arbitrary. (§358)

But, because samples are used to define concepts which are also normatively structured, there is in fact something wrong with saying that they belong to language as opposed to the world. That problem emerges from considering the relation between linguistic rules and metaphysical possibilities.

The *Tractatus* proposes one account of the connection between linguistic and metaphysical possibility. Its account of how language is possible requires, among other things, an isomorphism between the combinatorial possibilities of linguistic and worldly elements. Consequently, exploring the combinatorial properties of language serves as a guide to what is metaphysically possible (and impossible). This account, however, raises the question of the supposed origin and explanation of the harmony between language and the world. Does the structure of the world explain and determine the underlying combinatorial possibilities of language? Or does the priority run the other way?

In the *Investigations* there are also comments that suggest that linguistic rules and metaphysical possibilities go hand in hand and, indeed, that it is because of this that philosophical analysis is possible:

> We feel as if we had to *penetrate* phenomena: our investigation, however, is directed not towards phenomena, but, as one might say, towards the 'possibilities' of phenomena. We

remind ourselves, that is to say, of the *kind of statement* that we make about phenomena. (Wittgenstein 1953 §90)

Essence is expressed by grammar. (§371)

Consider: 'The only correlate in language to an intrinsic necessity is an arbitrary rule. It is the only thing which one can milk out of this intrinsic necessity into a proposition.' (§372)

Even without the Tractarian picture of language as a fixed and eternal structure, the later Wittgenstein can still be interpreted as claiming that linguistic and metaphysical possibilities mirror one another. But, given his attack on Platonic foundationalism, the answer to the question of explanatory priority which matches that raised for the *Tractatus* seems at first quite clear: it must be the second option. Examination of language reveals the structure of the world because what is possible depends (in some sense to be articulated) on our language. But that response would be a form of constructivism and thus would not be able to account for the necessity expressed in by, for example, the mathematical and logical rules.

I think that the correct moral to draw is that drawing a distinction in this way between mind or language and the world is as philosophically disastrous as the previous distinctions. Those distinctions were between understanding, construed as an internal state, and the applications one can make of it; and content-laden mental states in general, construed as free-standing representations, and what would satisfy them. Similarly, once a distinction is drawn between linguistic rules, construed as dependent only on human definitions and practice, and possibilities, construed as metaphysically given facts of the matter, the question of which has priority becomes pressing. Instead, no such distinction should be drawn. No useful principled distinction can be drawn between language and the world.

In Chapter 5 I shall return to the general question of the relation of language and the world in discussing Davidson's attack on scheme-content dualism. For now, what matters is that samples themselves should be regarded neither as bridging a gap between language and the world, nor as functioning within language construed in opposition to, and separate from, the world. They are, however, used as representational. They have content in virtue of the linguistic practices in which they are embedded. This suggests that Wittgenstein's externalism can invoke samples as part of a theory of sense rather than reference. I will briefly consider two cases. Frege's example of Hespherus and Phosphorus and Putnam's Twin Earth.

The classic argument against a referential theory of meaning is provided by consideration of identity statements such as that Hespherus is Phosphorus. (I put the point in this negative way rather than talking of the distinction between sense and reference because, on the Wittgensteinian account that I am suggesting, that opposition plays no important role. What matters is simply rejecting the claim that the meaning of a word is what it designates.) If meaning is reduced to reference then, because 'Hespherus' and 'Phosphorus' refer to the same thing, the statement should not be informative. But it is. Frege's solution is to introduce an extra tier to the account of meaning: senses. On Frege's account, senses are modes of presentation of referents, determine those referents and inhabit a Platonic realm. Clearly that picture is not compatible with Wittgenstein's hostility to epistemic intermediaries and to Platonism in the account of meaning. But the advantages of the distinction between sense and reference can be had without subscribing to an intermediary or Platonic conception of senses.

Given that samples act as samples only when so employed in representational practices, 'Hespherus' and 'Phosphorus' have different senses in that they are paradigmatically explained in different ways. The former can be explained by pointing to an object low in the evening sky; the latter by pointing in the morning. Explaining Hespherus by pointing to the morning sky is simply wrong. Given the role of practices in the use of samples it seems that Wittgensteinian externalism can still accommodate a theory of sense. But there is a further well-known case the moral of which is less clear cut.

Putnam's Twin Earth thought experiment presents the converse kind of case (Putnam 1975). In 1750, before the development of the atomic theory of elements, Oscar and his Twin-Earth *doppelgänger* have thoughts about the colourless, odourless fluid which surrounds them that both refer to using the word 'water'. But, according to the standard reading, while Oscar has thoughts about water – the substance found on earth – his twin has thoughts about the chemically different substance – call it 'twater' – found on Twin Earth. Referential externalism ascribes different contents in this case to words and thoughts, despite the fact that neither Oscar nor his twin could distinguish water and twater and neither would ascribe to it significantly different general properties.

But there is an important distinction between the standard reading of this thought experiment and the minimal externalist account so far described. The standard interpretation presupposes a fundamentally different role for samples from the Wittgensteinian account. In both cases, a sample of water, or twater, can be used to define the meaning of the word 'water' in utterances made by Oscar or his twin. In both cases the definition is supposed to be broader than the particular sample used. It is supposed to link the word 'water' with water, or twater, generally. The difference is how this generality is achieved. On the standard reading it is achieved through the fact that water is a natural kind and the definitional link to the sample spreads laterally – of its own accord – to other instances of the *same* kind. But this presupposes a notion of sameness that is antecedent to, and independent of, the rule the governs the use of the word 'water'. That is a form of Platonism that Wittgenstein has undermined. On

Wittgenstein's account, the sample of water is used to *represent* water generally depending on the way in which the sample is used by a speaker or speakers. This suggests the possibility of a different sort of interpretation.

One interpretation is that the use which both Oscar and his twin make of samples to define 'water' is the same. The descriptions and definitions they might offer sound the same. The practical claims and uses that they make of 'water' coincide. Thus, there are good reasons to say that the uses are the same and, consequently, that their utterances and mental states have the same contents. The obvious objection to this interpretation is that we know that water and twater are different substances. Thus, the use of samples on Earth and Twin Earth *must* be different because the substances are different. But this objection presupposes that Oscar and his twin use the word water to pick out the natural kinds that we recognise. It is as though they are in the position that we would be if we baptised two different colourless liquids with two different names saying that the names stood not just for these two test-tubes of liquid (as proper names) but for the kinds of liquids that they are, as might be picked out by chemical analysis. Given a rough knowledge of chemical composition this makes sense. But, prior to 1750, Oscar's use of samples is very different from ours. And it is that that determines what counts as the same and what as different without any appeal to such further tests. The development of an atomic theory thus changes the standards of sameness and difference. To insist that the question of what 'water' means can be answered by appeal to absolute classifications of sameness and difference is to fall back on a kind of Platonism that cannot mesh with the normativity of human practices.

This is not to say that Wittgenstein's minimal externalist account of content set out in this chapter has to interpret Putnam's Twin Earth thought experiment in this way. In a sense, the very lack of further foundations for meaning make absolute pronouncements about the interpretation of this case impossible. But the general moral of this section is clear. Wittgenstein's version of externalism allows samples to play a role in a theory of sense rather than reference, and is thus immune to some of the difficulties of externalist theories of content.

Chapter 5 will examine Davidson's theory of content. I shall argue that there are important similarities between the account he offers and that set out in this chapter. Davidson's own minimally externalist position helps clarify the conception of mental states and psychological explanation which can survive Wittgenstein's attack on explanatory mechanisms. But, by replacing the practical use of samples by merely causal links between language and the world, Davidson undermines the normativity of content.

Further Reading

Wittgenstein's account of first-person access is discussed in contrasting ways in McDowell (1991, 1992) and Wright (1991). It is also discussed at length in Pears (1988). The connection between language and pre-linguistic abilities is explored in Malcolm (1982).

Wittgenstein's account of third-person access is usually discussed via the idea of criteria. More general work on criteria include Baker (1974), McDowell (1981, 1982) and Wright (1987b: 357–402).

Clear general discussions of externalism can be found in Bilgrami (1992) and C. McGinn (1989). The *locus classicus* of work on the connection between singular thought and externalism is Evans (1982). But briefer expositions of some of the key claims can be found in McDowell (1984a, 1986, 1994).

CHAPTER 5

Wittgenstein and Davidson on Content

The previous chapter set out a Wittgensteinian theory of content. This chapter will compare it with Davidson's theory of content. Like Wittgenstein, Davidson can be seen as advocating a minimal form of externalism. By comparing their views, I hope to shed light on and to fill out the austere positive account that Wittgenstein provides and to criticise Davidson's claims about the relation between thought and the world from a Wittgensteinian perspective.

Davidson's philosophy of content combines two ingredients: the philosophy of language of the field linguist and the formal theory of meaning. The first follows from Davidson's fundamental assumption: there are no facts about meaning that are inaccessible from a third-person perspective. Consequently, by investigating the conditions of possibility of radical interpretation, Davidson aims to uncover the metaphysics of meaning. I shall argue that this approach can be understood as broadly consistent with Wittgenstein's account. The second ingredient, the formal theory of meaning, cannot, however, be reconciled with Wittgenstein. Nevertheless, the two need not be seen as interdependent. One can reject the latter while still taking up the perspective of the field linguist.

Having set out Davidson's account of radical interpretation, I shall examine the conclusions that he draws about the relation between language and the world and between thought and the world. These claims can be clarified by, and clarify, Wittgenstein's views. But Davidson also assumes that one consequence of the philosophy of language of the field linguist is that the idea of representational links between language and the world must be replaced by merely causal links. I shall argue that this does not follow and would have disastrous consequences for meaning.

1 Davidson's Theory of Interpretation

1.1   The philosophy of language of the field linguist

Davidson's approach to content is based on the thought experiment of radical translation. To clarify what we understand when we understand our home

language, Davidson considers the conditions of possibility of the radical interpretation of a foreign language. Radical interpretation is supposed to be
interpretation from scratch (Davidson 1993: 77). It is a philosophical abstraction from the kind of interpretation undertaken by a field linguist having first
contact with an alien tribe. Such interpretation – it is assumed – cannot appeal to
bilingual speakers or to dictionaries. It precedes those resources. Furthermore,
according to Davidson, it cannot make substantial use of the content of the
mental states of speakers. Whatever the connection between mental content and
linguistic meaning, radical interpretation must earn access to, and cannot simply
assume, facts about both. The intentional contents to which Grice appeals in the
analysis of linguistic interchange, for example, cannot be identified prior to the
interpretation of the agent's language. Thus, they cannot simply be appealed to
in radical interpretation.

Instead, interpretation must rely only on the evidence of correlations between
utterances and the circumstances that prompt them:

> [The radical interpreter] interprets sentences held true (which is not to be distinguished
> from attributing beliefs) according to the events and objects in the outside world that cause
> the sentence to be held true. (Davidson 1983: 317)

Davidson's account of radical *interpretation* is a development from Quine's
account of radical *translation*. But one key difference is its characterisation of
the evidence available:

> The crucial point on which I am with Quine might be put: all the evidence for or against a
> theory of truth (interpretation, translation) comes in the form of facts about what events or
> situations in the world cause, or would cause, speakers to assent to, or dissent from, each
> sentence in the speaker's repertoire. We probably differ on some details. Quine describes
> the events or situations in terms of patterns of stimulation, while I prefer a description in
> terms more like those of the sentence being studied; Quine would give more weight to a
> grading of sentences in terms of observationality than I would; and where he likes assent
> and dissent because they suggest a behaviouristic test, I despair of behaviourism and accept
> frankly intensional attitudes toward sentences, such as holding true. (Davidson 1984: 230)

Davidson takes the evidence available to radical interpretation to be worldly
facts and events in the environment of speakers together with the occasion of
their utterances. The role that evidence plays is important and I shall return to
this issue having sketched in the underlying purpose of radical interpretation.

Davidson's methodological claim for the philosophy of content is that one
can clarify the nature of both linguistic meaning and of mental content more
generally by examining how they are determined in radical interpretation.
'What a fully informed interpreter could learn about what a speaker means is
all there is to learn; the same goes for what the speaker believes.' (Davidson

1983: 315) Because it is intended to serve this philosophical purpose, Davidson concentrates on clear instances of radical interpretation – interpretation by field linguists – rather than the 'interpretation' that, he claims, takes place in daily life:

> All understanding of the speech of another involves radical interpretation. But it will help keep assumptions from going unnoticed to focus on cases where interpretation is most clearly called for: interpretation in one idiom of talk in another. (Davidson 1984: 125–6)

Nevertheless, Davidson also thinks that everyday understanding of language involves radical interpretation. That claim puts some strain on the initial characterisation of radical interpretation as interpretation from scratch because it undermines the contrast that such a description presupposes. If everyday 'interpretation' is also really from scratch, what example could there be of interpretation that was not? But, while Davidson makes this claim in part to defend his radical thesis that communal language plays no explanatory role in human understanding, it can also be seen as a reminder of the purpose of considering radical interpretation. (The radical claim is defended in Davidson 1986.) That is to shed light on what is understood when we understand speech and action generally. (I shall return to the question of whether everyday understanding can be called interpretation at all.)

Seen in this light, Davidson's account of radical interpretation serves as an example of reconstructive epistemology. It does not matter that our everyday understanding of other speakers does not proceed using the tools that Davidson describes. One might argue that everyday understanding works on the implicit and tacit assumption that others speak the same language as oneself. But radical interpretation does not aim at phenomenological accuracy. Similarly, it would not matter if real field linguists made use of interpretative heuristics less minimal than those Davidson describes. An example of that might be the assumption that any newly encountered human language has a good chance of being related to some previously encountered language. Such a principle would be useful if it turned out that all human languages sprang from a common source. Because radical interpretation is really a piece of reconstructive epistemology, it concerns the ultimate *justification* of ascriptions of content whatever the actual process of reasoning that gives rise to them. It concerns the evidence that could be used to justify the possible heuristic suggested above and also our everyday methods of understanding. Radical interpretation is supposed to explain what the assumption that other speakers speak the same language amounts to. (According to Davidson, one of its consequences is that such talk of shared languages is of no philosophical significance.) It is precisely because it plays a clarificatory – via a justificatory – role that radical interpretation is characterised in the austere terms that it is.

The early Davidson sometimes suggests that progress can be made only if the evidence used in radical interpretation is not described in question begging-terms:

> [U]ninterpreted utterances seem the appropriate evidential base for a theory of meaning. If an acceptable theory could be supported by such evidence, that would constitute conceptual progress, for the theory would be specifically semantical in nature, while the evidence would be described in non-semantical terms. (Davidson 1984: 142)

Because one of the obstacles to using Davidson's account of language to shed light on Wittgenstein's is precisely the question of evidence, it is worth taking this point slowly.

What reason did Davidson have for thinking that the evidence for a theory of meaning should itself be described in non-semantic terms? Two sorts of consideration suggest two related motivations. From the perspective of providing a general philosophical account of the nature of meaning, the motivation might run like this. If a philosophical account is to shed light on meaning by connecting it – albeit holistically – to the evidence that determines it, then that evidence should not be described in content-laden terms. If it is, no light will have been shed on what meaning is because facts about meaning will have been presupposed in the description of evidence.

The other consideration depends more specifically on Davidson's chosen approach to the general philosophical account of meaning. Light is shed on meaning in general by reflecting on how radical interpretation is possible. But what is the final justification for ascribing meanings to other people? One method an interpreter could adopt for testing her interpretations – which Davidson assumes will form part of an interpretative theory or 'theory of meaning' – would be to see whether, in individual cases, her interpretations agreed with those given by dictionaries or bilingual speakers. But in *radical* interpretation no such resources can be assumed because they merely postpone the question of how ascriptions of meaning can be justified. In this context it may seem that the evidence which is available must be characterised in non-semantic terms:

> In radical interpretation, however, the [interpretative] theory is supposed to supply an understanding of particular utterances that is not given in advance, so the ultimate evidence for the theory cannot be correct sample interpretations. To deal with the general case, the evidence must be of a sort that would be available to someone who does not already know how to interpret utterances the theory is designed to cover: *it must be evidence that can be stated without essential use of such linguistic concepts* as meaning, interpretation, synonymy, and the like. (ibid.: 128 italics added)

If either or both of these arguments were compelling, then Davidson's approach to the philosophy of content would run counter to that of

Wittgenstein. One of the morals of Wittgenstein's discussion is, as I have described, that no analysis of meaning can be given that turns on the interpretation of otherwise meaningless noises or movements. I shall argue shortly, however, that whatever Davidson's view of the matter, the thought experiment of radical interpretation can be pruned of any commitment to the neutral description in non-semantic terms of the evidence that supports interpretation. Briefly:

- The results of radical interpretation can still be supported or criticised by appeal to evidence even if that evidence cannot be described (*qua* evidence) in non-semantic terms. The evidence can still be used to test interpretation because of the systematicity and holism implicit in radical interpretation. Just because it is described in semantic terms does not undermine its independence of the theory for which it is evidence. Construing an utterance as a particular assertion will have consequences for how similar-sounding utterances are construed. (As will become clearer later in the chapter, Davidson's philosophical monism implies that evidence could *also* be described in non-semantic, meaning-free terms. But this would obscure its role as *evidence for* an interpretation.)
- It is wrong to assume that radical interpretation sheds light on meaning if the connection between meaning only and evidence is explicitly represented in the results of that interpretation. The nature and limits of possible evidence can play an implicit role. Davidson's key claim is that there are no facts about meaning that are *inaccessible* to the radical interpreter. But this connection between meaning and interpretation need not be encoded in the results of radical interpretation. Thus, there is no need to require that the input can be characterised in non-semantic terms.

In fact, Davidson himself realises that his project cannot escape all intentional notions and in later accounts drops the requirements about its non-semantic nature:

> My way of trying to give an account of language and meaning makes essential use of such concepts as those of beliefs and intention, and I do not believe it is possible to reduce these notions to anything more scientific or behaviouristic. What I have tried to do is give an account of meaning (interpretation) that makes no essential use of unexplained *linguistic* concepts. (Even this is a little stronger than what I think is possible.) It will ruin no plan of mine if in saying what an interpreter knows it is necessary to use a so-called intensional notion – one that consorts with belief and intention and the like. (ibid.: 175–6)

Given the strategic options for explicating linguistic meaning and mental content described in the first chapter, this distinction between intentional concepts and semantic concepts may suggest that Davidson advocates something like intention-based semantics. It may seem, in other words, that he is suggesting that linguistic meaning can be analysed in terms of mental content. But that is not the strategy he follows. The distinction between the narrowly semantic and the more broadly intentional marks his preferred strategy for coping with a general difficulty for radical interpretation.

Davidson thinks that, ultimately, facts about mental content have to be determined in the same way as facts about linguistic meaning. Meanings and contents are interdependent. This presents a principled difficulty for radical interpretation:

> A speaker who holds a sentence to be true on an occasion does so in part because of what he means, or would mean, by an utterance of that sentence, and in part because of what he believes. If all we have to go on is the fact of honest utterance, we cannot infer the belief without knowing the meaning, and have no chance of inferring the meaning without the belief. (ibid.: 142)

Thus, the interpreter faces the task of unravelling two sets of unknowns – facts about meaning and facts about beliefs – with only one sort of evidence: linguistic actions that depend on meaning and belief. How can the interpreter – to change the metaphor – break into this interdependent set of facts?

Davidson's solution has two ingredients. Firstly, he takes the evidential basis of radical interpretation to be the prompted assent of a speaker, which he characterises as 'the causal relation between assenting to a sentence and the cause of such assent' (Davidson 1983: 315). The reason for this is that it is possible to know that a speaker assents to a sentence without knowing what the sentence means and thus what belief is expressed by it (or vice versa). Characterising a speaker as holding a particular sentence true is an intentional interpretation of what is going on – the speaker is described by relation to a propositional content – but it does not *presuppose* a semantic analysis of the sentence. That will be derived later.

The second step is to restrain the degrees of freedom of possible beliefs in order to interpret linguistic meaning. The interpreter must impose his or her own standards of truth and coherence on ascriptions of beliefs and meanings. There must be a presumption that any utterance or belief held true really is true. Further, in a significant range of cases, the interpreter must assume that the object of an utterance, and the belief the utterance expresses, is the cause of the utterance and belief. (As Davidson remarks in a passage quoted above, the relevant cause is a worldly state of affairs rather than, as Quine suggests, proximal stimulation at the boundary of the body.) This complex of related assumptions governing the rationality imputed – generally briskly labelled the Principle of Charity – enables interpretation to get off the ground. If utterances are assumed by the interpreter to be generally true and to concern the worldly states of affairs that prompt them, then they can be correlated with those observed states of affairs. Their meaning can thus be determined. Given an overall interpretation, exceptional false beliefs can then be identified.

These a-priori constraints on interpretation operate in a general manner but allow exceptions. Thus, even the basic datum that a speaker holds a particular utterance true can be revised in the light of the subsequent interpretation of his or her other beliefs and meanings. The epistemology of interpretation is fallible and holistic. So the appeal to evidence should not be regarded as a foundational or reductionist account of meaning. The earlier prescription that evidence should be describable in theory-free non-semantic terms (while still being represented as evidence) does not fit easily with the holism that Davidson more generally emphasises.

Davidson's basic strategy can now be summarised as follows. On the assumption that radical interpretation has access to all the facts about content, content can be explicated by examining the conditions of possibility of radical interpretation. Thus, Davidson assumes that content can be captured by a third-person perspective and that it can be fully analysed through its connection to the action of agents in the world. In the weakest sense of the term, Davidson can be seen, in his philosophy of content at least, as promoting a form of philosophical behaviourism provided that this is not construed in its Quinean and reductionist sense. Meaning is explicated through its role in human behaviour. (In fact, he adds to this picture of content a token identity theory to explain the *causal* role of content to which I shall turn in Chapter 6.)

Rorty describes this basic approach as the 'philosophy of language of the field linguist' (Rorty 1991: 132). This is the aspect of Davidson's philosophy of content that he shares with Wittgenstein. I shall return to discuss the similarities that result. But, in addition to this general approach to the philosophy of content, Davidson advocates a particular formal structure for the results of radical interpretation which has nothing in common with Wittgenstein's approach.

1.2   The formal theory of meaning

Davidson suggests that the output of the process of radical interpretation can be regimented in a formal theory of meaning. There are two important points to note here with respect to the comparison of Davidson and Wittgenstein. Firstly, the very assumption that linguistic mastery can by regimented in any formal structure runs counter to Wittgenstein's view of language. Secondly, Davidson assumes that the theory can be extensional and employ merely the first-order logic used in Tarski's account of truth.

As I described in Chapter 4, there are two general Wittgensteinian arguments against regimenting linguistic abilities in a formal theory:

- Wittgenstein thinks that there is no reason for languages to possess the kind of systematicity that can be regimented into uniform formal patterns. There are no principled limits that can be placed on the number of different kinds of sentences, for example. There are countless kinds of use for what we call 'symbols', 'words' and 'sentences', and new uses can come into being. Wittgenstein uses the analogy of an ancient city with a maze of little streets and also regular new streets.
- More fundamentally, Wittgenstein rejects the kind of explanation for which the formal theory of meaning is devised. It is by no means clear how the provision of a formal theory, of which as yet no-one can have *explicit* knowledge, can explain our linguistic capacities. But nor does it seem a plausible candidate for *tacit* or *implicit* knowledge because it cannot be elicited by promptings, does not command assent when suggested and so forth. An example of the difference in approach of Wittgenstein and Davidson is exemplified by the latter's attitude to explanation of some standard deductions. Davidson thinks that the linguistic understanding which enables speakers to infer the fact that toast was buttered from the fact that toast was buttered with a knife can be explained by providing a model that uses only first-order logic but which quantifies over events. But, again, it is by no means clear how this underlying and hidden structure of events explains the abilities of ordinary speakers incapable of understanding the translation Davidson offers (Davidson 1980: 105–48).

Davidson fails to explain the purpose of the theory of meaning. He makes two comments on the subject. One is that knowledge of such a theory would *suffice* for understanding (Davidson 1984: 125). The other is that it is a necessary condition for languages to be learnable that a constructive or compositional account of the language could be given (ibid.: 3). But even taken together, these do not explain how provision of a theory of meaning helps the philosophical enterprise of clarifying linguistic and mental content.

He is more explicit in his reasons why such a theory should be extensional. Theories of meaning of the form: s means m – where m refers to a meaning of a word or sentence – have proved to be of little use in showing how the meaning of parts of a sentence structurally determines the meaning of the whole. Things can be improved by modifying the theory's structure to be: s means that p, where p stands for a sentence. But this still leaves the problem that 'wrestling with the logic of the apparently non-extensional "means that" we will encounter problems as hard as, or perhaps identical with, the problems our theory is out to solve' (ibid.: 22). The solution is to realise that what matters for such a theory is not the nature of the connection between *s* and *p* but that the right *s* and *p* are connected:

> The theory will have done its work if it provides, for every sentence *s* in the language under study, a matching sentence (to replace '*p*') that, in some way yet to be made clear, 'gives the meaning' of *s*. One obvious candidate for matching sentence is just *s* itself, if the object language is contained in the meta-language; otherwise a translation of *s* in the meta-language. As a final bold step, let us try treating the position occupied by '*p*' extensionally: to implement this, sweep away the obscure 'means that', provide the sentence that replaces '*p*' with a proper sentential connective, and supply the description that replaces '*s*' with its own predicate. The plausible result is
> (T) *s* is T if and only if *p*. (ibid.: 23)

Further reflection suggests that, if this is to serve as an interpretation, the appropriate predicate for T is truth. We want the sentence *s* to be *true* if and only if *p*.

The proposed theoretical schema has the further advantage (and motivation) that it dovetails with Tarski's account of truth. Tarski's account is pressed into service to show how the meanings of sentences are constructed from the meanings of words (which are themselves abstracted from the meanings of sentences). Davidson's use of Tarski inverts its normal explanatory priority. Tarski assumes that the notion of translation can be presupposed in the task of giving an extensional definition of truth in a language. By contrast, Davidson suggests that truth is a suitably primitive, transparent and unitary notion to shed light on meaning. With this change of emphasis, Davidson can then borrow Tarski's technical machinery to articulate the structure of a given language.

Without going into its details it is worth noting one result of this strategy. Davidson replaces the intensional connective 'means that' with the extensional form *s* is true if and only if *p*. Clearly, however, the fact that the truth values of the left- and right-hand side of this conditional agree does not in itself ensure that the right-hand side provides an interpretation of the sentence mentioned on the left. In Tarski's use of the T schema, it can simply be assumed or stipulated that the right-hand side provides an interpretation by being the same sentence as, or a translation of, the sentence mentioned on the left. But Davidson has to earn the right to that claim. His suggestion is that instances of the T schema should not be thought of as interpretative in themselves (ibid.: 61). Rather, it is the fact that each instance can be derived from an overall theory for the language that also allows the derivation of many other instances of the T schema with the right matching of truth values, which is interpretative.

Given this regimentation, meaning is fundamentally holistic. Because instances of the T schema are not interpretative in isolation, it makes no sense to ascribe meaning to elements of language in isolation from the rest. Only in the context of a language does a sentence (and therefore a word) have meaning. It is this, rather than the holistic epistemology of meaning ascription, which is the fundamental source of holism in Davidson.

Aside from the apparent benefits of escaping the intensionality of 'means that' and of the ability to make use of Tarski's formal machinery, Davidson's proposed structure for theories of meaning has another advantage. The formal machinery allows the derivation of a set of instances of the T schema. This seems to make it particularly apt for formalising the output of radical interpretation because, as I have sketched above, that begins by assuming that uninterpreted utterances are held true. Thus, it seems that this formal theory of meaning encapsulates the close relation between truth and meaning emphasised in radical interpretation.

It is worth noting here, however, that, although radical interpretation and the formal theory of meaning sit fortuitously together, they are independent. Even if radical interpretation did not rely on the basic evidence of assertions but on imperatives instead, for example, its output might still be formalised using a theory of meaning based on Tarski. Reciprocally, Davidson's account of radical interpretation might be used to explicate meaning in general – its connection to action in the world, the connection between meaning and belief – without adopting the formal theory of meaning as a representation of language. The latter option is what I advocate.

1.3   Interpretation in Davidson and Wittgenstein

I have suggested that Davidson's philosophy of language comprises two separable elements: the philosophy of language of the field linguist and the formal theory of meaning. While the latter runs counter to Wittgenstein's picture of language, the former has important similarities that help shed light on both projects. But this claim is threatened by arguments against Davidson inspired by Wittgenstein. These focus on the role that *interpretation* plays in the philosophy of language of the field linguist. In this section I shall sketch out those critical arguments. But I shall argue that they turn on an uncharitable interpretation of Davidson that is not obligatory. I shall then sketch out an alternative interpretation and show how the appeal to interpretation need not run counter to Wittgenstein's attack on interpretational explanations of content.

The two related criticisms of Davidson which have to be overcome if a parallel is to be drawn are:

- Davidson attempts to explicate linguistic understanding via the notion of interpretation. But, as Wittgenstein shows, that picture of understanding is, ultimately, incoherent.
- The evidence on which radical interpretation is based is brute, meaningless data that acquire meaning only on interpretation. Davidson denies that one

can experience meaning directly. But again Wittgenstein shows that that picture of the understanding of meaning is incoherent.

These two ideas dovetail. If understanding is really a form of interpretation, then there needs to be something that is interpreted. But, if understanding meaning always requires an act of interpretation, then it seems that what is interpreted is itself meaningless or meaning-free. If it were not, then interpretation would be unnecessary. If Davidson is guilty of either, it seems plausible that he is guilty of both. I shall begin by sketching out the Wittgenstein-inspired criticism of Davidson, which, I shall suggest, depends on a particular interpretation of Davidson's project.

Davidson's characterisation of understanding meaning as a process of interpretation is clearly no slip of the pen. It is frequently repeated throughout his work on the subject. What matters, however, is not the word he uses but the conception of understanding that this expresses. Light is shed on this by the connection he makes between interpretation and redescription:

> We interpret a bit of linguistic behaviour when we say what a speaker's words mean on an occasion of use. The task may be seen as one of *redescription*. We know that the words 'Es schneit' have been uttered on a particular occasion and we want to *redescribe* this uttering as an act of saying that it is snowing. (Davidson 1984: 141 italics added)

If understanding utterances requires interpretation or redescription, what is it that is redescribed? The one answer which Wittgenstein precludes as incoherent is that the input for such redescription should itself be characterised in content-less, non-intentional, non-normative terms. But that is precisely what Davidson sometimes seems to suggest. I have already set out two early quotations that insist that the evidence available to radical interpretation should be characterisable in non-semantic terms. But there are also more recent passages, discussing what it is that an interpretative theory has to achieve, in which Davidson still seems to characterise the input in precisely such terms:

> But although interpretable speeches are nothing but (that is, identical with) actions performed with assorted non-linguistic intentions (to warn, control, amuse, distract, insult), and these actions are in turn nothing but (identical with) intentional movements of the lips and larynx, this observation takes us no distance towards an intelligible general account of what we might know that would allow us to redescribe uninterpreted utterances as the right interpreted ones. (ibid.: 126)

> [A] method of interpretation can lead to redescribing the utterance of certain sounds as an act of saying that snow is white. (ibid.: 161)

> [S]peaker and hearer must repeatedly, intentionally and with mutual agreement, interpret relevantly similar sound-patterns of the speaker in the same way. (ibid.: 277)

That these passages imply that the input to an interpretative theory is bare and meaningless sound or movement is assumed by critics and supporters alike:

> Here, Davidson implies that what we *really* hear when we listen to another speaker (even an English speaker) is a sequence of sound-patterns . . . when a human being speaks to us, we hear sound-patterns; when he acts we see bare movements. The world we really perceive is radically devoid of any human significance, until we use our interpretative theorising to organise this primitive data into units of human meaning. (Mulhall 1990: 104–5)

> Events, in themselves, are opaque or meaningless. It is only when they are described in certain ways that we see them as intentional actions, mental events like beliefs or linguistic utterances. (Evnine 1991: 99)

But, if this is the correct interpretation of Davidson's account of the philosophy of language, then nothing can be salvaged for my purposes. To repeat one of the morals of Wittgenstein's discussion of content, any account of understanding which turns on the interpretation of bare meaningless data fails for a number of related reasons:

- It makes meaning incommunicable and inexpressible because what can be communicated – bare sounds and movements – cannot determine a unique meaning. Kripke's exegesis of Wittgenstein has at least the virtue of making this point very clear. Normative content cannot be extracted from a norm-free experience.
- Ascriptions of linguistic meaning and of mental content would be *hypotheses* about private or hidden states behind the denuded public phenomena. Shared practices would be in danger of breaking down because there would be no such thing as a shared pattern that determined correct future behaviour.
- No sense can be attached to the purely private conception of meaning which is a corollary of this picture. That would require something like possession of an internal sign or symbol. But, as I have argued, Wittgenstein demolishes that picture.

Despite the agreement by Davidson's exegetes and critics about the interpretation of these passages, it is not the only way in which these remarks and the general account of radical interpretation can be interpreted. Furthermore, I suggest that it is instructive – whatever Davidson's actual view of the matter – to provide a more charitable interpretation of the general approach to meaning through radical interpretation.

One defensive option is to discount these remarks as inessential to the general description of radical interpretation. In the case of his early insistence that the evidence for radical interpretation should be described in non-semantic terms, I think that this is the best that can be done. But a more charitable interpretation of the later comments is available that does not invite the Wittgensteinian criticism mentioned above. Statements that utterances are identical with sounds or meaningful actions with movements can instead be interpreted as merely expressing Davidson's anomalous monism. (In the next chapter, I shall set out Wittgensteinian arguments against anomalous monism. But these are not relevant in the present case. Davidson's anomalous monism explains his remarks here. But radical interpretation need not presuppose that view of the relation of mind and body.)

Davidson's metaphysical account of mind is a non-reductive form of physicalism which includes a token identity theory. Every mental event just is a physical event under a different description. But there is no systematic connection between *types* of mental event and types of physical event. Because it rejects the claim that the mental can exist independently of physical stuff, Davidson's account is a form of physicalism or monism. It is committed to an identity theory because mental and physical classifications classify the same entities. But it is non-reductive and anomalous because it denies that mental and physical types can be matched.

Given this basic metaphysical picture, Davidson's comment that speech is nothing but, or identical with, physical movement need not be seen as the beginning of a reductionist account of content. Furthermore, there is good reason not to make this claim because Davidson explicitly argues that no such reduction of mental terms to physical terms is possible (Davidson 1980: 207–27). No interpretative theory could be framed which connected bare inputs to meaningful outputs because that would require precisely the systematic interconnection between those two descriptions which Davidson argues is impossible. It would – impossibly – connect *types* of bare sounds to *types* of meaningful utterance, for example. Nevertheless, if the *token* identity theory is true, then speech acts just are (and are nothing more than) physical events. Each mental token is identical to a physical token.

A token identity theory of mind implies that the evidence available for radical interpretation can be described in non-semantic terms. Because, on Davidson's account, an action or utterance just is a physical event then it can also in principle be picked out by its physical properties. These will be non-intentional. But it does not follow that evidence can be described in non-semantic terms and still maintain its evidential or justificatory relations for the interpretation. It cannot be described *as evidence* in non-semantic terms. But that is not a claim that the later Davidson makes. The token identity theory is consistent with the basic Wittgensteinian claim that third-person access to content cannot generally comprise bare sounds mediated by interpretations. (I shall return to Wittgensteinian criticisms of the token identity theory in Chapter 6.)

1.3.1 Radical interpretation and aspect blindness

There is a further Wittgensteinian argument that has been advanced against Davidson's use of radical interpretation based on passages in the second part of the *Investigations* in which Wittgenstein discusses changes of aspect. According to Mulhall, Wittgenstein's discussion of aspect perception is of general importance (Mulhall 1990). It attempts to characterise the immediacy with which we experience the significance of pictures, themes, words, actions and the world more generally. The point of the discussion of cases of *changes* in aspect, such as Gestalt switches, is to illustrate the general nature of *continuous* aspect perception. The latter characterises our normal immediate response to words and to the world. Forging a link with the Heideggerian notion of the ready-to-hand, Mulhall suggests that our experiences of the world are usually immediately charged with significance. They do not have to be interpreted.

Wittgenstein describes this kind of immediate understanding of the meaning of a word in isolation as a form of understanding. But, while this is not a metaphorical use of the word 'understanding', it is nevertheless a *secondary* use (Wittgenstein 1953: 216). A secondary use is one which we find natural given the primary use, but which is discontinuous with, and could not be used to teach, the primary use. Nor is it metaphorical. An example is the use of 'fat' in the thought that Wednesday is fat. Clearly Wednesday cannot in any ordinary sense be compared with other fat or thin things. And it would be optimistic to attempt to teach the meaning of fat by giving Wednesday as an example. Nevertheless, many language users give spontaneous expression to the thought that Wednesday is a fat day.

Thus, although we may wish to say that a word or action can be immediately experienced as bearing a meaning in isolation, this does not contradict Wittgenstein's general connection of meaning with an extended practice or technique. The concept of meaning is used in its primary sense in the latter defining context and only in a secondary sense in the former. This distinction is important because Wittgenstein claims that, although as a matter of contingent fact it is not true of us, it would make sense to ascribe to someone understanding in the primary sense unaccompanied by the secondary aspect. He calls such a person 'aspect blind' (ibid.: 213).

Mulhall argues that Davidson's use of radical interpretation to explicate meaning must be fundamentally mistaken because it presupposes that language users are all aspect blind:

> [I]t is important to note that this metaphysics of the given – revealed as it is by Davidson's emphasis upon the concept of 'interpretation' – exemplifies to perfection the stance of the interlocutor in Section xi of the *Philosophical Investigations*. Incapable of finding a home for the notion of continuous aspect perception in his framework of thought, Davidson describes the everyday phenomenon of perceiving words and other human beings as if

aspect-blindness were the normal human state. His emphasis on processes of theorising as necessary in order to organise bare sounds and movements into words and actions . . . commits him implicitly to a general notion of visual perception as divided into what is really seen and what is interpreted, ie as divisible in precisely the way Wittgenstein rejects. (Mulhall 1990: 106)

This is not, however, a decisive criticism for three reasons:

- It presupposes the uncharitable – if common – interpretation of Davidson that I have suggested is not obligatory. While the early Davidson does indeed suggest that the evidence for radical interpretation should be described in neutral terms, the later Davidson explicitly criticises the picture of any evidence for a belief 'whose character can be wholly specified without reference to what it is evidence for' (Davidson 1989: 162). The division of perception into what is seen and what is interpreted is rejected as the third dogma of empiricism (see below).
- Furthermore, the comments which, I have suggested above, can be understood as expressions of Davidson's token identity theory, can be reconciled with Mulhall's criticism. The fact that meaningful utterances or actions – or even, according to Davidson, content-laden mental states – are identical with physical events or states does not imply that they are *experienced* as mere physical events and only subsequently interpreted.
- The connection between the primary and secondary sense of meaning is far from clear. The fact that we experience the 'meaning' of words in isolation – in the secondary sense of 'meaning' – is a contingent feature of the phenomenology of meaning. Consequently Davidson could simply reply that his account of radical interpretation is meant to capture only meaning proper, meaning in the primary sense. The phenomenology is a further matter. This fits with my interpretation of radical interpretation as merely *reconstructive* epistemology.

This third point may require a little more explanation. One of the problems of Mulhall's argument is that it is not clear what the presence or absence of the phenomenology amounts to. This is because it is difficult to describe what someone who is aspect blind lacks without impinging on the primary sense of meaning. According to Wittgenstein, such a person cannot see aspects change, cannot see a cube 'as a cube', but nevertheless can recognise a cube (Wittgenstein 1953: 213–14). Likewise, she cannot experience a word as bearing a meaning in isolation but can nevertheless learn its technique of use because blindness to the secondary sense of meaning is not blindness to the first. But the moral of this separation is clear. Whatever the secondary experience consists in, because it is possible to understand and use a word without it, it is not a part of content proper. Thus, it is not essential to the philosophy of content.

One can imagine a possible counter-argument to this that runs as follows. Although in any given case of primary understanding there need not be direct secondary understanding, all primary understanding must be traceable to some secondary understanding. The motivation for this argument can be illustrated as follows. Consider the case of someone who has an attitude to a line drawing of the face of her beloved as we recognise an electrical circuit diagram. Having some facility, she is able quickly to determine that some of the lines designate the eyes and nose, and on the basis of this, can deduce the meaning of any problematic smaller features. Now the counter argument runs thus. Her ability must depend in turn on some ability to take in the lines and circles which ground her *interpretation* of the picture without the need to interpret them.

This thought, however, does not support the counter claim. What it helps illustrate is the familiar Wittgensteinian point that understanding cannot be explicated in terms of interpretation. It shows that aspect blindness must not be explicated in terms of a need to *interpret* pictures because that picture of understanding is incoherent. If aspect blindness is to act as a meaningful contrast to some more immediate phenomenological description of our relation to language and the world, then it must be described in some other way. The apparent force of the counter argument relies on just what is captured by the right account of the *primary* sense of understanding meaning. To understand a meaning is to master a technique of application without an interpretation.

This digression on the secondary sense of 'meaning' and the immediate experience it is used to characterise suggests the following moral. Wittgenstein's account of the primary sense of meaning, described in this book, undermines any interpretation of Davidson in which understanding meaning depends on the interpretation of norm-free signs or sounds. But the further phenomenological objection that may be raised based on aspect perception adds nothing further to this objection and can be resisted.

So much then for Davidson's occasional claims that the input to radical interpretation comprises bare sounds or movements. I propose to neglect the early explicit claims that evidence for a theory of interpretation should be non-semantic as mistaken and to accommodate later claims that utterances are identical with sounds or meaningful actions with movements as expressions of his physicalism. But if the input to radical interpretation is, when considered as evidence, always meaningful, norm-laden, utterances or actions, of what philosophical significance is Davidson's account of radical interpretation?

The point that has been reached is this. Davidson's philosophy of content comprises two main aspects. One is the formal theory of meaning that is supposed, in some dark sense, to formalise in a regimented structure what is known by a speaker of a language. This runs counter to Wittgenstein's belief that language does not comprise any such organised structure and his metaphilosophical denial that philosophy should advance explanatory theories. The other aspect of Davidson's approach is the philosophy of language of the field linguist. Providing that this is not taken to depend upon the interpretation of bare norm-free and meaningless data – sounds and movements – this position has informative similarities to Wittgenstein's account. In the rest of this chapter I shall examine some of the consequences of this similarity. This will answer the question about the significance of radical interpretation.

1.3.2 Third-person access in Davidson and Wittgenstein

The key assumption which Wittgenstein and Davidson share is that 'what a fully-informed interpreter could learn about what a speaker means is all there is to learn; the same goes for what the speaker believes' (Davidson 1983: 315). 'The nature of language and thought is such as to make them interpretable' (Davidson 1989: 166). Davidson takes a third-person approach to meaning. There are no facts about the contents of mental states and utterances that cannot, in principle, be discovered from this standpoint. The third-person perspective contrasts with a first-person stance and with an idealised, metaphysical stance outside linguistic practices. The former is the perspective of Cartesian philosophy that makes the normativity of mental content impossible. The latter perspective is motivated by the thought that philosophy can provide further explanatory insight into meaning that goes beyond the resources available to language users. Wittgenstein's philosophical minimalism amounts to a rejection of this possibility. A similar rejection is enshrined in Davidson's choice of the radical interpreter to elucidate meaning.

A second similarity concerns the role of context in the understanding of speech and action. Davidson suggests that radical interpretation takes account of the context of utterances to pin down their meaning and the background beliefs of speakers. He also suggests that all interpretation is a form of radical interpretation. For my purposes, these comments are best thought of as a piece of reconstructive epistemology designed to reveal the relational constitution of content together with its essentially rational and normative structure. Davidson suggests that the results of radical interpretation could be formalised as a theory. If this were so, then the theory could not characterise the input to interpretation in norm-free terms. But, in fact, talk of a theory here is unhelpful given that it cannot explain linguistic abilities. It is better to say, as in the previous chapter, that content is essentially normatively structured without reference to an interpretative theory at all.

With these basic connections between Davidson and Wittgenstein established, there are three further issues that will help shed light on the account of Wittgenstein given in previous chapters:

- Davidson's rejection of the dualism of scheme and content has close parallels to Wittgenstein's minimalist account of the connection between language and the world.
- Davidson's denial of the role of mental objects present to consciousness in the metaphysics of thought helps clarify the close connection between mental states and behaviour that Wittgenstein emphasises. This sheds light on Wittgenstein's account of false thought and on the general shape of a plausible Wittgensteinian account of singular thought.
- Davidson and Rorty take the attack on representational theories of mind to be an attack on the idea that beliefs can represent the world. Representation is replaced by a merely causal connection. But as McDowell suggests, this cannot account for the normativity of thought.

2 Davidson and Wittgenstein on the Distinction between Scheme and Content

This section will compare the general picture of the connection between language and the world offered by Davidson and Wittgenstein. To do this, I shall examine Davidson's criticism of the dualism of conceptual schemes and their contents. The account which follows from Davidson's criticisms of that dualism resembles and sheds light on Wittgenstein's philosophically minimalist account.

Scheme-content dualism is a philosophical theory of the relation of language and the world. The word 'content' here is used in a special philosophical sense. Elsewhere in philosophy it refers to meaning, in the case of language, and something closely related to meaning, in the case of beliefs and other mental states. But, in the context of this specific debate, it stands for one half of a two-ingredient theory of how everyday content comes about. The (everyday) content of a belief results from the combination of a conceptual *scheme* and an unconceptualised *content*. Content in this special sense refers either to what is given in a pure and unconceptualised experience of the world or to the world itself, again conceived of as unconceptualised. Conceptual schemes organise this data to produce fully fledged conceptualised beliefs.

Davidson calls the dualism of scheme and content the third and final dogma of empiricism. He claims that it can survive even in a post-Quinean environment that rejects the first two dogmas. By calling it the third dogma, Davidson suggests that the argument against this dogma continues the same philosophical trajectory as Quine's arguments against the first two (Quine 1951). The reason is this. Quine characterises the first dogma, the analytic-synthetic distinction, as one between sentences that are true in virtue of meaning alone and those that are true in virtue of the joint contribution of their meaning and the world. Given hard facts about meaning, the second dogma of empiricism claims that the world's contribution to the truth of synthetic sentences can be apportioned sentence by sentence. Quine, however, denies the determinacy of meaning. He thus denies that a class of analytic sentences can be isolated and that 'empirical significance' can be ascribed to individual synthetic sentences. But he still accepts, according to Davidson, that there is a distinction, at the level of the whole of science 'between the invariant content and the variant conceptual trappings . . . world-view and cues, theory and data: these are the scheme and content of which I have been speaking' (Davidson 1989: 162).

> The dualism of the synthetic and the analytic is a dualism of sentences some of which are true (or false) both because of what they mean and because of their empirical content, while others are true (or false) by virtue of meaning alone, having no empirical content. If we give up the dualism, we abandon the conception of meaning that goes with it, but we do not have to abandon the idea of empirical content: we can hold, if we want, that *all* sentences have empirical content. Empirical content is in turn explained by reference to the facts, the world, experience, sensation, the totality of sensory stimuli or something similar. (Davidson 1984: 189)

If the third dogma can survive *even without* the first two dogmas, it seems strange that one might want to reject the third dogma while asserting the first. That, however, is more or less the Wittgensteinian position that I shall advocate shortly.

Davidson provides four kinds of arguments against scheme-content dualism:

- An argument in 'On the very idea of a conceptual scheme' against the intelligibility of the scheme side of the dichotomy (Davidson 1984: 183–98). This deconstructs the metaphors used to substantiate the idea of conceptual schemes. It focuses primarily on the relation between language and the world.
- An argument that attacks the idea of schemes from the perspective of the radical interpreter. This argument reflects, I suggest, Davidson's underlying motivation for rejecting this dualism.
- An argument in 'A coherence theory of truth and knowledge' that criticises the content side of the dichotomy, arguing that pure unconceptualised content cannot play the explanatory philosophical role it is supposed to (Davidson 1983). It focuses primarily on the relation of thought and experience.

- An argument that attacks the idea of contents from the perspective of the radical interpreter.

I shall focus first on the relation between language and the world, and then make some brief comments on the relation between concepts and experience.

2.1   Scheme-content dualism and the relation of language and the world

Davidson's criticism of *schemes* runs like this. The idea of a dualism of organising conceptual scheme and content which awaits organisation has to be substantiated. Davidson suggests that, if it really makes sense, then so must the idea of an alternative scheme that organises the same unorganised content in a different way. (Alternative conceptual schemes are the stuff of conceptual relativism which is often the motivation for thinking of schemes in the first place.) He thus suggests that one will have succeeded in making sense of the idea of a conceptual scheme if and only if one can make sense of an alternative scheme that is true but not translatable into our own terms.

This talk of translation marks the connection that Davidson makes between schemes and languages. For the purposes of argument, Davidson suggests that, if speakers employ different conceptual schemes, then they must employ different languages. The converse implication does not hold because different languages might share the same conceptual scheme. But, because schemes are said to be largely true while languages can be neither true nor false, they cannot simply be assimilated. Schemes correspond to world-views expressed in languages. Davidson's tendency to assimilate them derives in part from his view that the identification of belief and meanings cannot be separated. This complication does not, however, undermine the basic insight into the connection between language and the world which the discussion of this dualism provides.

To return to the argument, Davidson suggests that there are only a limited number of underlying metaphors available to substantiate the idea of schemes that are true but not translatable. A scheme either *organises* or *fits* something. Examples of the former include systematising and dividing up. The latter includes predicting, accounting for and facing. What is organised or fitted is either *reality* (the universe, the world, nature) or *experience* (the given, sense-data, sensory promptings). This leaves four possible permutations. None of these, however, can be used to fill out what is being claimed. Briefly, one cannot organise a single object such as reality or the world. Organising requires a plurality. But whatever plurality experience comprises will be individuated according to familiar principles, and whatever scheme organises, these entities will be translatable into our own.

Moving to the idea of fitting requires consideration of whole sentences rather than sub-sentential referential devices. But the idea of fitting all the evidence, or the facts, or even the world adds nothing to the more basic idea of being true. Thus, according to Davidson, the attempt to fill out the idea of an alternative conceptual scheme collapses into the claim that there could be a scheme which is true, or largely true, but not translatable into ours. He then argues that we cannot separate our conception of truth from that of translation because that connection is explicit in Tarski's Convention T and that embodies our best intuition about the use of the concept of truth. Thus, we cannot make sense of the idea of an alternative conceptual scheme and therefore of a single universal scheme.

One of the key assumptions behind the last stage of this argument is that there is no alternative way of making sense of truth independently of translation. One such alternative might be a correspondence theory. Davidson rejects the correspondence theory on the grounds that there is nothing to which the vehicles of truth can correspond:

> Nothing, however, no *thing* makes sentences and theories true: not experience, not surface irritations, not the world, can make a sentence true. *That* experience takes a certain course, that our skin is warmed or punctured, that the universe is finite, these facts, if we like to talk that way, make sentences and theories true. But this point is put better without mention of facts. The sentence 'My skin is warm' is true if and only if my skin is warm. Here there is no reference to a fact, a world, an experience, or a piece of evidence. (Davidson 1984: 194)

One challenge to Davidson's conclusion might accept the claim that truth must be linked to translation or translatability but deny that this implies translation into *our* scheme. Such a challenge helps to make explicit Davidson's underlying assumption: that is, that the full facts about meaning are available to a mundane third-person perspective that, in principle, we could adopt. This is an assumption which those who insist on the possibility of a true but untranslatable scheme will not accept. But it is the basic assumption that guides Davidson's approach to content.

(This approach is also shared by Wittgenstein. It is implicit in the connection he makes between meaning and practice and in the thought experiment of the anthropological interpretation of language (Wittgenstein 1953: §206-7). But there are some comments in the *Investigations* and elsewhere that may seem to qualify or undermine Wittgenstein's support of Davidson's claim. These are the passages where he suggests that there might be people, or animals, with whom we might not find our feet. Such claims can be limited to particular concepts or practices (e.g., Wittgenstein 1956: 38). Or they may apply across the board (Wittgenstein 1953: 223). But, although I will not argue for this claim here, I think that these are generally consistent with Davidson's claim. Firstly, the suggestions that there might be tribes who measure using elastic rulers or count using non-standard rules are supposed to undermine any conviction we may have that our concepts are the *right* concepts (ibid.: 230). But, in so far as Wittgenstein is successful in filling out these non-standard practices to make them genuine alternatives to our practices, they are accessible to us. Secondly, the context of the claim of *general* scope that if a lion could speak we would not understand it suggests that this also does not contradict Davidson. The context implies that Wittgenstein's suggestion is that we might understand the lion's language but not understand its manners. But that is consistent with the claims advanced here.)

Given his underlying assumption that facts about content are available to a mundane third-person perspective, Davidson sometimes deploys a much quicker argument against the dualism of scheme and content or world (an example of the second argument listed above):

> In my opinion we do not understand the idea of such a really foreign scheme. We know what states of mind are like, and how they are correctly identified; they are just those states whose contents can be discovered in well-known ways. If other people or creatures are in states not discoverable by these methods, it can be, not because our methods fail us, but because those states are not correctly called states of mind – they are not beliefs, desires, wishes, or intentions. The meaninglessness of the idea of a conceptual scheme forever beyond our grasp is due not to our inability to understand such a scheme or to our other human limitations; it is due simply to what we mean by a system of concepts. (Davidson 1989: 160)

If there are no facts about meaning which are unavailable to radical interpretation then there cannot be untranslatable conceptual schemes because that would involve inaccessible meanings.

So much then for the arguments against scheme-content dualism that concern the relation of language to the world. But what positive account of that relation does this leave? Davidson claims that the denial of dualism puts us in unmediated touch with the world:

> In giving up dependence on the concept of an uninterpreted reality, something outside all schemes and science, we do not relinquish the notion of objective truth – quite the contrary. Given the dogma of a dualism of scheme and reality, we get conceptual relativity, and truth relative to a scheme. Without the dogma, this kind of relativity goes by the board. Of course truth of sentences remains relative to language, but that is as objective as can be. In giving up the dualism of scheme and world, we do not give up the world, but re-establish unmediated touch with the familiar objects whose antics make our sentences and opinions true or false. (Davidson 1984: 198)

The threat to objectivity which Davidson counters here results directly from the denial of the dualism of organising scheme and uninterpreted world. As he comments elsewhere, this dualism is an expression of a more general dualism of the subjective and the objective (Davidson 1989: 163). The scheme or language side of the distinction coincides with subjectivity. The world or content side coincides with objectivity. From this perspective it might seem that denying that the world plays this objective role involves a denial that utterances or beliefs are *objectively* true or false in virtue of something properly independent of our utterances or beliefs. Davidson attempts to provide some reassurance that this is not so. But, because the detailed argument considered so far criticises the scheme side directly and thus the content side only indirectly, it is not clear what account of objectivity this leaves. (Davidson's third argument, against the content side of the distinction, concentrates on unconceptualised *experience* and thus does not answer this question.) Wittgenstein's minimalist account of the connection between rules and their applications – and thus of meaning and use and mental states and their fulfilments – provides a model for the conception of objectivity that is rejected by Davidson and thus what notion remains.

A central claim of the minimalist interpretation of Wittgenstein is that no substantial answer can be given to any of the following questions:

- What connects one's understanding of a word with its correct future application?
- What connects an intentional mental state with the event or events that satisfies or satisfy it?
- More generally, what is the relation between thought or language and the world?

Each of these questions presupposes that a distinction can be drawn – between meaning and use, thought and its objects – that corresponds to a gulf which has to be crossed. But no explanatory mechanism can successfully bridge any of these gaps. Wittgenstein's conclusion is that there is something wrong with attempting this kind of philosophical explanation. Rather than attempting to provide an underlying mechanism which makes meaning or thought possible, the initial presuppositions which lead to the need for this kind of answer should be rejected.

This minimalist response was illustrated by the opposition of Platonism and constructivism. The fundamental difference between these positions can be summarised by the different interpretations they provide to the biconditional, discussed in Chapter 3, which links the practice of applying concepts in rule-guided judgements to the extension of those concepts. Like the Euthyphro paradox, this conditional can be read in two ways: either the antecedent extension determines correct judgement; or correct judgement determines the extension. On the former reading, judgements latch on to pre-existing extensions, series, similarities or groupings. By tracking those extensions, judgements succeed in being true. This is a form of Platonism, broadly construed. On the latter interpretation, the extensions are constructed by the ongoing practice of judging. The correctness of judgements is an internal matter, guided by a rule that is characterisable independently of its extension.

Wittgenstein rejects both these interpretations. Neither successfully accounts for the normativity of judgement. Constructivism undermines the everyday notion that rules determine correctness and incorrectness in advance. Platonism presupposes an external source for the normativity of judgement, separated from human practice. But, even on the doubtful assumption that such external extensions could exist, they could not function as standards for judgement without presupposing further standards for their correct selection and application. Because these further standards would likewise require yet further standards, the account of following such fundamentally external standards cannot be given without vicious regress. But, instead of accepting that these two interpretations exhaust the space of logical possibility, Wittgenstein is best interpreted as rejecting the assumption that constructivism and Platonism share. The assumption at fault is that a distinction can be drawn between a purely internally structured practice of judging and a purely external extension or series. The correct moral is that the practice of judging cannot be characterised except by reference to what is judged and the extension cannot be specified except by appeal to human practice.

Wittgenstein's conclusion thus resembles Davidson's claim that the distinction between organising conceptual scheme and unconceptualised content cannot be drawn. The dogma that Davidson rejects puts the full responsibility for organising on the scheme side, the side of language-users. Content awaits organisation. Thus the third dogma resembles constructivism rather than Platonism (which is unsurprising because it is the third dogma of *empiricism*) and so Davidson's suggestion that rejecting it is no threat to objectivity becomes much clearer. The constructivist way of drawing the distinction between human judgement and worldly extension minimises the world's contribution to the objectivity of the truth of judgements. Denying this account makes judgement *more* objective, *more* world-involving, rather than less so.

If this connection between Davidson's attack on scheme-content dualism and Wittgensteinian minimalism is correct it suggests a surprising possibility. Davidson presents his arguments against conceptual schemes as a continuation of Quine's argument against the analytic-synthetic distinction. Wittgenstein shares Quine's hostility to the reification of meaning, which Quine claims underpins the distinction. Wittgenstein agrees that there are no true sentences the truth of which can be explained by the interconnection of cog-like meaning-bodies. But Wittgenstein does uphold a distinction that plays a similar role to the analytic-synthetic distinction. That is the distinction between grammatical rules, which determine how words can correctly be used, and linguistic moves made according to those rules. While the explanatory baggage which has traditionally accompanied the analytic-synthetic distinction is a target of Wittgenstein's criticism, something like the distinction survives in a post-Wittgensteinian environment.

There is a number of differences between analytic truths and expressions of rules or grammatical propositions. Glock, for example, lists four (Glock 1996b: 131–2):

- The class of normative rules is greater than the traditional model of analytic sentences because Wittgenstein recognises non-truth-functional claims such as white is lighter than black.
- Analytic truths are defined as sentence types, but expressions of rules are context dependent.
- Rules by contrast with analytic truths determine the meaning of constituent words rather than following from them.
- Rules are normative prescriptions and not descriptive truths.

But these differences do not matter to the point being made here. A minimalist interpretation of Wittgenstein resembles Davidson's attack on the third dogma of empiricism while preserving something like the first. One consequence of this is that Wittgenstein, unlike Davidson, can preserve a principled distinction between a-priori philosophical inquiry and natural science. Philosophy can investigate the 'possibilities of phenomena' through conceptual analysis. Such analysis examines grammatical rules. But, given the attack on scheme-content dualism, this is not *merely* an investigation of language but also of what is possible and impossible.

2.2   Scheme-content dualism and the relation of thought to experience

In addition to the affinities between Davidson's and Wittgenstein's accounts of the relation of language and the world there are also some affinities in their account of the connection between thought and experience. Davidson provides two sorts of argument against a dualism of concepts and unconceptualised experience. One attempts to undermine the intelligibility of unconceptualised content 'from within' by showing that it cannot fulfil its supposed philosophical purpose. The second attacks the idea of content from the external perspective of radical interpretation.

The first argument is given in 'The coherence theory of truth and knowledge' (Davidson 1983). This criticises the content side of scheme-content dualism by criticising the idea that thoughts about the world are interpretations of an unconceptualised given. The problem is that unconceptualised contents – sense-data, sensations – cannot stand in justificatory relations to fully interpreted thoughts:

> Introducing intermediate steps or entities into the causal chain, like sensations or observations, serves only to make the epistemological problem more obvious. For if the

intermediaries are merely causes, they don't justify the beliefs they cause, while if they deliver information, they may be lying. The moral is obvious. Since we can't swear intermediaries to truthfulness, we should allow no intermediaries between our beliefs and their objects in the world. Of course there are causal intermediaries. What we must guard against are epistemic intermediaries. (Davidson 1983: 312)

In addition to this argument, Davidson also argues that, given the perspective of radical interpretation, there is no theoretical use for unconceptualised content. He argues that one of the consequences of the connection between content and what is available to the radical interpreter is that:

[T]he details of the mechanisms which constitute the causal chains from speaker to speaker, and spoken-of object to speaker to language learner, cannot in themselves matter to meaning and reference. The grasp of meanings is determined only by the terminal elements in the conditioning process and is tested only by the end product: use of words geared to appropriate objects and situations . . . The reason the senses are of no primary theoretical importance to the philosophical account of knowledge is that our ears, eyes, taste buds, and tactile and olfactory organs play a causal role in the formation of beliefs about the world. The causal connections between thought and objects and events in the world could have been established in entirely different ways. (Davidson 1989: 163–5)

This undercuts any dualism in which thoughts about the world are supposed to be the result of concepts being applied to unconceptualised sense-data. Sense-data are merely contingent intermediaries in the causal chains between thought and its objects. Thus, according to the above argument, whatever sense-data are experienced, they can have at most causal significance in the formation of beliefs and cannot either provide normative support for, or partially constitute, those beliefs. Because scheme and content were defined together, the uselessness of the one implies the uselessness of the other for the metaphysics of thought. 'Content and scheme . . . came as a pair; we can let them go together.' (Davidson 1989: 165)

My purpose in comparing these Davidsonian claims with Wittgenstein is largely negative. It might be thought that the fact that experience cannot be broken down into two factors is established in Wittgenstein's account of aspect perception in the second part of the *Investigations*. When Wittgenstein is invoked in the philosophy of science to support the claim that all observation is theory-laden, this is the section that is typically discussed (e.g., Hanson 1958). The changing aspects of the duck-rabbit resist description in a language of pure sense-data. But, in fact, as the discussion of Mulhall above suggested, Wittgenstein's hostility to such a two-component picture runs much deeper. It does not depend merely on the phenomenological fact that we experience some things under aspects [it is worth noting that Wittgenstein *denies* that we experience *everything* in this way (Wittgenstein 1953: 195)]. It follows from the attack on interpretational accounts of understanding. Because judgements stand in normative relations to experience and since interpretational accounts sever normative connections, experiences cannot comprise an unconceptualised given which is then interpreted.

3 Davidson and Wittgenstein on the Rejection of Internal Mental Objects

Two of the arguments against a dualism of scheme and content, discussed in the last section, are directed against the idea of an independent or autonomous scheme defined in opposition to the corresponding idea of content. (The third and fourth arguments attack the other side of the dichotomy: the idea of an unconceptualised content, or the given, defined in opposition to a conceptual scheme.) While Davidson's arguments against internal mental objects differ in details, the picture against which they are directed is related. Davidson, like Wittgenstein, rejects the conception of content-laden mental states as free-standing states, independent of the world. (I shall argue in Chapter 6, however, that Davidson does not succeed in escaping that picture. Anomalous monism, his ontological account of the mind, is in fact committed to just such a picture.)

Like his attack on the dualism of scheme and content, Davidson deploys two kinds of argument against the role of internal mental objects in the metaphysics of thought. One concerns the *identification* of the inner object, and I shall comment on it shortly. Effectively, it attempts to deconstruct the idea of mental representations from within. The other, which I will tackle first, relies on the third-person perspective of radical interpretation.

Davidson suggests that the argument against the dualism of concept and unconceptualised experience also undercuts the motivation for postulating mental objects. He claims that the only motivation for postulating reified *interpreted* propositional objects before the mind's eye is as part of a picture in which they result from the application of concepts to immediately experienced private or subjective data. Thus, once sense-data are rejected 'no *objects* will be left with respect to which the problem of representation can be raised' (Davidson 1989: 165). As an observation about philosophical motivation, this is not convincing. There is no reason why representationalism should be committed to the claim that mental representations result from, or can be analysed into, contributions from scheme and content.

But, whether or not the only motivation for postulating mental objects is commitment to a picture of unconceptualised private contents, the central role of radical interpretation in the determination of belief and meaning provides a direct argument against mental representations. Because the facts that constitute meaning are, according to Davidson, essentially relational, they cannot be purely subjective. They cannot be independent of the world in any way that allows them to 'be identified and described without reference to "what goes on around us"' (Davidson 1989: 162). But that is precisely the kind of free-standing world independence that mental representations are supposed to have. Thus, whatever internal mental representations might exist would be irrelevant to the constitution of meaning.

Davidson's second argument is directed against the coherence, the general picture of the mind which includes internal mental objects. The picture Davidson criticises is this. To have a propositional attitude is to have an object, a propositional object, before, or present to, the mind. These objects have two roles: '[T]hey *identify* a thought by fixing its content; and they *constitute* an essential aspect of the psychology of the thought by being grasped or otherwise known by the person with the thought' (Davidson 1991: 198). Davidson argues that these two roles cannot be reconciled. The problem is that we take it for granted that we have authority over the content of our own mental states. But, if their content is fixed by an object which is known to the thinker, then to know the content of one's own thoughts requires that one knows which object is before the mind: 'The trouble is that ignorance of even one property of an object can, under appropriate circumstances, count as not knowing which object it is.' (ibid.: 198) It is this difficulty that leads to the philosophical postulation of special objects, such as Fregean senses, which must be what they seem and seem what they are. But, as Davidson points out, there simply are no such objects. Thus:

> If the mind can think only by getting into the right relation to some object which it can for certain distinguish from all others, then thought is impossible. If a mind can know what it thinks only by flawlessly identifying the objects before it, then we must very often not know what we think. (ibid.: 201)

This argument clearly differs from Wittgenstein's argument against inner mental objects. Wittgenstein's argument, as set out in Chapter 2, turns, not on problems with the identification of such inner objects, but on the impossibility of them serving their supposed function in constituting thoughts. No object before the mind could have the normative connections that content-laden mental states have to their fulfilment conditions. But, despite this difference in argument, the end result is the same. Thinking a thought is not a matter of having an internal object before the mind's eye. This convergence of critical views is more than just a matter of interest. The obvious question which follows from the negative result is: what then is it to have a content-laden mental state? Davidson's positive account can be compared with, and used to shed light on, Wittgenstein's account set out in the previous chapter.

Davidson's response to the critical arguments is to accept the first role of objects and reject the second:

> It does not follow, from the facts that a thinker knows what he thinks and that what he thinks can be fixed by relating him to a certain object, that the thinker is acquainted with, or indeed knows anything at all about the object. It does not even follow that the thinker knows about any *object* at all. Someone who attributes a thought to another must . . . relate that other to some object, and so the attributer must, of course, identify an appropriate object, either by pointing to it or describing it. But there is no reason why the attributer must stand in any special relation to the identifying object; all he has to do is refer to it in the way he refers to anything else.
>
> We specify the subjective state of the thinker by relating him to an object, but there is no reason to say that this object itself has a subjective status, that it is 'known' by the thinker, or is 'before the mind' of the thinker. (ibid.: 203)

He suggests that the ascription of propositional attitudes to people functions like the ascription of weights to objects. Objects stand in various relations of the form: weighing more than, weighing less than, weighing twice as much as. For simplicity, these relations and ratios can be represented by the use of a standard. This enables weights to be ascribed to objects directly using numbers. Thus, one can say of an object that it weighs 5 kg. But this does not require the addition of *kilogrammes* into our ontology in addition to weighty objects. On this picture, numbers are in no sense *intrinsic* to the objects that have weight or *part* of them:

> What are basic are certain *relations* among objects: we conveniently keep track of these relations by assigning numbers to the objects . . . In thinking and talking of the weights of physical objects we do not need to suppose there are such things as weights for objects to have. Similarly in thinking and talking about the beliefs of people we needn't suppose there are such entities as beliefs. (ibid.: 205)

The last sentence might be taken to imply some form of eliminativism. But I think that it is clear from the context that that is not the position that Davidson supports. Instead he offers a picture which clarifies what should replace mental representations or internal objects in the metaphysics of thought. The answer is in keeping with Wittgenstein's philosophical minimalism as described in earlier chapters. No objects come before the mind's eye. Nor are there internal states that encode propositional attitudes. But this implies neither eliminativism nor any crude behaviourism in which mental states can be identified one to one with dispositions to act. To be in a mental state with a certain content is for one's behaviour to be explicable from a third-person perspective using a system of propositional attitudes. (This is a necessary condition. To rule out things which do not need to be so described but which could be – such as planets – Davidson would have to add some further condition. One such further condition might be that using the system of propositional attitudes must have pragmatic advantage over a merely physical description (cf. Dennett 1987: 23). But the formal project of specifying necessary and sufficient conditions is not Davidson's purpose.)

The general picture, which Davidson suggests, resembles the Wittgensteinian account, given in the previous chapter, in which behaviour is explained by reference to system of content-laden states governed by normative and rational relations. It can also be coupled with Wittgenstein's claim that one learns new behaviour when one learns a language. One learns behavioural repertoires that essentially turn on one's linguistic abilities. And one also learns to describe oneself in the language of propositional attitudes. Thus, there is no prospect of reducing content-laden mental states to behavioural dispositions which could be described without the resources of the language of propositional attitudes. But all that is essentially involved in having content-laden mental states is the possession of complex practical abilities and behaviour. (I say 'essentially' because Davidson focuses here on the connection between the content of propositional attitudes and behaviour. But having such states may also involve a range of experiences. As Wittgenstein repeatedly emphasises, the experiences, which may or may not occur when one understands, expects or imagines something, do not themselves *constitute* the state of understanding, expecting, imagining and so forth. One of the differences, however, between Wittgenstein and Davidson is that the latter simply does not discuss inner experiences.)

Having set out the similarity between the pictures of mental content offered by Davidson and Wittgenstein, I shall now examine two consequences. Davidson's alternative to internal mental objects sheds light on Wittgenstein's brief characterisation of false thought – mentioned in Chapter 3 – and the general shape of a Wittgensteinian account of singular thought – touched upon in Chapter 4. I shall consider these in turn.

Davidson claims that beliefs, whether true or false, do not involve psychological relations to objects. There is, of course, a sense in which this claim is obviously false. Tautologically to have a mental state with a particular content is to be in a relational psychological state and thus psychologically related to something. Davidson's point, however, is that this tautological claim cannot be *explained* by reference to, or broken down into, a relationship to an object that could be characterised in independent, and thus explanatory, terms. For this reason it might be better to say that possession of a propositional attitude does not consist in a *psychologistic* relation to an object. Instead, to have a belief is just for one's behaviour to be explicable by a network of propositional attitudes. One stands, not in a psychologistic relation to an object, but in an explanatory relation to other behaviour from the third-person perspective.

Given this picture, having false thoughts presents no particular philosophical difficulty. The attitude that explains one's behaviour can be one which is described using a sentence that is false. Beliefs about non-existent objects can be similarly accommodated. One's behaviour may be best explained by ascribing an attitude which contains reference to something that does not actually exist. Because, according to Davidson, thinkers do not have to be in psychological relations to objects to think thoughts, there is again no particular philosophical problem in either case. This fits Wittgenstein's claim that 'The agreement, the harmony, of thought and reality consists in this: if I say falsely that something is *red*, then, for all that, it isn't *red*' (Wittgenstein 1953: §429). As I commented in Chapter 3, Wittgenstein treats true and false thoughts symmetrically. But there remains an intuitive temptation to regard the content of true thoughts as worldly facts, and regard the content of false thoughts as internal surrogates or mere shadows of facts. Davidson helps show why this is unnecessary. To form an intentional mental state is never to get oneself into a psychologistic relation to a fact but to fit one's behaviour into a rational and explanatory system that can be described using propositional attitudes.

Davidson's picture also suggests how a Wittgensteinian account of content might best accommodate singular or demonstrative thought. Davidson states that his argument against the need for objects of thought to be present to the mind also applies, to and undermines, accounts of singular thought (Davidson 1991: 200). Because Davidson says little on the subject and Wittgenstein says nothing, my comments will be brief and inconclusive. But it seems likely that Wittgenstein would again favour only a minimalist account of the connection between thought and the world in the case of singular thought. As a result the constitution of singular thoughts does not present the key grounds for Wittgenstein's externalism.

Davidson's claim that thought does not require a psychological or psychologistic relation between a thinker and an object dovetails with Wittgenstein's minimalist externalism. Wittgenstein argues that the connection with the world achieved in a thought does not require any further simultaneous explanatory relation. As I described in Chapter 4, in thinking that King's College Chapel is on fire, a person stands, in virtue of that thought, in a relation to that very chapel (and not merely to a shadowy object of thought). But there need be no further simultaneous and underlying relation between thinker and object that explains that connection. Provided that she can express her thought in such a way that connects it to the chapel, by naming it, describing it or pointing to it, for example, she can think it. But, in the case of singular thought, it may seem that a further connection is required.

The motivation for such a claim is this. Consider the case of someone in a bookshop looking at a book in front of them and thinking 'That looks an interesting book!'. As is now well known, this thought cannot be captured by any paraphrase that replaces the indexical element of the thought with a different sort of referring device such as a description. The buyer could rationally take different attitudes to thoughts which could be expressed as 'That book looks interesting' and 'The cheapest book in the biggest bookshop in Leamington looks interesting'. Thus, these cannot express the *same* thoughts (or senses) even if both are uniquely true of the same book (Evans 1982: 7–41). One consequence is that singular thoughts cannot be linguistically codified. The book itself has to play a role in the individuation of the thought. This is another reason for denying representationalism. But there are two further conclusions that are often drawn.

One is that singular thought requires a further connection between thinker and object than the connection which is implicit in the thought. One such claim is that singular thought requires that there is a causal connection or 'information link' between thinker and object (e.g., ibid.: 121–42). The other conclusion is that if, as a result of illusion or hallucination, a thought which a thinker would express as a singular thought turns out not to have an appropriate object, then it cannot be a singular thought after all. It must instead be a different sort of thought, such as a descriptive thought (ibid.: 170–9).

This externalist strategy for accounting for singular thought does not fit with Wittgenstein's merely minimalist externalism. A causal connection or information link which *must* exist is just the sort of underlying explanatory mechanism that Wittgenstein rejects. It runs counter to the connection which Wittgenstein emphasises between meaning and practice because its existence plays no part in the practice. One might nevertheless argue that singular thoughts provide particularly powerful support for externalism because the very possession of a singular thought requires the existence of a worldly object. But there is an alternative strategy which Wittgenstein's and Davidson's general accounts of mental states suggest.

This alternative is to say that even radically unsuccessful singular thoughts – where there is no appropriate object – are still singular thoughts although false. A Davidsonian argument for this view is that the ascription of a singular thought might be the best explanation of behaviour from a third-person perspective. A Wittgensteinian account would emphasise the fact that this is what is self-ascribed. Provided that a person has a *general* ability to self-ascribe mental states, including singular thoughts, then a singular thought can be ascribed even under radically unsuccessful circumstances. In such circumstances there is a problem specifying the thought. One cannot say, for example, that Macbeth has a belief about *that* dagger when there is no such thing for thought to latch on to. But, clumsy though such ascriptions are, one might say that he has a singular thought which he would express by saying 'That dagger . . .'.

These are merely speculative comments on how best to accommodate singular thought into a Wittgensteinian account of content. But one point is clear. Wittgenstein, like Davidson, opposes any account in which linguistic meaning or mental content is explained by appeal to free-standing internal objects of thought or mental representations. (In fact I shall argue in Chapter 6 that Davidson does not entirely escape this picture.) Instead, content depends on, and is partly constituted by, the use of samples. Thus, Wittgenstein supports a form of externalism. But this form of externalism does not depend for its support on a particular conception of singular thoughts. They, like thought in general, must be given an externalist account but they do not present particular support for a minimalist version of externalism that shuns philosophical *explanation*.

4 Davidson, Wittgenstein and McDowell on the Connection of Thought and the World

Davidson's account of mental states, set out in the previous section, resembles Wittgenstein's minimalist account in two important respects. Firstly, he denies that mental content depends on internal objects of thought. Instead, he explicates propositional attitudes through their systematic relation to behaviour. They comprise a systematic framework for the explanation of speech and action. There is no deeper *internal* explanation of thought. (There remains a difference in their willingness to talk about 'inner' experiences, however.) Secondly, there is no rich explanation to be given of the connection between thoughts and the *worldly* facts that they concern. Propositional attitudes are ascribed to make sense of behaviour from a *mundane* third-person perspective. There is no *philosophical* perspective from which more elaborate causal or mechanical connections between thoughts or words and things could be articulated. The details of any such causal connections are irrelevant to meaning. But Davidson sometimes suggests, and is interpreted as making, two further and stronger claims.

Firstly, he rejects not only the claim that the content of mental states, such as beliefs, can be explained by reference to underlying mental representations, but also that beliefs *represent* at all. He does not simply reject an explanatory account of mental representations but also the very idea of representation: 'Beliefs are true or false, but they represent nothing' (Davidson 1989: 165–6). Secondly, he thinks that the minimal links between mental states and the world are just causal links. Representation is replaced by causation: '[S]tates of mind, including what is meant by a speaker, are identified by causal relations with external objects and events' (ibid.: 170–1). '[W]e can't in general first identify beliefs and meanings and ask what caused them. The causality plays an indispensable role in determining the content of what we say and believe' (Davidson 1983: 317). 'The relation between a sensation and a belief cannot be logical, since sensations are not beliefs or other propositional attitudes. What then is the relation? The answer is, I think, obvious: the relation is causal. Sensations cause some beliefs' (ibid.: 311).

I shall return shortly to the question of whether Davidson should be interpreted as *replacing* rational links with causal links in this way. But this is the interpretation of him that Rorty gives:

> [W]e have no suitable items to serve as representations, and thus no need to ask whether our beliefs represent the world accurately. We still have beliefs, but they will be seen from the outside as the field linguist sees them (as causal interactions with the environment) or from the inside as the pre-epistemological native sees them (as rules for action). To abjure tertia is to abjure the possibility of a third way of seeing them – one which somehow combines the outside view and the inside view, the descriptive and the normative attitudes. To see language in the same way as we see beliefs – not as a 'conceptual framework' but as the causal interaction with the environment described by the field linguist, makes it impossible to think of language as something which may or may not (how could we ever tell?) 'fit the world'. (Rorty 1991: 139)

> [T]he inferential relations between our belief that S and our other beliefs have nothing in particular to do with the aboutness relation which ties S to its objects. The lines of evidential force, so to speak, do not parallel the lines of referential direction . . . the causal roles played by their linguistic behaviour in their interaction with their environment. (ibid.: 148)

This is also the interpretation of Davidson that McDowell criticises (McDowell 1994). I shall argue that Davidson's account of content – though not his anomalous monist account of the metaphysics of mind – can be defended against McDowell's criticism but this, in turn, undermines Davidson's attack on representation.

In *Mind and World* McDowell raises two sorts of objections to Davidson's account of the connection between mental states and reality. One is an epistemological objection. Causal, as opposed to rational, connections between beliefs and the world do not comprise the right kind of external constraint on thought. They do not prevent thought from being merely a frictionless spinning in the void. More fundamentally, in the absence of the right sort of connection, McDowell claims that there is no reason to think of mental states as having content at all. Mere causal connections leave a picture in which internal states remain dark:

> Davidson's picture depicts our empirical thinking as engaged in with no rational constraint, but only causal influence, from outside. This just raises a worry as to whether the picture can accommodate the sort of bearing on reality that empirical content amounts to, and that is just the kind of worry that can make an appeal to the Given seem necessary. (McDowell 1994: 14)

> We seem to need rational constraints on thinking and judging, from a reality external to them, if we are to make sense of them as bearing on a reality outside thought at all. Davidson denies that there is any such need, and proposes that we make do with nothing but causal constraints. (ibid.: 25)

Davidson embraces . . . the renunciation of rational control from independent reality. He thinks a merely causal, not rational, linkage between thinking and independent reality will do, as an interpretation of the idea that empirical content requires friction against something external to thinking. But it will not do. Thoughts without intuitions would be empty. (ibid.: 68)

Why does a merely causal connection between mental states and the world leave the mind in darkness? McDowell himself offers no further explicit explanation of just what is wrong, assuming instead that the onus of argument lies with the causal theorist to explain how mental states acquire their contents (this also holds of McDowell 1986). But Wittgenstein's critical arguments, discussed in the second chapter, help diagnose what is wrong with mere causal links and help explain the connection between McDowell's two criticisms. Mental content is essentially relational and normative. Mental states *prescribe* what accords with them. But these normative connections cannot be captured by appeal to causal mechanisms or dispositions. Because that is so, no account of content is possible that connects free-standing internal states with the world through causal relations. The possibility of content and its rationality and normativity go hand in hand.

But in fact, it is by no means clear that the philosophy of language of the field linguist is committed to the picture McDowell criticises. That depends on the role that causation plays in the determination of content and the underlying metaphysics of mental states. Consider again how causal connections are employed in the framework in which Davidson approaches the philosophy of content. Beliefs and meanings are ascribed from the third-person perspective of the radical interpreter. Causal connections are invoked to pin down the contents of beliefs and meanings. But these connections do not form atomic and foundational links for interpretation. They are instead ingredients of a holistic interpretative enterprise and thus subject to correction in the light of the overall interpretation.

Thus, causal connections impact on content only *via* the process of radical interpretation. Because of this, Davidson's account of content is consistent with a theory of sense in the way that that is characterised in Chapter 4. The right interpretation of an utterance or belief depends not only on what causes it but also what description of the cause best fits the overall pattern of other beliefs and meanings. That pattern includes the rational and normative interconnection of beliefs. Thus, Rorty's distinction between two accounts of belief – from within and from without – is wrong. The holism which characterises Davidson's position requires that these two perspectives are united. But it also suggests that McDowell's worry is misplaced. Beliefs are not tied to the world by merely causal connections but by rational and explanatory connections as viewed from the third-person perspective. They are part of the rational and normative system of propositional attitudes that keep track of, explain and extend the behaviour of language-users.

Given the basic role that radical interpretation plays in Davidson's account of content, I think that his abandonment of the very idea of representation is premature. His comment that beliefs are true and false but not representations continues:

> It is good to be rid of representations, and with them the correspondence theory of truth, for it is thinking there are representations that engenders thoughts of relativism. Representations *are* relative to a scheme; a map represents Mexico, say – but only relative to a mercator, or some other projection. (Davidson 1989: 165–6)

The argument here seems to be this. Where it makes sense to talk of representation, it makes sense to talk about the scheme that makes that representation possible, the rules of projection. So, if beliefs are representations, then there must be some such scheme. But that reintroduces the dualism of scheme and content which cannot be substantiated, and a threat of conceptual relativism. This argument repeats Wittgenstein's point that content cannot be explained by postulating internal states or mental representations because that either simply postpones the problem of how they should be interpreted or fails to account for the normativity of content. The moral should not be that beliefs cannot be representations. Rather, they cannot be explained as *internal* representations. The scheme or rules of projection which make belief possible are not internal causal mechanisms but public linguistic and representational practices using samples.

I have argued in this final section that the account of content implied by Davidson's philosophy of language of the field linguist need not fall prey to McDowell's criticism. But Davidson does not rest content with this behaviourist account of mental content. He attempts to combine it with a physicalist identity theory. I shall argue in Chapter 6 that no such reconciliation is possible. It turns on just the conception of mind which Wittgenstein rejects – that of free-standing internal states.

Further Reading

There are three books on Davidson's philosophy of content. Evnine (1991) provides a general account of Davidson's philosophy of language and philosophy of mind. Ramberg (1989) focuses solely on the philosophy of language, especially the formal theory of meaning. Malpas (1992) provides a different, hermeneutic perspective. Useful critical essays can be found in LePore (1986).

In addition to Mulhall's Wittgensteinian criticisms of Davidson (Mulhall 1990), Glock (1996a) contrasts Wittgenstein's use of anthropological interpretation with Quine and Davidson.

Davidson's general account of the relation between ·mind and world is discussed in Child (1994), McDowell (1994) and Rorty (1991). McDowell attempts to reconcile a neo-Fregean account of sense with Davidson's account of meaning in McDowell (1976).

CHAPTER 6

Content and Causality

So far I have examined Wittgenstein's account of the relation of language or thought and the world, how thought can capture reality in its net. That is one aspect of the relation of mind and world. It is the central issue for any account of content. But there is another kind of relation of mind and world. This concerns the ontology of mind. How are minds in or part of the world? How are minds and bodies related?

The mind-body problem is a substantial philosophical issue a thorough treatment of whichlies outside the scope of this book. But this final chapter will touch on it for the following reason. While the majority of Wittgenstein's discussions of mind concern the first problem, the problem of content, there are also a number of passages that touch on the mind-body problem. The discussion of content has some implications for the relation of mind and body, but these other passages appear to support a more extreme position. They appear to go beyond the arguments discussed so far – that content cannot be reduced to causal mechanisms – to deny that there need be *any* causal processes that underpin thought and language.

The strategy in this chapter will be to examine Davidson's causal theory of mind. As I have already described, Davidson's account of linguistic and mental content has important similarities to Wittgenstein's account. Centrally, both deny a role to inner mental representations and both deny that reduction (via a type-identity theory) is possible. But Davidson combines that view of the irreducibility of content with a causal theory of mind. He argues that reasons are causes and also provides a model of the mind that explains how this in turn is possible. Thus, it may seem that Wittgenstein's move from an attack on reductionism to a denial of the causal role of mental states is premature and based on an oversight. It may appear that Wittgenstein simply failed to spot the possibility of reconciling these two claims in the way that Davidson suggests.

Despite the plausibility of that claim, I shall argue that Davidson's reconciliation of the normative and the causal role of mental states is not successful. I shall argue that Wittgenstein can resist the assimilation of reasons and causes and also that anomalous monism is incompatible with Wittgenstein's account of content.

While Davidson's account of content is broadly consistent with Wittgenstein, his account of the underlying metaphysics of mind is not. Finally, I shall make some comments on the general picture of the relation of mind and world which Wittgenstein advocates. While by no means compelling, Wittgenstein's comments are at least intelligible.

1 Wittgenstein on Physicalism

The later Wittgenstein makes a number of comments on the connection between mind and body. One claim, however, follows from the discussion of linguistic and mental content that has already been discussed in earlier chapters. Content cannot be given a reductionist explanation by appeal to brain processes. There is no deeper explanation of understanding meaning or forming an intentional mental state to be had by appealing to physical states of the brain. This follows from Wittgenstein's criticisms of causal and dispositional explanations. As the discussions of real and ideal machines imply, the attempt to explain rules by appeal to mechanisms is either question begging or fails to sustain their normativity. Thus, no account can be given in which thought-processes might be read off from brain-processes. Such considerations might be thought to motivate the following claim in *Zettel*:

> No supposition seems to me more natural than that there is no process in the brain correlated with associating or with thinking; so that it would be impossible to read off thought-processes from brain-processes. I mean this: if I talk or write there is, I assume, a system of impulses going out from my brain and correlated with my spoken or written thoughts. But why should the *system* continue further in the direction of the centre? Why should this order not proceed, so to speak, out of chaos? (Wittgenstein 1981: §608)

> It is thus perfectly possible that certain psychological phenomena *cannot* be investigated physiologically, because physiologically nothing corresponds to them. (§609)

These passages could be interpreted as merely denying that the systematicity of thought can be explained as resulting from an underlying systematicity in the brain. In other words, they could be interpreted as a denial of representationalist explanations of mental content.

This interpretation would also be consistent with another passage:

> Imagine the following phenomenon. If I want someone to take note of a text that I recite to him, so that he can repeat it to me later, I have to give him paper and pencil; while I am speaking he makes lines, marks, on the paper; if he has to reproduce the text later he follows those marks with his eyes and recites the text. But I assume that what he has jotted down is not *writing*, it is not connected by rules with the words of the text; yet without those jottings

he is unable to reproduce the text; and if anything in it is altered, if part of it is destroyed, he sticks in his 'reading' or recites the text uncertainly or carelessly, or cannot find the words at all. – This *can* be imagined! – What I called jottings would not be a *rendering* of the text, not so to speak a translation with another symbolism. The text would not be *stored up* in the jottings. And why should it be stored up in our nervous system? (§612)

This passage does not establish that the marks on paper do not form a system. It is just that they do not form a system of the same sort as writing. That is why they are not a *rendering* of the text. They are not connected by *rules* to words. But in that case, what is their connection to the text supposed to be? Given that this is supposed to be an analogy for the connection between the nervous system and our linguistic abilities, one suggestion is that the marks are connected to written or spoken words *causally* rather than normatively. If this were the case, while the internal system could not be used to *explain* content, it could still play a necessary causal role.

But, in fact, Wittgenstein goes further than this. He suggests that there need be *no* cause of a memory in the nervous system. Nothing need be stored 'up there' in any form. There need be no physiological regularity or order causing psychological order. Mental order could proceed out of chaos:

The case would be like the following – certain kinds of plants multiply by seed, so that a seed always produces a plant of the same kind as that from which it was produced – but *nothing* in the seed corresponds to the plant which comes from it; so that it is impossible to infer the properties or structure of the plant from those of the seed that it comes out of – this can only be done from the *history* of the seed. So an organism might come into being even out of something quite amorphous, as it were causelessly; and there is no reason why this should not really hold for our thoughts, and hence for our talking and writing. (§608)

I saw this man years ago: now I have seen him again, I recognise him, I remember his name. And why does there have to be a cause of this remembering in my nervous system? Why must something or other, whatever it may be, be stored up there *in any form*? Why *must* a trace have been left behind? Why should there not be a psychological regularity to which *no* physiological regularity corresponds? If this upsets our concepts of causality then it is high time they were upset. (§610)

And now suppose that in the foregoing example someone had at last succeeded in discovering a difference between the seed of an A-plant and the seed of a B-plant: he would no doubt say: 'There, you see, it just isn't possible for *one seed* to grow into two different plants.' What if I were to retort: 'How do you know that the characteristic you have discovered is not completely irrelevant? How do you know *that* has anything to do with which of the two plants grows out of the seed?' (Wittgenstein 1993: 375–7)

In these passages, Wittgenstein suggests not just that content cannot be *explained* by appeal to underlying mechanisms, but that there need be no such mechanisms. This is a much stronger claim. It amounts to the suggestion that the mental might not supervene on the physical or even that the supervenience of macroscopic properties and processes on the microscopic which physicalism generally takes for granted is questionable: 'Why should there not be a natural law connecting a starting and a finishing state of a system, but not covering the intermediary state? (Only one must not think of *causal efficacy*)' (Wittgenstein 1981: §613). The thought in this passage seems to be this. A natural law which connected two states without covering the intervening process could not be causal because causal processes are mechanical. (This claim runs counter to his own discussion of causation, which I will discuss later in this chapter, by suggesting a single form of causal relation.) If so, then this claim might augment what also motivates his denial that reasons are causes. That other argument turns on the normativity of content. Because the structure of content cannot be captured within, or explained by, a network of physical laws – because any attempt undermines its essential normativity – Wittgenstein rejects any identification of mental states with causal mechanisms. This thought could combine with the above claim about causation. Reasons cannot be causes in any sense because causation presupposes mechanism, and the normativity of reasons means they cannot be mechanical.

But there is a further independent argument against a causal account of reasons:

> The proposition that your action has such and such a cause, is a hypothesis. The hypothesis is well-founded if one has had a number of experiences which, roughly speaking, agree in showing that your action is the regular sequel of certain conditions which we then call causes of the action. In order to know the reason which you had for making a certain statement, for acting in a particular way, etc, no number of agreeing experiences is necessary, and the statement of your reason is not a hypothesis. The difference between the grammars of 'reason' and 'cause' is quite similar to that between the grammars of 'motive' and 'cause'. (Wittgenstein 1958: 15)

Here the argument is not directed against the philosophical attempt to explain content in causal terms. It is instead an argument to the effect that an assimilation of reasons and causes runs counter to the practices that give the concepts of 'reason' and 'cause' sense.

Thus, Wittgenstein appears to make all of the following claims:

- There can be no deeper explanation of content by appeal to underlying physical mechanisms. This is a denial of psychologism: the attempt to explain rationality itself through mental mechanisms.
- There need be no physiological regularity that corresponds to or is isomorphous with psychological regularity. This is a denial of any attempt to explain how thinking is possible in terms of underlying internal mental representations or brain states.

- There need be no physiological regularity that underpins psychological regularity at all. This is a denial of physicalism.
- Mental states or reasons are not causes. This denies any 'causal theory of mind'.

In the preceding chapters I have outlined Wittgenstein's arguments for the first two claims. But can either of the final pair be justified? Or are these merely groundless expressions of the dark side of Wittgensteinian philosophy?

2 Davidson's Causal Theory of Mind

2.1   Why reasons are causes

Davidson's arguments in favour of the causal status of reasons are directed against a Wittgensteinian position. He thus attempts to do two things. The first is to undermine any Wittgensteinian arguments for denying that reasons are causes. The second is to provide positive argument for a causal interpretation of reasons.

Davidson relies on two key distinctions that underpin his attempt to reconcile reasons and causes. One is a distinction between ontological and conceptual reduction, or what there is and how it is described. The other is a distinction between the epistemology and the ontology of reasons. The first distinction plays an important role in disarming Wittgenstein-inspired objections to the identification of reasons and causes. Davidson argues that causal relations are natural relations the existence of which does not depend on how they are described. They are *extensional* not intensional. This basic claim underpins two counter arguments (Davidson 1980: 3–19):

- The normative connection between mental states and behaviour is no obstacle to a causal account. Reasons have to be described in a suitable way to display their rationalising powers. But, even if this implies that there is an analytic connection between reason and action, that fact does not preclude a causal connection. The analytic connection depends on how the facts are *described*. But the causal relation does not. The fact that an analytic connection can be made by a suitable choice of description cannot preclude a causal connection because any given causal relation can be so described. Suppose event A causes event B. Event A could be described as 'the cause of B' in the analytically true statement: the cause of B caused B. But this does not contradict the assumption that A caused B.
- The statement that someone acted in a particular way because of a particular reason does not imply that reasons of that type generally lead to actions of that type. But again that does not preclude a causal relation between reason and

action. A Humean or nomological account of causation requires that some description of the two events, which connects them as a matter of law is possible . But it does not require that the descriptions used to pick out cause and effect are suitable for inclusion in the law. It may be that the cause of an event which is reported on page 13 of *Tribune* is itself reported on page 5 of *The Times*. But that does not imply that there is a linking law that uses the descriptions: 'events reported on page 13 of *Tribune*' and 'events reported on page 5 of *The Times*'. Ignorance of the actual law does not, however, eliminate causal explanation.

Having cleared the ground, Davidson then puts forward a positive argument to construe reasons as causes. Causality is needed in the analysis of what it means to say that someone acted *because of* or *for* a reason.

The role of causality in the analysis can be brought out by asking: what is the difference between *a* reason for an action and *the* reason? The problem is to explicate the difference between a case in which someone has a reason for an action *and* carries out that action – where the 'and' is read purely conjunctively – from cases where they act *because* of the reason, where the reason is 'active':

> [A] person can have a reason for an action, and perform the action, and yet this reason not be the reason why he did it. Central to the relation between a reason and an action it explains is the idea that the agent performed the action *because* he had the reason. (ibid.: 9)

The philosophical issue here is to explain what this distinction amounts to. What constitutes the reason for an action as *the* reason?

This problem is not a matter of epistemology. It is not a question of how one *knows* which reason is *the* reason for an action. Davidson's implicit assumption is that epistemology is little guide to ontology here. How in practice one knows what the reason for an action is, either in one's own case or for others, plays no part in the discussion. A philosophical account of the distinction need not postulate facts that help *guide* practical knowledge. (On the other hand, the account should not make knowledge here utterly mysterious or impossible.) Nor is the objection that one may always act for a number of reasons relevant. Provided that it is possible to act, and to have even one reason for that action which is inactive, then an account is owed as to what the difference between an active and an inactive reason is.

This distinction between epistemology and ontology is also what enables Davidson to ignore Wittgenstein's practice-based argument in favour of distinguishing reasons and causes. He can simply concede that how we typically discover causes differs from the special case of reasons. But he can also argue that this is merely an epistemological issue which is irrelevant to the metaphysical question of whether reasons are causes.

Davidson argues that the rationalising aspect of reasons is no help here. The rationalising role of reasons is to make sense of action through contextualisation:

> When we ask why someone acted as he did, we want to be provided with an interpretation. His behaviour seems strange, alien, outré, pointless, out of character, disconnected; or perhaps we cannot even recognize an action in it. When we learn his reason, we have an interpretation, a new description of what he did, which fits it into a familiar picture. The picture includes some of the agent's beliefs and attitudes; perhaps also goals, ends, principles, general character traits, virtues or vices. Beyond this, the redescription of an action afforded by a reason may place the action in a wider social, economic, linguistic, or evaluative context. (ibid.: 9–10)

This rationalising power can be regimented in the syllogistic model of practical reasoning which dates back to Aristotle and provides the first condition on reasons:

> C1. R is a primary reason why an agent performed the action A under the description d only if R consists of a pro attitude of the agent towards actions with a certain property, and a belief of the agent that A, under the description d, has that property. (ibid.: 5)

But, if the rational power of reasons is understood and formalised in this way, it cannot constitute the difference between *a* reason and *the* reason. To be *a* reason is already to be a reason that is held by the person who acts and that rationalises the action. Rationality has already been used in distinguishing between such reasons for action and mental states that have no bearing on the action whatsoever. It cannot also provide the extra ingredient sufficient for being the actual reason why someone acted.

Davidson suggests that one might augment the characterisation of rational power so as simply to include the extra ingredient, whatever it is. But the cost of that assumption would be to make the rationalising role of reasons mysterious. Davidson suggests that the rationalising role should instead be construed in the transparent way already described and that something has to be added to the rationalising role of reasons to answer the question.

Davidson's proposal is that the extra ingredient is causal efficacy. *The* reason for an action is the reason that causes it. Thus, reasons have to meet a second non-rational condition:

> C2. A primary reason for an action is its cause. (ibid.: 12)

Thus, the argument which Davidson puts forward is of the following form. Something needs to be added to the rationalising force of reasons to distinguish between *a* reason for an action and *the* reason. The only candidate for this extra ingredient is causation. One way of putting this is that Davidson points out that there is second necessary condition on reason explanation. But he gives no reason to believe that it is more than contingently true that this condition is satisfied by causation.

There is a second general argument that points more directly to why reason explanation must be causal (Child 1994: 90–100). Reason explanation not only reveals the purpose and pattern in action, it also explains *why* it happened. The only general model we have of explanations of why events occur is explanation by citing causes. Thus, reason explanation must implicitly be a species of causal explanation. This argument clearly turns on the claim that the only way of explaining why an event occurs is giving a causal explanation. Such a claim certainly fits with some models of explanation more familiar from the philosophy of science (see Lewis 1986). But consistency with a model that (arguably) fits one context – scientific explanation – does not ensure that, in the context of folk psychology, this is the only method of explaining why an action took place. This premiss can, however, be made more compelling through a challenge that also shows that this argument is not so distinct from the first argument.

The challenge is this. Consider a non-causal explanation of an action which, for example, characterises it as an addition in accord with the rules of arithmetic. While any such explanation might help make sense of the action, it does not explain why the event occurred. (Had an action of that sort taken place, it would have been an addition, but that does not explain why it did take place.) To get an explanation of why the event actually occurred, further information has to be added, and that information is causal. This challenge reflects the need to add the causal condition C2 to the rationalising condition C1 in the first argument. What the challenge brings out is that Davidson's appeal to causation is not merely a move of unprincipled desperation: what else can it be other than causation that transforms *a* reason into *the* reason? There is also a strong general intuition to back the selection of causation in particular as the extra ingredient.

The conclusion of these two arguments is that when one acts for or because of a reason, the reason is also the cause of the action. But there is a danger that this slogan merely repeats the initial pre-philosophical characterisation without shedding light on it. What does it mean to say that the reason is the cause of an action over and above the fact that it is *the* reason why someone acted? Davidson avoids the charge of vacuity by connecting causality to underlying laws. He comments: 'Causality is central to the concept of agency, but it is ordinary causality between events that is relevant' (Davidson 1980: 53).

The focus of the next section is Davidson's reconciliation of a nomological account of causation with anti-reductionism of the mental. But it is worth noting in advance that if that fails – as I argue it does – then the claim that reasons are causes may not be shown to be false, but rather vacuous.

2.2   How reasons are causes

What makes Davidson's attempted reconciliation of reasons and causes relevant to the assessment of Wittgenstein's views on the relation of mind and body is that Davidson shares with Wittgenstein the view that content cannot be reduced to causal processes. It is unnecessary to spell out again the details of his argument but it can be roughly summarised as follows.

The starting assumption is that reasons are ascribed to people in order to make sense of their speech and behaviour from a mundane third-person perspective. The conditions imposed for this to be possible can be identified by consideration of radical interpretation: interpretation of language, beliefs and behaviour from scratch. Such interpretation is possible, according to Davidson, only on the assumption of the overall rationality, broadly construed, of the beliefs of the interpretee. Because rationality is an essential precondition of the ascription of reasons for a radical interpreter, and because the information available to the interpreter is all the information concerning reasons that there is, reasons are essentially governed by rationality. Rationality plays a constitutive role in the mental realm. But there is no echo of rationality in the physical realm. Law-like relations are possible only between realms governed by the same constitutive principles. Thus, there cannot be laws connecting the mental and physical (ibid.: 207–44).

Davidson's argument for the irreducibility of mental and linguistic content to a network of causal laws is thus different from Wittgenstein's. But the conclusion is the same. Davidson does not, however, combine the denial of reduction with a rejection of a causal theory of mind. Instead, he argues, against Wittgenstein, that the two can be reconciled. That is the purpose of his account of the metaphysics of mind: anomalous monism.

Anomalous monism attempts to reconcile three principles:

- the causality of mental states,
- an underlying nomological account of causation,
- the anomalism of mental.

At first sight, these three principles appear to be in tension. If mental states cause action, and causal relations require that exceptionless causal laws exist, then mental states must be subject to causal laws. But the third principle – that the mental is anomalous – appears to deny just that. Davidson's solution again turns on the extensionality of causal relations. The claim that some mental states cause actions asserts a causal relation. But that does not imply that the *law* whose existence it implies picks out cause and effect in the same vocabulary as the causal *statement*. Thus, the fact that there are no laws framed using mental predicates is consistent with the claim that mental states can play a causal role provided that those same states can, in principle, be picked out in a vocabulary suitable for stating exceptionless laws.

Davidson can thus achieve a harmony between these three principles provided that an identity theory is possible which does not require that mental predicates or types play a role in laws. The anomalousness of the mind rules out type-identity theories of the mind such as type physicalism or functionalism. But it does not preclude a merely token identity theory. Davidson's positive account of how mental causation is possible is thus a token identity theory. Every mental event is identical with a physical event – it just is a physical event – although there is no systematic relation between types of mental event and types of physical event. An event can be picked out by a mental description in order to display its rational role. But it can also be picked out by a physical description to explain its causal role. The exceptionless laws which connect events of that type are physical laws using physical descriptions.

Davidson's token identity theory concerns events. Mental *events* are identified with physical *events*. This reflects his general commitment to an ontology of events. Davidson has two reasons for taking events to be fundamental:

- Events are invoked to give a systematic treatment of the inferential relations between adverbs. By postulating events as a basic ontological category alongside things and properties, Davidson hopes to provide a theory of meaning that makes use only of first-order logic but still captures their inferential relations. Consider: Jones buttered the toast slowly, deliberately in the bathroom, with a knife, at midnight. From this it can be inferred that Jones buttered the toast slowly. Davidson suggests the analysis: there was a buttering event; and it was by Jones; and it concerned the toast; and it was slow . . . Given this analysis then the adverbial inferential relations can be modelled as simple conjunction elimination (ibid.: 105–48).
- Events underlie Davidson's account of the metaphysics of causation. Under-lying all causal explanation is a causal relation. That relation connects *events*. This account contrasts with, for example, accounts that claim that causation is a fact about the connection of two further facts. (One advantage of the alternative is that it allows for iterated connections. The second-level causal fact can in turn be causally connected at a higher level to other facts allowing an easier story to be told of how we can come to know about causal relations (cf. Mellor 1991).)

The fact that Davidson's version of anomalous monism relies on an ontology of events suggests a prima facie difficulty. It can only serve as an accurate model for reconciling Wittgenstein's anti-reductionism if Wittgenstein's account of the mind can be translated into a series of events. Given Wittgenstein's attack on the assimilation of all mental phenomena to datable events or states, this seems implausible (Wittgenstein 1953: §154). But I propose to ignore this for the moment. I shall assume that a token identity theory can be flexible about the mental and physical elements it identifies. They might be events, states or facts.

There is another important feature of Davidson's anomalous monism. In addition to the token identity theory, Davidson also claims that the mental *supervenes* on the physical (Davidson 1980: 214). Supervenience provides an additional constraint on the relationship between the mental and the physical. Supervenience is the claim that physical facts determine mental facts but not vice versa. Thus, there could not be two people completely alike in physical properties but differing in mental properties. This allows some general dependence of the mental on the physical while also allowing that mental states could be realised in different physical structures. Davidson has made different and contradictory claims about the connection between anomalous monism and supervenience (compare Davidson 1980: 214, 1987: 453, 1989: 164). But his general position appears to be that the mental supervenes on bodily states together with their causal histories. Whatever the exact position, it is clear that this runs counter to Wittgenstein's apparently wild claims that there need be no connection between states of the brain and states of mind. Wittgenstein's seed analogy, for example, denies that the behaviour of the seed supervenes on its microstructure but instead on its history alone.

Davidson thus asserts a much tighter connection between the mental and the physical than Wittgenstein allows. He does this in a way that at least appears to be consistent with a denial that facts about content can be reduced to or explained by facts about physical states. Thus, it appears that Wittgenstein's radical claims do not follow from the account of content set out so far in this book. Nor do they seem intrinsically plausible. Nevertheless, in the second half of this chapter I will argue that Davidson's position is not a coherent middle ground that Wittgenstein could occupy. Furthermore, there are at least metaphilosophical grounds for Wittgenstein's claims about the relationship between mind and body.

3 A Non-causal Theory of Mind?

I have presented Davidson's anomalous monism as an explanation of how the claim that reasons are causes can be reconciled with a broadly Wittgensteinian claim that mental types cannot be regimented into laws and the claim that causality presupposes laws. In the next section I shall argue that a token identity theory is not a coherent account of the metaphysics of mind. While this will not justify Wittgenstein's strikingly negative claims, it will help to make them more intelligible. In this section I shall attempt to shake Davidson's anti-Wittgensteinian claim that reasons are causes. Again the argument will not be conclusive.

But it will connect Wittgenstein's position here to his more general meta-philosophical claims.

Two arguments reported earlier in the chapter supported the claim that reasons are causes (whatever account might be given of *how* reasons are causes). They were:

- Causality explains the difference between *a* reason and *the* reason for an action.
- Because reason explanation explains *why* an action takes place, it must be a form of causal explanation.

I shall begin by examining the first of these two arguments.

In brief, that argument ran as follows. There is a pre-philosophical distinction which is drawn between having a reason and acting and acting *for* that reason. That difference stands in need of explanation and analysis. It cannot consist in differences between the rationalising powers of reasons because all reasons for an action rationalise it. So the difference must consist in the presence or absence of something else. A causal connection fits that bill. The reason for an action, the reason why one acts, must be the cause of the action.

Before examining the underlying assumptions behind this argument and contrasting them with Wittgenstein's approach to philosophy, it is worth noting one preliminary limitation. Despite his earlier optimism, Davidson himself realised that the simple addition of a causal condition to the rationality of reasons (C1 and C2 above) does not provide a sufficient condition for acting for or because of a reason. The problem is that a reason may cause an action but cause it in the wrong way:

> Let a single example serve. A climber might want to rid himself of the weight and danger of holding another man on a rope, and he might know that by loosening his hold on the rope he could rid himself of the weight and danger. This belief and want might so unnerve him to loosen his hold, and yet it might be the case that he never *chose* to loosen his hold, nor did he do it intentionally. It will not help, I think, to add that the belief and the want must combine to cause him to want to loosen his hold, for there will remain the *two* questions *how* the belief and the want caused the second want, and *how* wanting to loosen his hold caused him to loosen his hold. (Davidson 1980: 79)

Thus, while causality was invoked as the element that distinguishes having a reason and acting from acting *for* that reason, it turns out that in some cases it will not be enough to make the difference. A person may have a reason, and the reason may cause the action while not being the reason *why* he or she acted. There may be no reason (and thus on some accounts no action). Cases of deviant causation present problems for an analysis in terms of necessary *and sufficient* conditions of acting for a reason. They do not, however, contradict the claim that causality is a *necessary* ingredient in reason explanation.

There are, however, two further related points to note about Davidson's argument:

- The possibility that the difference between *a* reason and *the* reason is an unanalysable *sui generis* fact receives short shrift from Davidson. He assumes that the difference can be explained in independent terms. He realises that the prospect of a complete analysis of reason explanation is unlikely but he still thinks that the connection might be given some further analysis in causal terms.
- The argument is a form of philosophical explanation. It attempts to explain what *must* be going on behind or beneath the practice of explaining actions by reasons. The difference between *a* reason and *the* reason is explained by the absence or presence of a causal relation. Given this explanatory purpose, Davidson has to draw a sharp distinction between the epistemology and ontology or metaphysics of reasons. He has to argue that the fact that his method of explaining actions differs from more paradigmatic instances of determining causes is irrelevant to the underlying ontology. The fact that the causal mechanisms described by the token identity play no role in the everyday determining of reasons for action does not count against this philosophical explanation.

These two broad assumptions – that reason explanation can be analysed and that the analysis will constitute an *explanation* or justification of a pre-philosophical distinction – run counter to Wittgenstein's meta-philosophical injunctions. This suggests that a Wittgensteinian answer to the question 'What is the difference between *a* reason and *the* reason?' cannot take the same line as Davidson's explanatory theory. Before outlining the sort of positive account open to Wittgenstein, I shall examine the sort of *methodological* objection that Wittgenstein raises against this type of philosophically explanatory strategy.

3.1   Philosophical minimalism vs philosophical realism

As I described in Chapter 4, Wittgenstein argues that philosophy should not attempt to offer explanations. Philosophical problems should instead be dissolved. This is a corollary of the claim that philosophical problems arise from misunderstanding the rules of grammar. As speakers, we have a practical grasp of the rules that govern language but our understanding of them is distorted, for various reasons, when doing philosophy. One common source of distortion is a false assumption that language is more uniform than it is. Philosophical insight is achieved by gaining a clearer insight into the workings of language through careful attention to language use, perspicuous representations of grammar and comparisons that reveal the true workings of language. Wittgenstein encapsulates this view in the injunction: don't think, *look* (Wittgenstein 1953: §66).

This descriptive methodology has been reflected in the minimalist account of content described in this book. Wittgenstein does not provide an explanatory mechanism to connect meaning to use or mental states to their fulfilments. Instead he argues that those connections cannot be further analysed or explained. They constitute the basic datum which has to be presupposed in any account of the capacities and practices of language users. Furthermore, one can see that everyday explanations which can be given of the meaning of words or the content of mental states are quite sufficient. One does not generally have to *guess* what such explanations are really trying to communicate. Explanation does not have to *point* to something ineffable. The resources available to everyday accounts of meaning stand in need of no further philosophical explanation, justification or buttressing.

In an early passage in the *Investigations* Wittgenstein suggests that a failure to pay attention to the details of language and practice is not simply the result of carelessness:

> If I am inclined to suppose that a mouse has come into being by spontaneous generation out of grey rags and dust, I shall do well to examine those rags very closely to see how a mouse may have hidden in them, how it may have got there and so on. But if I am convinced that a mouse cannot come into being from these things, then this investigation will perhaps be superfluous. But first we must learn to understand what it is that opposes such an examination of details in philosophy. (§52)

Philosophical theory may lead one to ignore practical details because of a prior belief that they cannot be relevant. But, the suggestion goes, the details might contain just what was needed to resolve one's philosophical difficulty.

Diamond provides an extended discussion of Wittgenstein's meta-philosophy which includes an interpretation of this passage (Diamond 1991). Following a gnomic comment from Wittgenstein, she suggests that the tendency to be blinded to important details by philosophical theory is a mark of philosophical *realism*. This is a surprising remark because, in philosophical debates about the reality of the past, or distant spatio-temporal points, or mathematics, realism is usually thought of as the non-revisionary position, the position that most fits everyday language. Nevertheless, realism fails to be *realistic* when it goes beyond the everyday phenomena and instead attempts to explain them by postulating underlying processes or mechanisms. Diamond suggests that the central ambition of Wittgenstein's philosophy is to be realistic while eschewing, on the one hand realism and, on the other, empiricism which is closely related to constructivism.

Diamond uses two examples from outside Wittgensteinian philosophy to clarify the distinction between realist and realistic philosophy. One is Berkeley's discussion of matter in his *Three Dialogues*. Hylas, the philosophical realist, argues that the distinction between real things and chimeras – mere hallucinations or imaginings – must consist in a fact that goes beyond all experience or perception. For this reason, philosophy has to invoke the philosophical concept of *matter* to explain the difference. The presence or absence of matter is beyond direct perception or experience, though perception can provide evidence of its presence or absence. This, however, presents Philonous, who speaks on behalf of a realistic approach, with an opening for a criticism. Because of its independence from perception, matter cannot explain the distinctions that we *actually* draw between reality and chimeras. But nor, given our actual practices of drawing a distinction, is such a further philosophical explanation necessary. The practical or epistemological distinctions which Hylas can rely on are also available to Philonous without commitment to the philosophical account of matter. The mouse, in this case, is the distinction, and the rags, which Hylas is convinced cannot explain the distinction, are the practical distinctions actually made.

The second example concerns a more recent case of philosophical realism. The distinction here is that between laws of nature and merely accidentally true generalisations. Peirce argues that this distinction must consist in the presence or absence of active general principles in nature (Hartshorne and Weiss 1965: 93–101). These can be used to explain the reliability of predictions based on laws. But:

> The reply of a realistic spirit is that an active general principle is so much gas unless you say how you tell that you have got one; and if you give any method, it will be a method which anyone can use to distinguish laws from accidental uniformities without having to decorate the method with the phrase "active general principle". Peirce of course knows that there are such methods, but assumes that his mouse – properly *causal* regularity – cannot conceivably come into being from the rags: patterns of observed regularities. (Diamond 1991: 48)

In both these cases, realist explanation is rejected. This rejection does not depend on nominalist scruple, however. Diamond suggests that closer attention shows that realist explanations are wheels that can be turned although nothing else moves with them. They cannot serve as explanations of what the prephilosophical difference in either case really comprises since their presence or absence is not connected to the practices which they were supposed to explain. Their presence or absence could make no difference.

There is, however, an obvious objection which needs to be countered if Diamond's exegesis of philosophical minimalism is to shed light on the distinction between *a* reason and *the* reason for action. The problem is that an opposition to philosophical realism might be thought to comprise a form of idealism, anti-realism or, more relevantly in this case, constructivism. I shall examine shortly whether a Wittgensteinian approach to reasons in particular need be constructivist. But first here is the general danger.

Diamond's account of the realistic spirit has idealist connotations for two reasons. Firstly, and most obviously, she selects Berkeley to illustrate a realistic approach to philosophy. Despite Berkeley's own claims to the contrary, his opposition to matter is not simply a rejection of one philosophical explanatory theory which leaves everything else, including our normal views of the world, unchanged. Instead, he advocates a revisionary idealist metaphysics. Secondly, Diamond characterises Peirce's account of active principles as a 'belief in a connection supposed to be *real*, in the sense of independent of our thought, and for which the supposed regularity is evidence' (ibid.: 50). This suggests that the object of Diamond's criticism is the *mind-independence* of Peirce's conception of active principles. In both cases the examples of a realistic opposition to philosophical realism appear to support a form of idealism.

While Diamond's account may encourage an idealist interpretation, idealism is not a necessary ingredient of Wittgenstein's opposition to philosophical realism. What matters in both these cases, if they are to illustrate philosophical minimalism, is the opposition to realist *explanations*. But anti-realist or idealist explanations are just as much to be rejected. Wittgensteinian minimalism opposes speculative metaphysical explanation and only thus realism (or anti-realism). I shall clarify this by examining one further passage from Diamond's account.

This is how Diamond characterises the realist account of matter which should be rejected as unrealistic:

> For Hylas, real existence is existence distinct from and without any relation to being perceived; and so if the horse we see (in contrast to the one we merely imagine) *is* real, it is because its sensible appearance to us is caused by qualities inhering in a material body, which has an absolute existence independent of our own. The judgment that the horse is real and not imaginary, not a hallucination, is thus a hypothesis going beyond anything we might be aware of by our senses, though indeed it is clear on Hylas's view that we must use the evidence of our senses in trying to *tell* what is real. Still, it is not what we actually see or hear or touch that we are ultimately concerned with in such judgments; and this because *however* things appear to us, it is quite another matter how they *are*. (ibid.: 47)

This passage contains two characterisations of what it is for something to be real rather than imaginary. One is the claim that reality has 'an absolute existence independent of our own'. The other is that reality goes 'beyond anything we might be aware of by our senses'. It is 'not what we actually see or hear or touch' and 'however things appear to us, it is quite another matter how they are'. Ignoring for the moment the qualification 'absolute', denying that reality has an existence independent of our own – the first characterisation – would amount to idealism. By contrast, the second characterisation goes beyond an everyday affirmation of the mind independence of the real. It presupposes a philosophically charged and revisionary account of perception in which reality always lies beyond our senses. Thus its rejection is merely the rejection of a philosophical explanatory theory and not itself a piece of revision.

Thus, a minimalist or realistic criticism of philosophical realism need not succumb to the criticism that it confuses epistemology and ontology. The rejection of realist explanations of the distinction between real things and illusions or between causal laws and accidentally true generalisations does not imply that these distinctions are *constituted* by the discriminations we make, by their epistemology. On the other hand, the distinctions are not matters that lie beyond our ways of detecting them. They are not independent of our practices in that complete and absolute sense. (If this is what Diamond means by denying *absolute* independence, then neither rejection is tainted with idealism or constructivism.)

Having plotted at a general level the kind of Wittgensteinian criticism of explanatory theory which is relevant here, I will now turn to Davidson's account of reasons.

3.2   A minimalist approach to the distinction between *a* reason and *the* reason for action

Davidson's causal account of reasons is an example of explanatory philosophical realism. He attempts to account for reason explanation by postulating a structure that lies behind that practice. Causality is invoked to explain a distinction that is drawn pre-philosophically between *a* reason and *the* reason for an action. It does not, however, form part of the epistemology of reason explanation. Facts about causation do not add to the evidence used to determine which, from a range of possible reasons, is the reason why someone acted. Instead, their role is to explain the nature of the distinction normally made. Discovering the causal ingredient deepens our understanding of reason explanation but does not make it any easier to give reasons.

But as in the two examples of philosophical realism described above, this account fails to engage with our practice of reason explanation. The same sort of response that Diamond makes to Peirce can be made in this case to Davidson. To paraphrase the quotation above:

> The reply of a realistic spirit is that an underlying causal connection (via a token identity thesis) is so much gas unless you say how you tell that you have got one; and if you give any method, it will be a method which anyone can use to distinguish *a* reason from *the* reason for an action without having to decorate the method with the phrase 'underlying causal

connection'. Davidson, of course, knows that there are such methods, but assumes that his mouse – *the* reason for an action – cannot conceivably come into being from the rags: practices of ascribing reasons.

There are therefore Wittgensteinian metaphilosophical objections to Davidson's causal construal of reasons. There is no need to explain the difference between *a* reason and *the* reason for an action by invoking an underlying causal machinery. That distinction is a *sui generis* distinction that cannot be further broken down. In learning to ascribe reasons to oneself, one learns to identify the reason (or reasons) for an action in one's own case and in others. Furthermore, one learns connections between this notion and that of moral responsibility and agency (which lie outside the scope of this book). In other words, one learns why the distinction is important. But this is not to say that the distinction can be defined either in terms of how in practice one determines the reason or the consequences of the distinction.

If this minimalist response is to provide a satisfactory account of reason explanation, it will have to escape the charge of idealism, to maintain a distinction between epistemology and ontology. If so, then it should not be interpreted as saying that being the reason for an action consists in being judged to be the reason. Unfortunately that may seem, at first sight at least, the best interpretation of a key passage in the *Investigations*:

> 'I am leaving the room because you tell me to.'
>   'I am leaving the room, but not because you tell me to.'
>   Does this proposition *describe* a connexion between my action and his order; or does it make the connexion?
>   Can one ask: 'How do you know that you do it because of this, or not because of this?' And is the answer perhaps: 'I feel it'? (§487)

The response to Davidson and the interpretation of this passage can go hand in hand. Davidson briefly considers and rejects the thought that the relation between reason and action is *sui generis*. But, I suggest, that is the best interpretation of Wittgenstein. It is not that the facts are constituted by ways of finding out the reasons for actions, but that those ways are responsive to the facts that are otherwise unanalysable. The connection is thus as unanalysable as facts about content, on which Davidson and Wittgenstein agree.

This interpretation is not, in fact, undermined by the passage from Wittgenstein above. In it he re-emphasises his critique of any model of self-knowledge based on inner perception. One neither perceives the connection by introspection nor does one construct it by an act of interpretation, perhaps of one's behaviour. First-person reports are of central importance in the ascription of reasons but they no more rely on reading off reasons from inner states or from behaviour than do self-ascriptions of content more generally.

This might be thought to leave a third option which construes the connection between reasons and reports of reasons as itself causal on the model of representationalism. But that would presuppose that reasons were internal free-standing states that could stand in causal relations. Instead the ability to report why one acted cannot be broken down into constituent parts at all. It does not provide any support for a causal construal of reasons either by reference to its epistemology or its underlying metaphysics.

3.3   Wittgenstein on causation

I have been discussing the first of two arguments for a causal construal of reasons. That argument can be defused by providing an alternative candidate to make the difference between *a* reason and *the* reason for an action. The second argument, by contrast, provides explicit support for a causal conception. Reason explanations explain why actions take place. But the only method of explaining why events occur is by providing causal information. Thus, reason explanation must be a form of causal explanation. Again, however, Wittgenstein has a response to this sort of argument which is motivated by his general views on language. While not decisive, it suggests that Wittgenstein's refusal to assimilate reasons and causes is, at least, a credible position.

As I suggested earlier, the second argument is only as strong as the premiss that the only way of explaining why an event occurs is to provide causal information. But it can be given some intuitive further support. While non-causal information can give insight into the nature of events – why they are the events they are, for example – it is always insufficient to explain why they occur. Despite the general plausibility of that thought, however, it does not compel the conclusion that reason explanation must be causal.

The assumption on which the argument really depends is that all forms of event-explanation must be the same. But that assumption is again a form of philosophical realism of the form described above. It is an example of philosophical legislation resulting from the craving for generality which is, according to Wittgenstein, a key source of philosophical error. Once one frees oneself from the prior conviction that all forms of event-explanation must be the same, then one can follow Wittgenstein's injunction to examine our practices rather than prejudge how they must be. Once we do that, according to Wittgenstein, we discover that the practices of ascribing reasons and causes differ. In this context, the differences between reason explanation and causal explanation become important.

Thus, I think that Wittgenstein provides principled reasons for rejecting the claim that reason explanation *must* be a form of causal explanation. The assumption that it must relies on a dubious principle that all forms of event-explanation must be the same and on playing down the differences in the practices of ascribing reasons and causes. There is, however, another response that might be made. This is to concede that reason explanation is causal explanation but deny that any substantial metaphysical consequences follow.

The claim that reason explanation is a form of causal explanation serves only to unify explanation if a uniform account of causation is available. That was the assumption that led Davidson to advocate a token identity theory. The theory was supposed to explain how a uniform Humean account of causation could also be applied to causal relations between mental events. But, in fact, Wittgenstein himself denied that a uniform account of causation could be given:

> Don't we recognize immediately that the pain is produced by the blow we have received? Isn't this the cause and can there be any doubt about it? – But isn't it quite possible to suppose that in certain cases we are deceived about this? . . .
> Certainly there is in such cases a genuine experience which can be called 'experience of the cause'. But not because it infallibly shows us the cause; rather because *one* root of the cause-effect language-game is to be found here, in our looking out for the cause.
> *We react to the cause.*
> Calling something 'the cause' is like pointing and saying: '*He's* to blame!'
> We instinctively get rid of the cause if we don't want the effect. We instinctively look from what has been hit to what has hit it. (I am assuming that we do this.)
> Now suppose I were to say that when we speak of cause and effect we always have in mind a comparison with impact; that this is the prototype of cause and effect? Would this mean that we had *recognized* impact as a cause? Imagine a language in which people always said 'impact' instead of 'cause'. (Wittgenstein 1993: 373)

> Someone has followed the string and has found who is pulling at it: does he make a further step in concluding: so that was the cause – or did he not just want to discover if someone, and if so who, was pulling at it? Let's imagine once more a language-game simpler than the one we play with the word 'cause'. (ibid.: 387)

> Consider two procedures: in the first somebody who feels a tug on a string, or has some similar sort of experience, follows the string – the mechanism – in this sense finds the *cause*, and perhaps removes it. He may also ask: 'Why is this string moving?', or something of the sort. – The second case is this: He has noticed that, since his goats have been grazing on that slope, they give less milk. He shakes his head, asks 'Why?' – and then makes some experiments. He finds that such and such a fodder is the cause of the phenomenon. (ibid.: 389)

Wittgenstein suggests that our concept of causation is made up from a number of distinct prototypes. These include:

- immediate bodily reaction to causes (when, for example, pushed over in the snow);
- traction (following a tugging string);

- causal mechanism (or nexus);
- impacts between bodies;
- experimentally determined correlation.

These different prototypes cannot be unified into a single fundamental account. They collectively make up a composite notion of cause. Thus, even if one grants that reason explanation is a species of causal explanation it does not follow that it depends on underlying correlations or laws. It is not, in other words, the first step in explaining reason explanation through underlying processes.

One might object to this claim that all Wittgenstein really asserts is that we do not, in practice, identify correlations in all cases of causation. Nevertheless, in all these cases it would be possible to go on to establish relevant correlations. But Wittgenstein's point is that no such 'facts' are relevant to the concept of causation. Its correct use in any of the first four senses is independent of whatever future correlations may be discovered. Thus, whether or not correlations could be discovered underpinning psychological explanation, they *need* not for such explanation to be classed as causal. If we do class reason explanation as causal – for whatever reason – it does not follow that it must have a hidden underlying similarity to explanation that presupposes correlations.

I have argued in this section that:

- Wittgenstein has principled metaphilosophical objections to the kind of philosophical explanation which Davidson offers of reason explanation.
- Davidson's ground-level argument that the difference between *a* reason and *the* reason for an argument must consist in the fact that the latter is causal can be side-stepped.
- The argument that reason explanation must be a form of causal explanation because it explains *why* events occur turns on the unjustified assumption that linguistic practices can be given a unified account. Even if it is conceded that reason explanation is causal, since Wittgenstein argues that there is more than one notion of cause, no substantial metaphysical claims follow.

Thus, Wittgenstein has principled objections to two of the premises for Davidson's anomalous monism: that reasons are causes and that causes presuppose laws. This undermines the motivation for Davidson's position. But it might still be thought that anomalous monism presents an attractive alternative to Wittgenstein's claims about the relation of mind and body. But, as I shall argue in the next section, there is also something wrong with that position.

4 An Objection to Anomalous Monism

Davidson's anomalous monism attempts to reconcile an anti-reductionist account of linguistic and mental content with a causal theory of mind. It thus attempts to provide a middle ground between Wittgenstein's anti-causal claims in *Zettel* and representationalist attempts to provide a reductionist explanation of mental content. Because Davidson acknowledges the anomalousness of mental predicates and rejects type identity theories, he escapes Wittgenstein's attack on reductionist explanations of content. But, by advocating a token identity theory, he can diverge from Wittgenstein's dark claims that there need be no relation between mind and body.

Nevertheless, I shall argue that Davidson's position is unstable. Roughly speaking, what enables a token identity theory to escape Wittgenstein's attack on reductionism makes it susceptible to a related attack. The conclusion for which I shall argue is that a token identity theory is hopelessly implausible and fails to harmonise the rational and causal roles that it ascribes to mental states. The underlying problem is that it presupposes just the picture of the mind, which Wittgenstein opposes, in which mental states are free-standing internal states. Davidson ties a relational account of content (described in the previous chapter) which is similar to Wittgenstein's account to a non-relational account of the metaphysics of mind that runs counter to Wittgenstein. I shall, however, approach these claims in a slightly round-about way by examining first Davidson's account of irrationality.

Davidson notes that irrationality is by its very nature paradoxical. The paradox results from the fact that our most basic ways of characterising and explaining mental states and behaviour using folk psychological descriptions locate them within a network of rational and normative relations. Irrational beliefs or actions are failures *within* that space of reasons. In virtue of being beliefs and actions, irrational beliefs and actions are subject to description and explanation by reason. They are thus subject to the in-built rationality of folk psychology. In virtue of being irrational, however, they are subject to merely *partial* reason explanations: reason explanations that fail to be fully rational. The philosophical difficulty is to account for this half-way house.

Davidson's solution turns on the two-fold nature that he ascribes to reasons: causality and rationality. He suggests that irrationality is the result of reasons the causal efficacy of which pathologically exceeds their rationalising force. Taking the case of a man who goes far out of his way to replace a branch he had earlier moved in a park, irrationally against his overall assessment of its worth:

> [T]he man who returns to the park to replace the branch has a reason: to remove a danger. But in doing this he ignores his principle of acting on what he thinks best, all things

considered. And there is no denying that he has a motive for ignoring his principle, namely that he wants, perhaps very strongly, to return the branch to its original position . . . Irrationality entered when his desire to return made him ignore or override his principle. (Davidson 1982: 297)

Whereas in normal cases, beliefs stand in rational and in causal relations to one another and to actions, in cases of irrationality some of the rational relations are distorted or overridden by merely causal factors. In the case described, the desire to return to the park causally overpowers the general desire to act on what the man thinks best. In the case of wishful thinking, for example, the wish to have a particular belief can be causally sufficient or act as a reason for *holding* the belief despite failing to offer it rational support. It is a reason to *hold* the belief but not a reason *for* the belief. Irrational behaviour of this sort is sufficiently intelligible for interpretation, via rational reasons. The relevant causes of behaviour are still mental states – reasons – with intentional content, as displayed by their other rational connections. But the causal power of some of these reasons exceeds their rational power.

Thus, Davidson accounts for irrationality by suggesting that the two components of reasons – their causality and their rationality – can, on occasion, come apart. In cases of irrationality, the causal relations connecting mental states remain while the rational relations are missing or distorted. But this theory of irrationality highlights a general problem with Davidson's reconciliation of reasons and causes. He provides no answer of why it is *generally* the case that the rational power and the causal power of reasons stand in the right relations. Why should the causal power of reasons stand in proportion to their rational force?

Representationalists can give an answer to this question by appeal to the computer analogy discussed in the Chapter 1. By suitable engineering, the physical properties of the physical states (computational states or mental representations) which encode mental content can be designed so that the causal powers of mental representations match, as a matter of law, their rational powers. The human brain, the argument continues, must be similarly designed (perhaps as a result of natural processes). But this kind of answer presupposes a rich set of laws linking types of mental content with types of structured physical states and types of mental state with other types of mental state – laws of thought. Because Davidson rejects psychological and psycho-physical laws, there are simply no resources in his account to explain the general harmony of the rational and causal powers of mental states. Normative powers are determined by the constitutive principle of rationality while causal powers are determined by different and independent physical constitutive principles. Given this general independence, why should the two sorts of property stand in harmonious relations?

In other words, Davidson's rejection of psychophysical laws helps ensure that his version of physicalism does not fall prey to Wittgenstein's attack on representationalism. But, instead, it leaves him open to the charge that he relies on an unexplained pre-established harmony. I shall now try to spell out the general problem which Davidson's account faces and its relation to Wittgenstein's criticism of reductionist type identity theories.

Representationalism attempts to naturalise intentionality by providing (necessary and) sufficient conditions for representational content. It aims at something of the form: 'R represents S' is true iff C where the vocabulary in which condition C is couched contains neither intentional nor semantic expressions. In general, this takes the form of stipulating *mechanisms* the operation of which is supposed to explain intentionality.

Wittgenstein's key criticism of this approach is that it either illicitly presupposes, or fails to account for, the normativity of content. A mechanistic explanation of content can only make use of the causal dispositions of the mechanism. But as Wittgenstein points out, this fails to account for the normative dimension of meaning. It fails to distinguish between dispositions to use a word correctly and incorrectly. Any real mechanism could break down. But invoking an abstract or ideal mechanism cannot help either. That will beg the question of how the ideal mechanism is supposed or intended to work. A token identity theory can escape this sort of objection to mechanism because it does not aim at reductionist explanation of content. It does not set out to explain normative concepts using non-normative terms in the form of reductionist equations of the sort set out above. A token identity theory of Davidson's sort identifies an instance of being in a mental state, or understanding a meaning, at a particular time, with being in a particular token physical state at that time. It does not owe an account of the *right* causal dispositions because it does not attempt to define the meaning or content of the physical state or disposition in physical terms. Nevertheless even a nonreductive, merely token, identity theory falls to a related criticism of a mechanistic approach.

The problem is this. If the dispositions of physical states described in causal terms do not *define* or *set* the normative standard, then they must instead *conform* to that standard. Thus, if a token mental state is identified with a token physical state, the causal role of that mental state when physically described must match its normative role when described in intentional terms. By abandoning the responsibility for attempting to *explain* how the content of a state arises in physical terms, token identity theories have instead the duty of explaining how the physical and mental properties of states keep in step. I shall illustrate why this is a problem.

One of the pre-philosophical characteristics of content, identified in the Chapter 1 was that mental contents and linguistic meanings are structured. They stand in rational relations, for example, justificatory and confirmatory. And they are also internally structured according to the Generality Constraint. Both these features of content impose a structure on mental states when they are described in content-laden terms. At a more fundamental level, mental states have normative consequences for other states and actions. If one understands the series of even numbers, one knows the correct continuation for arbitrarily high numbers. The latter knowledge or ability is partially constitutive of the former. If one understands the meaning of a word, one understands how to use it in a potentially unlimited number of possible future occasions. And if one forms a content-laden mental state, one (generally, to take account of self-deception) knows what would satisfy it. Thus, there are many normative connections that govern mental states.

Because the token identity theory identifies token mental states or events – such as understanding the meaning of a word in a flash, forming an intention or grasping a series – with particular dated physical states or events, and because the states are the states they are in virtue of their normative relations to other states and events, the causal role of the states described in physical, causal terms will have to match their normative, systematic and rational role. But, in the absence of psychophysical laws, there is no explanation of this harmony (cf. Child 1994: 80–9).

If understanding the thought that Simon loves Lesley is a particular physical state, the connections between that state and some state corresponding to understanding that Lesley loves Simon must be part of the causal role of the state described physically. Representationalism has an account of this because it explains the structure of content through a corresponding structure in the mental representations that encode that content. It is thus a matter of causal law – corresponding to the rules of inner syntax – that, if one can think the one thought, one embodies the right mechanism to think the other. But, for a merely token identity theory, there is no account of why the one state should enable the other.

It may be objected that this is not a pressing problem for a merely token identity theory. Token identity theories impose much weaker constraints on the physical realisation of mental states than type identities. Thus, there are no principled limits placed on the number of different physical states that could realise the mental ability: understanding the thought that Simon loves Lesley. This response will not do, however. Whatever state does realise that mental state will have physical and mental properties. Its mental properties will have to be appropriate for it to be an instance of the type: understanding the thought that Simon loves Lesley. This means that it will have to enter into the right normative relations to other mental abilities and states. But this places constraints on its physical properties which will have to be such that its causal role fits its rational role such that it is causally related to other token states that realise those other mental abilities and states. The normative relations constitutive of content impose general constraints on the physical level.

This point can be made in counter-factual terms. The identification of mental and physical states replaces the essential and unmediated connection between mental states and their fulfilments by causal mediation. But because causal connections are contingent, they could have failed to obtain. Consider the physical state that is identical to the mental state of understanding a series. Because it is only a contingent matter, it might not have led to the states that actually – according to the theory – correspond to making the right applications.

Again, this may not seem to present a difficulty for a merely token identity theory. After all, in other possible worlds, the states which are causally connected to the state corresponding to understanding a series might themselves, in those worlds, correspond to instances of the application of the ability that understanding gives. For a token identity theory, different types of physical state might still correspond to instances of the same type of mental state. (The same mental state can be multiply realised.) But this response will not do. Again there is no reason to believe that the states which could physically have been so caused would have corresponded to the right mental states in the absence of appropriate psychophysical laws.

The moral of this argument is that the token identity theory is an unstable middle ground between two more stable positions. One is a reductionist type identity theory that does offer some – albeit unsatisfactory – explanation of what keeps the mental and physical in step. The other position denies that any identification can be made between mental and physical states. Davidson's position has the initial attraction that it promises to reconcile anti-reductionism about content with an account of how mental states can be causal in just the same way as physical events. But it is not a stable middle ground because the identification of mental and physical elements requires a harmony which it no longer has the resources to explain.

In addition to this argument, it is worth noting a general difficulty for combining Wittgenstein's account of content with an identity theory of this sort. In fact, the general difficulty helps bring out why the above criticism applies and demonstrates the fundamental difference between Wittgenstein and Davidson's pictures of the mind.

I mentioned earlier a basic incompatibility between Davidson's and Wittgenstein's account of mental states. Davidson presupposes that the mental side of the mind-body identity is a series of mental events. Wittgenstein, however, casts doubt on any such tidy regimentation of the mind. Understanding, for example, comprises an ability and not the constant or interrupted entertaining of mental signs or symbols. This suggests a prima-facie difficulty for an identity theory. But there is a more fundamental difficulty with the attempt to combine an identity theory in the metaphysics of mind with an account of content like

Wittgenstein's. Because content is normative and relational, it is hard to see what possible physical candidate there is for the body side of an identity of mental and bodily states.

Davidson is aware of this sort of objection and dismisses it:

> It should be clear that it doesn't follow, simply from the fact that meanings are identified in part by relations to objects outside the head, that meanings aren't in the head. To suppose this would be as bad as to argue that because my being sunburned presupposes the existence of the sun, my sunburn isn't a condition of my skin . . . Individual states and events don't *conceptually* presuppose anything in themselves; some of their *descriptions* may, however. (Davidson 1987: 451–2)

But this response marks out a fundamental difference between the view of mind in Davidson and Wittgenstein. Davidson here characterises mental states as non-relational free-standing states which can be referred to by relational mental descriptions and by non-relational physical descriptions. On Wittgenstein's account, by contrast, mental states are essentially relational and normative. The states themselves, rather than their descriptions, are relational. Consequently, Wittgenstein cannot, whereas Davidson can, identify these with non-relational physical states.

But, in this respect, Davidson's picture shares a defect of representationalist theories. What ensures that free-standing states stand in the right normative relations? This is the criticism that I have explored above. It stems from the assumption, which Wittgenstein rejects, that mental states are free-standing internal states. In Chapter 5 I defended Davidson's philosophy of language of the field linguist against McDowell's criticism on this score. McDowell suggested that Davidson was there committed to just such a view and consequently undermined the very possibility of mental content or intentionality. While his account of the philosophy of content does not imply such a picture, Davidson's account of the metaphysics of mind does. This is why the attempt to combine that account of content with the explanatory metaphysics of anomalous monism falls to Wittgensteinian criticism. Even a token identity theory must be rejected.

Abandoning the token identity theory has the disadvantage that there is no longer a uniform explanation of how reasons can be causes. But, for a Wittgensteinian position, this is acceptable because there is no good reason to believe that reasons are causes in any sense that requires a unificatory metaphysical account of causes.

5 Concluding Remarks

I said at the start of this chapter that my aim was not to defend Wittgenstein's radical remarks about the relation of mind and body in *Zettel* but to place them in the context of other aspects of his philosophy and metaphilosophy. In this context they seem less bizarre and unmotivated. I can now make some concluding remarks.

Wittgenstein makes two counter-intuitive claims about mental states. Reasons and causes should not be assimilated. And there need to be no corresponding physical or physiological order that either explains or causes psychological order. But, as I have argued, both of these claims can be given some support by appeal to Wittgenstein's metaphilosophical views. The claim that reasons must be causes and that there must be an underlying mechanism to explain how this is possible are both instances of the kind of philosophical explanatory theory that Wittgenstein rejects.

Once the dubious assumption that philosophy should hypothesise unifying explanatory theories is rejected, the distinctions between giving reasons and determining causes can instead be noted. Two options are then open. One can either: simply resist the claim that reason explanation is a form of causal explanation; or one can accept it but resist the assumption that all forms of causal explanation are alike. Wittgenstein argues instead that there are several distinct prototypes for the concept of cause that cannot be reduced to a single form.

Whether or not reason explanation is a form of causal explanation, a mechanical model of reasons acting as causes is false. Wittgenstein's criticisms of representationalist reduction have been charted in earlier chapters. This chapter has argued that even a weak identity theory such as Davidson's token identity theory cannot be sustained. There does not seem space for a weaker identity theory than this. Thus, there can be no deeper explanation of content by appeal to underlying physical mechanisms and there need be no physiological regularity that *corresponds* to psychological regularity even at the level of tokens.

The denial of even such a weak identity theory as Davidson's token identity theory does not, however, support Wittgenstein's most radical claims about the relation of mind and body. Wittgenstein suggests that there need be no cause of a memory, for example, in one's nervous system, no trace in any form. This amounts to a denial of the supervenience of the mind on the body which does not follow from the denial that mental and physical elements can be correlated, or that psychological and physiological regularities can be aligned. But, while this remains an unattractive claim, three points can be made in its partial defence.

Firstly, Wittgenstein's claim is not that there are no such mechanisms but that there *need* not be any. It is a modal claim. Many contemporary supporters of supervenience would accept its merely contingent status and thus ought to accept Wittgenstein's claim. Secondly, Wittgenstein's denial of the necessity of supervenience of the mental on the physical is part of a broader denial of the necessity of the claim that the micro-structural determines the macro-structural. Again this is a modal claim. It is a reflection of the claim that, despite our current deep commitment to looking for mechanical and micro-structural explanations, it is neither a metaphysical truth nor a rule of grammar that large-scale behaviour is fixed by small-scale mechanisms.

Finally, Wittgenstein's key claim is that an appeal to mechanisms can provide no deeper explanation of linguistic meaning and mental content than can be given by everyday explanations of meaning. The claim that there need be no such mechanisms can thus be seen in two lights. On the one hand, it might seem to be an example of Wittgenstein forgetting his criticism that metaphysics obscures the distinction between physical and conceptual investigations. In this case, the metaphysical claim reflects a properly philosophical claim that intentional explanations are conceptually independent of underlying mechanical explanations. On the other hand, as a metaphysical claim about logical possibility, it has the virtue, like most of Wittgenstein's remarks, of being true.

Further Reading

Davidson's causal theory of mind is discussed in Child (1994) and Evnine (1991). A useful collection of critical essays is LePore and McLaughlin (1985). The claim that reasons are causes is disputed in Tanney (1995).

As well as in the above, the issue of whether Davidson is successful in accounting for the causal relevance of the mental is discussed in many of the essays in Heil and Mele (1993).

Accounts of physicalist theories of mind which do not presuppose an identity theory are given in Dennett (1987) and Haugeland (1982).

Bibliography

Arrington, R. L. (1991) 'Making contact in language: the harmony between thought and reality', in Arrington, R. L. and Glock, H.-J. (eds) (1991) *Wittgenstein's Philosophical Investigations*, London: Routledge.

Arrington, R. L. and Glock, H.-J. (eds) (1996) *Wittgenstein and Quine*, London: Routledge.

Baker, G. P. (1974) 'Criteria: a new foundation for semantics', *Ratio* 16.

Baker, G. P. and Hacker, P. M. S. (1980) *Wittgenstein: Understanding and Meaning*, Oxford: Blackwell.

Baker, G. P. and Hacker, P. M. S. (1983) *Wittgenstein's Philosophical Investigations*, Oxford: Blackwell.

Baker, G. P. and Hacker, P. M. S. (1984a) *Language, Sense and Nonsense*, Oxford: Blackwell.

Baker, G. P. and Hacker, P. M. S. (1984b) *Scepticism, Rules and Language*, Oxford: Blackwell.

Baker, G. P. and Hacker, P. M. S. (1985) *Wittgenstein: Rules, Grammar and Necessity*, Oxford: Blackwell.

Bilgrami, A. (1992) *Belief and Meaning*, Oxford: Blackwell.

Blackburn, S. (1984a) 'The individual strikes back', *Synthese* 58.

Blackburn, S. (1984b) *Spreading the Word*, Oxford: Oxford University Press.

Block, N. (1980) 'What is functionalism', in *Readings in Philosophy of Psychology*, London: Methuen.

Boghossian, P. A. (1989) 'The rule-following considerations', *Mind* 98.

Brentano, F. (1995) *Psychology from an Empirical Standpoint*, London: Routledge.

Brown, D. (1996) 'A furry tile about mental representation', *Philosophical Quarterly* 46.

Budd, M. (1989) *Wittgenstein's Philosophy of Psychology*, London: Routledge.

Child, W. (1994) *Causality, Interpretation and the Mind*, Oxford: Oxford University Press.

Churchland, P. (1989) *A Neurocomputational Perspective: The Nature of Mind and the Structure of Science*, Cambridge, Mass.: MIT Press.

Davidson, D. (1980) *Essays on Actions and Events*, Oxford: Oxford University Press.

Davidson, D. (1982) 'Paradoxies of irrationality', in Wollheim, R. and Hopkins, J. (eds) (1982) *Philosophical Essays on Freud*, Cambridge: Cambridge University Press.

Davidson, D. (1983) 'A coherence theory of truth and knowledge', in LePore, E. (ed.) (1986) *Truth and Interpretation*, Oxford: Blackwell.

Davidson, D. (1984) *Inquiries into Truth and Interpretation*, Oxford: Oxford University Press.

Davidson, D. (1986) 'A nice derangement of epitaphs', in LePore, E. (ed.) (1986) *Truth and Interpretation*, Oxford: Blackwell.

Davidson, D. (1987) 'Knowing one's own mind', *Proceedings and Addresses of the American Philosophical Association* 60.

Davidson, D. (1989) 'The myth of the subjective', in Krausz, M. (ed.) (1989) *Relativism, Interpretation and Confrontation*, Notre Dame: University of Notre Dame Press.

Davidson, D. (1991) 'What is present to the mind?' in Villanueve, E. (ed.) (1991) *Consciousness*, Oxford: Blackwell.

Davidson, D. (1993) 'Reply to Jerry Fodor and Earnest Lepore', in Stoecker, R. (ed.) (1993) *Reflecting Davidson*, Berlin: de Gruyter.

Dennett, D. (1987) *The Intentional Stance*, Cambridge, Mass.: MIT Press.

Diamond, C. (1991) *The Realistic Spirit: Wittgenstein, Philosophy and the Mind*, Cambridge, Mass.: MIT Press.

Dretske, F. I. (1981) *Knowledge and the Flow of Information*, Oxford: Blackwell.

Edwards, J. (1992) 'Best opinion and intentional states', *Philosophical Quarterly* 42.

Evans, G. (1982) *Varieties of Reference*, Oxford: Oxford University Press.

Evnine, S. (1991) *Donald Davidson*, Oxford: Polity.

Fodor, J. (1975) *The Language of Thought*, Hassocks: Harvester.

Fodor, J. (1987) *Psychosemantics: The Problem of Meaning in the Philosophy of Mind*, Cambridge, Mass.: MIT Press.

Fodor, J. (1991) *A Theory of Content and Other Essays*, Cambridge, Mass.: MIT Press.

Fodor, J. (1994) *The Elm and the Expert*, Cambridge, Mass.: MIT Press.

Frege, G. (1964) *The Basic Laws of Arithmetic*, Berkeley: University of California Press.

George, A. (ed.) (1989) *Reflections on Chomsky*, Oxford: Blackwell.

Glock, H.-J. (1996a) 'On safari with Wittgenstein, Quine and Davidson', in Arrington, R. L. and Glock, H.-J. (eds) (1996) *Wittgenstein and Quine*, London: Routledge.

Glock, H.-J. (1996b) *A Wittgenstein Dictionary*, Oxford: Blackwell.

Godfrey-Smith, P. (1989) 'Misinformation', *Canadian Journal of Philosophy* 19.

Goldberg, B. (1991) 'Mechanism and meaning', in Hyman, J. (ed.) (1991) *Investigating Psychology*, London: Routledge.

Goldfarb, W. (1983) 'I want you to bring me a slab: remarks on the opening sections of the *Philosophical Investigations*', *Synthese* 56.

Goldfarb, W. (1985) 'Kripke on Wittgentstein on rules', *Journal of Philosophy* 82.

Goldfarb, W. (1989) 'Wittgenstein, mind and scientism', *Journal of Philosophy* 86.

Grice, H. P. (1957) 'Meaning', *Philosophical Review* 66.

Grice, H. P. (1969) 'Utterer's meaning and intentions', *Philosophical Review* 78.

Hacker, P. M. S. (1972) *Insight and Illusion*, Oxford: Oxford University Press.

Hacker, P. M. S. (1987) *Appearance and Reality*, Oxford: Blackwell.

Hacker, P. M. S. (1990) *Wittgenstein: Meaning and Mind*, Oxford: Blackwell.

Hacker, P. M. S. (1996) *Wittgenstein: Mind and Will*, Oxford: Blackwell.

Hanson, N. R. (1958) *Patterns of Discovery*, Cambridge: Cambridge University Press.

Hartshorne, C. and Weiss, P. (1965) *Collected Papers of Charles Sanders Peirce* vol. 5, Cambridge, Mass.: Harvard University Press.

Haugeland, J. (1982) 'Weak Supervenience', *American Philosophical Quarterly* 19.

Heal, J. (1989) *Fact and Meaning*, Oxford: Blackwell.

Heil, J. (1981) 'Does cognitive psychology rest on a mistake?', *Mind* 90.

Heil, J. and Mele, A. (eds) (1993) *Mental Causation*, Oxford: Oxford University Press.

Hopkins, J. (1975) 'Wittgenstein and Physicalism', *Proceedings of the Aristotelian Society* 75.

Hyman, J. (ed.) (1991) *Investigating Psychology*, London: Routledge.

Jones, O. R. (ed.) (1971) *The Private Language Argument*, London: Macmillan.

Krausz, M. (ed.) (1989) *Relativism, Interpretation and Confrontation*, Notre Dame: University of Notre Dame Press.

Kripke, S. (1980) *Naming and Necessity*, Oxford: Blackwell.

Kripke, S. (1982) *Wittgenstein on Rules and Private Language*, Oxford: Blackwell.

Lear, J. (1982) 'Leaving the world alone', *Journal of Philosophy* 79.

Lear, J. (1984) 'The disappearing "we"', *Proceedings of the Aristotelian Society* supplementary volume 58.

Lear, J. (1986) 'Transcendental anthropology', in Pettit, P. and McDowell, J. (eds) (1986) *Subject Thought and Context*, Oxford: Clarendon Press.

LePore, E. (ed.) (1986) *Truth and Interpretation*, Oxford: Blackwell.

LePore, E. and McLaughlin, B. (eds) (1985) *Actions and Events*, Oxford: Blackwell.

Lewis, D. (1986) 'Causal explanation', in *Philosophical Papers* vol. 2, Oxford: Oxford University Press.

Luntley, M. (1991) 'The transcendental grounds of meaning and the place of silence', in Puhl, K. (ed.) (1991) *Meaning Scepticism*, Berlin: de Gruyter.

McCulloch, G. (1995) *The Mind and its World*, London: Routledge.

Macdonald, C. and Macdonald, G. (eds) (1995) *Philosophy of Psychology*, Oxford: Blackwell.

McDonough, R. (1989) 'Towards a non-mechanistic theory of meaning', *Mind* 98.

McDonough, R. (1991) 'Wittgenstein's critique of mechanistic atomism', *Philosophical Investigations* 14.

McDowell, J. (1976) 'On the sense and reference of a proper name', in Platts, M. (ed.) (1976) *Reference, Truth and Reality*, London: Routledge.

McDowell, J. (1981) 'Anti-realism and the epistemology of understanding', in Parrot, H. and Bourveresse, J. (eds) (1981) *Meaning and Understanding*, Berlin: de Gruyter.

McDowell, J. (1982) 'Criteria, defeasibility and knowledge', *Proceedings of the British Academy* 68.

McDowell, J. (1984a) 'De re sense', *Philosophical Quarterly* 34.

McDowell, J. (1984b) 'Wittgenstein on following a rule', *Synthese* 58.

McDowell, J. (1986) 'Singular thought and the extent of inner space', in Pettit, P. and McDowell, J. (eds) (1986) *Subject Thought and Context*, Oxford: Clarendon Press.

McDowell, J. (1989) 'One strand in the private language argument', *Grazer Philosophische Studien* 33/34.

McDowell, J. (1991) 'Intentionally and interiority in Wittgenstein', in Puhl, K. (ed.) (1991) *Meaning Scepticism*, Berlin: de Gruyter.

McDowell, J. (1992) 'Meaning and intentionality in Wittgenstein's later philosophy', *Midwest Studies in Philosophy* 17.

McDowell, J. (1994) *Mind and World*, Cambridge, Mass.: Harvard University Press.

McGinn, C. (1984) *Wittgenstein on Meaning*, Oxford: Blackwell.

McGinn, C. (1989) *Mental Content*, Oxford: Blackwell.

McGinn, M. (1989) *Sense and Certainty*, Oxford: Blackwell.

McGinn, M. (1997) *Wittgenstein and the Philosophical Investigations*, London: Routledge.

Malcolm, N. (1982) *Wittgenstein: The Relation of Language to Instinctive Behaviour*, · Swansea: University College of Swansea.
Malcolm, N. (1995) *Wittgensteinian Themes*, Ithaca: Cornell University Press.
Malpas, J. E. (1992) *Donald Davidson and the Mirror of Meaning*, Cambridge: Cambridge University Press.
Mellor, D. H. (1991) 'The singularly affecting facts of causation', in *Matters of Metaphysics*, Cambridge: Cambridge University Press.
Millikan, R. G. (1984) *Language, Thought and Other Biological Categories*, Cambridge, Mass.: MIT Press.
Millikan, R. G. (1993) *White Queen Psychology*, Cambridge, Mass.: MIT Press.
Millikan, R. G. (1995) 'A bet with Peacocke', in Macdonald, C. and Macdonald, G. (eds) (1995) *Philosophy of Psychology*, Oxford: Blackwell.
Mullhall, S. (1990) *On Being in the World*, London: Routledge.
Papineau, D. (1987) *Reality and Representation*, Oxford: Blackwell.
Parrot, H. and Bourveresse, J. (eds) (1981) *Meaning and Understanding*, Berlin: de Gruyter.
Peacocke, C. (1992) *A Study of Concepts*, Cambridge, Mass.: MIT Press.
Pears, D. (1988) *The False Prison* vol. 2, Oxford: Oxford University Press.
Pettit, P. (1990) 'The reality of rule-following', *Mind* 99.
Pettit, P. and McDowell, J. (eds) (1986) *Subject Thought and Context*, Oxford: Clarendon Press.
Platts, M. (ed.) (1976) *Reference, Truth and Reality*, London: Routledge.
Popper, K. (1959) *The Logic of Scientific Discovery*, London: Hutchinson.
Puhl, K. (ed.) (1991) *Meaning Scepticism*, Berlin: de Gruyter.
Putnam, H. (1975) 'The meaning of meaning', in *Mind Language and Reality*, Cambridge: Cambridge University Press.
Quine, W. V. O. (1953) 'Two dogmas of empiricism', in *From a Logical Point of View*, Cambridge, Mass.: Harvard University Press.
Quine, W. V. O. (1960) *Word and Object*, Cambridge, Mass.: MIT Press.
Ramberg, B. T. (1989) *Donald Davidson's Philosophy of Language*, Oxford: Blackwell.
Rorty, R. (1991) *Objectivity, Relativism and Truth*, Cambridge: Cambridge University Press.
Ryle, G. (1949) *The Concept of Mind*, London: Hutchinson.
Searle, J. (1992) *The Rediscovery of the Mind*, Cambridge, Mass.: MIT Press.
Shanker, S. (1991) 'The enduring relevance of Wittgenstein's remarks on intentions', in Hyman, J. (ed.) (1991) *Investigating Psychology*, London: Routledge.
Sober, E. (1984) *The Nature of Selection*, Cambridge, Mass.: MIT Press.
Sterelny, K. (1990) *The Representational Theory of Mind*, Oxford: Blackwell.
Stoecker, R. (ed.) (1993) *Reflecting Davidson*, Berlin: de Gruyter.
Summerfield, D. (1990a) 'On taking the rabbit of rule-following out of the hat of representation: a response to Pettit's "The reality of rule following"' *Mind* 99.
Summerfield, D. (1990b) '*Philosophical Investigations* 201: a Wittgensteinian reply to Kripke', *Journal of the History of Philosophy* 28.
Tanney, J. (1995) 'Why reasons may not be causes', *Mind and Language* 10.
Travis, C. (ed.) (1986) *Meaning and Interpretation*, Oxford: Blackwell.
Villanueva, E. (ed.) (1991) *Consciousness*, Oxford: Blackwell.
Williams, B. (1982) 'Wittgenstein and idealism', in *Moral Luck*, Cambridge: Cambridge University Press.

Wittgenstein, L. (1922) *Tractatus Logico-Philosophicus*, London: Routledge.

Wittgenstein, L. (1953) *Philosophical Investigations*, Oxford: Blackwell.

Wittgenstein, L. (1956) *Remarks on the Foundations of Mathematics*, Oxford: Blackwell.

Wittgenstein, L. (1958) *The Blue and Brown Books*, Oxford: Blackwell.

Wittgenstein, L. (1981) *Zettel*, Oxford: Blackwell.

Wittgenstein, L. (1993) *Philosophical Occasions*, Indianapolis: Hackett.

Wollheim, R. and Hopkins, J. (eds) (1982) *Philosophical Essays on Freud*, Cambridge: Cambridge University Press.

Wright, C. (1984) 'Kripke's account of the argument against private language', *Journal of Philosophy* 81.

Wright, C. (1986) 'Rule-following, meaning and constructivism', in Travis, C. (ed.) (1986) *Meaning and Interpretation*, Oxford: Blackwell.

Wright, C. (1987a) 'On making up one's mind: Wittgenstein on intention', in Weingartner, P. and Schurz, G. (eds) *Logic, Philosophy of Science and Epistemology: Proceedings of the 11th International Wittgenstein Symposium*, Vienna: Holder-Pichler-Tempsky.

Wright, C. (1987b) *Realism, Meaning and Truth*, Oxford: Blackwell.

Wright, C. (1988a) 'Moral values, projection and secondary qualities', *Proceedings of the Aristotelian Society* supplementary volume 62.

Wright, C. (1988b) 'Realism, antirealism, irrealism, quasi-realism', *Midwest Studies in Philosophy* 12.

Wright, C. (1989a) 'Critical notice: Colin McGinn, *Wittgenstein on Meaning*', *Mind* 98.

Wright, C. (1989b) 'Wittgenstein's rule-following considerations and the central project of theoretical linguistics', in George, A. (ed.) (1989) *Reflections on Chomsky*, Oxford: Blackwell.

Wright, C. (1991) 'Wittgenstein's later philosophy of mind: sensation, privacy and intention', in Puhl, K. (ed.) (1991) *Meaning Scepticism*, Berlin: de Gruyter.

Wright, C. (1992) *Truth and Objectivity*, Cambridge, Mass.: Harvard University Press.

Index

analytic-synthetic distinction, 157, 162–3
animals, 97
anomalous monism, 151, 165, 172, 176, 184–6, 196–202
Arrington, R. L., 68
aspects, 152–5, 164
asymmetric dependence theory, 25–6, 60–3; *see also* Fodor

Baker, G. P., 8, 68, 99, 138
behaviourism, 14, 105, 119–20, 140, 145, 167
belief *see* content-laden mental state
Berkeley, G., 190–1
Bilgrami, A., 115–18, 123, 138
Blackburn, S., 33, 74
Block, N., 14–15, 121
Blue Book, 30, 57, 129–30, 179
Boghossian, P. A., 60, 68, 76, 85–6
Brentano, F., 4, 13
Brown, D., 66

causal theories of content, 13–17, 21–6, 59–67, 105–8, 112, 171–4
    descriptive theories, 13, 19, 22, 25–6, 29, 59–63
    teleological theories, 13, 19, 22, 29, 56, 60, 63–7
causes
    nomological account, 180–1, 183–6
    and reasons, 180–8, 192–4
    Wittgenstein's account, 194–6
character, 121–2
Child, W., 175, 183, 200, 204
Churchland, P., 108
communication, 115, 125–7
compositionality, 146
computers, 15, 24, 58–9, 198
constructivism, 70, 80–8, 95–6, 98, 111, 119, 121, 130–1, 135, 161–2, 189, 191–2

content-laden mental state, 1–10, 27–9, 31, 48–53, 92–9, 101, 106, 107–10, 112, 117–18, 122, 127, 135, 153, 165–6, 168, 200
cube, 28, 36

Davidson, D.
    on causality, 176–8, 192–4, 204
    on content, 9, 125, 139–75
    on events, 146, 185
    on irrationality, 197–8
    see also anomalous monism, radical interpretation
demonstrative thought *see* singular thought
Dennett, D., 64, 105–6, 168, 204
Descartes, R., 14, 21, 57–8, 82, 103, 112, 123, 155
Diamond, C., 99, 189–92
disjunction problem, 25–6, 60–7; *see also* falsity, normativity
dispositional accounts of normativity *see* normativity
Dretske, F. I., 25, 60

Edwards, J., 86
Evans, G., 7, 22–3, 61, 117, 124, 138, 170
Evnine, S., 150, 174, 204
expectation, 3, 48–52, 92–4, 118, 128; *see also* content-laden mental state, fulfilment condition
explanatory role of content, 5–6, 118–22, 167–71, 180–3
externalism vs internalism, 101, 123–37, 139, 169–71; *see also* free-standing inner state

falsity, 5, 25, 32–3, 60–1, 94–5, 112, 123–4, 127–9, 145, 156–7, 161, 168–71; *see also* disjunction problem, normativity
field linguist, 9, 125–6, 139–41, 145, 148, 155; *see also* radical interpretation
first-person access, 8–9, 81–3, 110–12